CAN DELICIOUS, TRADITIONAL ~~~ REINVENTED FOR A LOWFAT DIET WITHOUT SACRIFICING FLAVOR?

Sí! At last there's a cookbook with all your favorite Latin recipes, revamped for today's health-conscious America. Maria Dolores Beatriz has helped over 50,000 Hispanic women shed big pounds with a huge smile. Now she shares her secrets for achieving health and fitness without giving up treasured traditional foods. This is the first book of its kind in English or Spanish. Anybody who loves Mexican, Cuban, and Latin foods from all over the world will love these mouthwatering, healthy recipes. Part lowfat Hispanic cookbook, part diet plan, LATINA LITE COOKING gives modern lovers of Latino cuisine everything they need to stay sleek, svelte, and *sensacional.*

"Now you can have your flan and eat it too! Beatriz provides lowfat alternatives and recipe makeovers for many of your favorite Latin dishes—without sacrificing authentic Latin flavor."
> —LAURA MILERA, food editor, *Latina Magazine,* author, *The Flavor of Cuba*

"Move over, Jenny Craig and Weight Watchers—now there's a weight-loss program for Latinos!"
> —*Profiles*

"LATINA LITE COOKING gives Americans of all origins tasty ideas for sensible, nutritious eating from around Latin America."
> —FAYE LEVY, author, *30 Low-Fat Vegetarian Meals in 30 Minutes* and *Faye Levy's International Vegetable Cookbook*

LATINA LITE COOKING

200 Delicious Lowfat Recipes from All Over the Americas

Maria Dolores Beatriz

WARNER BOOKS

A Time Warner Company

Neither this diet nor any other diet program should be followed without first consulting a health care professional. If you have any special conditions requiring attention, you should consult with your health care professional regularly regarding possible modification of the program contained in this book.

Copyright © 1998 by Maria Dolores Beatriz

Warner Books, Inc., 1271 Avenue of the Americas, New York, NY 10020
Visit our Web site at http://warnerbooks.com

 A Time Warner Company

Printed in the United States of America

First Printing: February 1998

10 9 8 7 6 5 4 3 2 1

Library of Congress Cataloging-in-Publication Data

Beatriz, Maria Dolores.
    Latina lite cooking : 200 delicious lowfat recipes from all over
  the Americas / Maria Dolores Beatriz.
       p.   cm.
    Includes index.
    ISBN 0-446-67297-1
    1. Cookery, Latin American.   2. Low-fat diet—Recipes.   I. Title.
  TX716.A1B42   1998   97-27741
  641.5'638—dc21   CIP

Book design and text composition by L&G McRee
Cover design by Diane Luger
Cover illustration by Melanie Marder Parks

To Jim White, the light of my life, who promised me the sun would shine on cloudy days.

CONTENTS

Acknowledgments

Latina Lite Cooking is my dream come true. But I can only accept partial credit since many special people contributed to this book.

First, I want to thank all of the *gente maravillosa*—wonderful folks who have lost weight with Esbeltez during the last thirty years. I appreciate the affection and trust we share.

Next, I would like to *brindarles*—offer a special low-calorie toast to the personnel of Esbeltez who have tolerated me while I was writing this book. Immersed in computer limbo, I had scant time to acknowledge their support and encouragement.

A special thank you is sincerely directed to Madeleine Morel and Barbara Lowenstein of Lowenstein-Morel Associates, my agents. In our initial telephone conversation Madeleine's enthusiasm convinced me to begin this project. Her unfaltering confidence guided me through the tough times. In her gentle, firm way she forced me to explore my mind and systematically organize my thoughts. Barbara, a crystal geyser of energy, exudes success. Whenever I became scared and worried her image motivated me to be better than I am. Thanks, Madeleine and Barbara.

Without some special people this book could not have become a reality. Carolyn Fireside, my first editor, is an extraordinarily warm human being and an extremely competent professional. Carla Fine, my succeeding editor, painstakingly listened to my thoughts and ideas and through her logical expertise the contents of this book were *pulido*—polished. Diane Stockwell, my editor at Warner Books, and I share a love for *todo Latino*. She has contributed knowledge, guidance, understanding, and direction to bring this project to fruition.

Muchas gracias, también to Felipe Baron, M.D., Herman Froeb, M.D., Helen Froeb, and Alan Schoengold, M.D., all of whom have a passion to help Latinos avoid endangering their health by obesity. I would also like to thank West Publishing Company for facilitating the analysis of the recipes and menus by providing the Direct Analysis Plus program.

My gratitude also extends to my children, Susana and Esteban, my stepdaughter, Summer, and my *nuera*, Marcia, and *yerno*, Wayne. So many times when they wanted their mom available I was busy writing.

I could not have done this without the helping hands of Susana and Maria Rocha, the experimental kitchen team. We have chopped, blended, and stirred our way through hundreds of bubbling recipes rejecting, modifying, and upgrading.

More than anyone, Jim has been at my side. He has helped me live through every computer glitch; held my hand and consoled me when we lost eight hours' work on a bad disk; discussed every word in every chapter with me; sacrificed our beloved ski trips; and, in general, has demonstrated exceptional love, friendship, dedication, and loyalty.

In summing up, I reflect upon my good fortune in having Jim and a loving family at my side plus a host of other people who through their generosity have afforded me the privilege of knowing and caring for them.

MARIA DOLORES BEATRIZ, 1998

INTRODUCTION

I remember the afternoons I spent as a little girl visiting my *abuelita*. My grandmother's kitchen was so cozy—warm, homey, and wonderful. She would give me chocolate to drink, tell romantic stories about her native Mexico, stroke my cheek, and offer *tacos*, *carnitas*, or sweet desserts that she was preparing. "Try this, *gordita linda*," she would say. With every bite I felt infused with love and comforting calories.

It was not until my teens and early twenties that being overweight began to interfere with my life. I looked in the mirror and hated what I saw—folds, flaps, and bulges. In my pain, I turned to the familiar comforts of food. With every bite, I heard my *abuelita*'s soothing voice: "Eat, *mi gordita*, eat." And with every bite, I got fatter.

I struggled with my weight for many years, going through one vicious cycle after another. Initially I lost pounds by denying myself normal eating, only to reach a point of unbearable stress each time. Invariably I gained every lost pound back plus a few more in a matter of months. I became convinced that I could never sacrifice my beloved foods and would always be fat.

After one of these fasting episodes, slimmer but feeling particularly apprehensive, I looked for comfort in a big bowl of *guacamole*, urgently dipping one *tostada* chip after another. I ate breathlessly, desperately. I had never experienced such desperation before, and it frightened me. I stopped in midbite; for the first time, I wanted to understand why I was gorging myself. I became aware that my gluttony was really a desire to satisfy the void created by my need for love and comfort. Now, with the nearly empty bag of chips and scraped-clean bowl of *guacamole* in front of me, I realized that all my life I had equated the beloved foods from my childhood with love and security. That was why dieting had always been such torture—it felt like I was depriving myself of love and affection. I realized I had to change my way of thinking but also find a way to prepare my adored security-oozing *platillos*—dishes—in healthier, nonfattening ways. I named the voice inside my head that told me that food is love my *mente gorda*, fat mind-set. I knew that daydreaming about the familiar foods of my childhood gave me warm and fuzzy feelings, while visions of nothing more in my future than dull salads, wilted vegetables, and tasteless boiled chicken or fish depressed me.

To lose weight, to look and feel the way I wanted, I was forced to develop a *mente delgada*, a lean mind-set, to guide me through weak moments. Through much hard work and discipline, I taught myself that food is nourishment for the body and love is nourishment for the soul, and they can be combined! I experimented enthusiastically in my kitchen, redesigning the heritage of familiar foods that had been handed down to me. I successfully modified the old recipes. I no longer felt deprived when I substituted lean skinless chicken for fatty meats, because I cooked and seasoned the chicken in the same way that my mother and grandmother had. Best of all, as I slowly lost weight and kept it off, my sense of accomplishment and pride and my growing confidence nourished my soul, making it easier for me to control my *mente gorda*.

This was the sixties, and I was living in Mexico City. In my struggle to lose weight, I searched for support. There were a few doctors who prescribed diet pills, and in the markets, *brujas*—female medicine men—sold foul-smelling concoctions guaranteeing enough weight loss to attract your Mr. Right and live happily ever after. But while there seemed to be two bakeries and three *taco* stands on every block, there was not a single weight-loss center that offered a sensible plan. As I thought about this, it struck me that the Latino mind-set not only predisposes many of us to being overweight but also makes it difficult to slim down. Not only are our diets saturated with fat, our cultures are replete with conventions that feed our *mentes gordas*—from the belief that a chubby child is a healthy child to the idea that a "proper" married woman should not be too alluring. The answer was a weight-loss plan specifically designed for Latinos. And since no such program existed, I decided to develop one.

In 1972, I founded *Pierda Peso* in Mexico City. My first clients were several women friends with whom I had met regularly for afternoon chats, usually accompanied by luscious snacks. I shared my newly discovered secrets, and they learned how to recognize and conquer their *mentes gordas*. Each worked on honing the tools needed to strengthen her resolve to lose unwanted pounds, and together we developed a support network to help overcome the obstacles to permanent weight loss. Willing support replaced negative disapproval. Old-wives' tales were replaced with carefully researched nutritional information. A list of healthful foods was printed and distributed as a shopping guide. We developed and shared recipes for preparing traditional dishes in new, healthful ways. We took long walks instead of meeting to eat. Within a few months, my first clients had lost an average of seventeen pounds.

That was the beginning of *Esbeltez*, the weight-loss system designed around Latino cultures, Latino needs, and Latino food. By 1989, we had centers across many states of Mexico, as well as in California and Arizona. For more than a quarter of a century, I have been controlling my own *mente gorda* and helping others govern theirs with the bonus of eating delicious Latin foods. The results? For over 100,000 people, permanent weight loss and a dramatic positive change in their lives.

In addition, I have traveled extensively across North America, speaking to Latinas who are frustrated by weight-reduction programs that do not understand their special needs. That is why I decided to share with you the recipes and secrets of the *Esbeltez* system in *Latina Lite Cooking*.

This book will help you learn everything you need to know to maintain a healthy diet without giving up the delicious Latin foods you love. In Part One, you will find over 200 lowfat, nutritious "recipe makeovers" for your favorite Latin dishes from around the world. Whether you're trying to lose weight or just want to establish a healthier diet, these mouthwatering recipes will prove that, yes, lowfat can be luscious!

Here you'll find lowfat versions of your favorite recipes for every meal of the day, including:

Spanish *tortillas*
Empanadas
Colombian Chicken and Potato Soup
Costa Rican Black Bean Soup
Basque-style Cod
Brazilian-style fish
Cuban Chicken and Rice
Spanish-style Chicken Fricassee
Paella
Venezuelan Black Beans
Nicaraguan Rice and Beans
Puerto Rican–style Rice Pudding

Soon you'll discover how easy it is to prepare healthy, lowfat meals the Latina Lite way without sacrificing any of the flavor found in traditional high-fat recipes!

In Part Two, *Latina Lite Cooking* will help you answer the questions so familiar to anyone who has gone through the painful struggle to lose weight:

Why can't I control my eating?
Why do I invent elaborate excuses to put off losing weight?
What is that special something that will motivate me to lose weight?
How does my body function?
What are reasonable expectations for slimming down?
What is the best diet for me and my family?
Is there a sensible plan that will help me lose weight and not leave me feeling constantly hungry?
What can I do to keep weight off permanently?
Is it possible to lose weight quickly without jeopardizing my health?
How can I overcome my family's objections to healthier eating?
How do I stay committed to my diet if my family tries to sabotage my efforts?

In *Latina Lite Cooking* you will learn how to:

Experiment with familiar foods prepared in a new way. If you are like me, your favorite foods came from your grandmother's table. Who wants to give that up? Not many of us. With Latina Lite menus there are no deprivations. You can enjoy *platillos sabrosos*, delicious dishes, by learning how to prepare them using our lowfat, low-calorie "recipe makeovers." Change to a more nutritious way of eating.

Recognize and learn to control your *mente gorda*, the part of your mind that tells you to stuff yourself when you feel frustrated, angry, unhappy, depressed, bored, or even content. Your *mente gorda* is a gremlin that pushes you to act against your own best interests. "Eat! Eat! You deserve it!" it insists. But you can learn to tune out these messages, and even replace them with thoughts that will help you stick to a healthier diet.

Develop your *mente delgada*, the part of your mind that tells you not to stuff yourself when you feel frustrated, angry, or unhappy. Conquer your emotional dependence on fattening foods and control unreasonable eating. Examine your reflection in the mirror and glory in what you have accomplished— your new, slimmer self. Self-pride will strengthen your resolve and make you feel more secure.

Yes, it is difficult to change old habits, but *Latina Lite Cooking* will show you how to become the slimmer, fitter person you want to be. Yes, it is difficult to resist instant gratification in favor of long-term rewards, but *Latina Lite Cooking* will help you stay focused and motivated. Yes, it is difficult to start exercising, but *Latina Lite Cooking* will prove to you that as little as thirty minutes a day of an activity you enjoy will greatly improve your looks and your health.

Over one hundred thousand people have lost weight and kept it off using our system, while enjoying healthy, delicious meals. *Sí, se puede.* You can, too.

LATINA
LITE
COOKING

Part
ONE

· ·

RECETAS TIPICAS— TRADITIONAL LATIN RECIPE MAKEOVERS

Lowfat Latin dishes *que te antojan con su sabor*, that tempt you with their flavor.

When you think of going on a "**Diet**," you probably imagine yourself dying of hunger. You do not think of tasty dishes served in generous portions. The Latina Lite menus furnish the Recommended Daily Allowances (RDA) of vitamins, minerals, and other nutrients. They are inexpensive, easy to prepare, and, of course, *sabrosas*—very tasty!

The following recipes maintain traditional flavor but are prepared in a more nutritious way. Culinary art, like painting and sculpture, depends on the artist's palette. Spices, flavorings, and ingredients determine the taste. Latino cuisine is a mix of Spanish, Indian, Arabic, African, Chinese, and Caribbean foods.

Many of these foods are deep-fried in grease because it makes them taste better. Try a little test. Put a dab of lard or a drop of oil on your tongue. It may be tasteless or have a disagreeable flavor. How can fat make food taste good? It really doesn't. Insoluble in saliva, it lubricates and holds the flavor of the salt (sodium chloride), sugar, spices, and other seasonings on your tongue. In reality these flavorings are added to mask the true taste of fat.

Latino recipes usually contain too much fat and salt. My "Lite" recipes teach you to cook differently. Always measure oil in place of just adding a splash; a measured tablespoon means that 0.9 tablespoons of fat actually reach the food. When the cook splashes a little from the bottle into the pan without measuring, the "little bit" always becomes two to three tablespoons.

Instead of adding salt to the recipe during the cooking and tasting phase, wait and add it last, after the dish is served. Fill your shakers with a mixture of equal parts of salt and salt substitute and allow everyone to season to their individual taste. The final flavor remains the same, but the dish contains much less sodium.

You can learn to prepare *tostadas* without fat by browning tortillas in your toaster-oven. They actually taste better than when they're fried the greasy old way.

One more admonition: Granulated consommé or bouillon cubes provide an easy, rapid chicken or beef broth. You may continue to utilize these shortcuts but be sure to read the label before buying the product. Select consommé or bouillon without monosodium glutamate (MSG). MSG, a white crystalline salt taste enhancer, triggers an allergic reaction in many people. The symptoms include light-headedness, tightness in neck, jaw, and back.

At the end of each recipe you will find a heading, "Each Latina Lite serving contains," where the food value per serving is found. If you are following a menu presented in Part Two, calculate the foods consumed as part of your daily allotment.

NOTE: Some recipes utilize Sauces or Seasonings presented in another recipe. Every recipe title included in the ingredients of another recipe appears with its page number for cross-referencing.

BREAKFASTS— DESAYUNOS

Years ago, breakfast had to tide you over for six or seven hours, until *comida*—the big meal. Breakfast consisted of meat, three or more eggs, beans, *tortillas*, fruit, *pan dulce*, coffee, and unhurried conversation. Times have changed, as has our knowledge of good nutrition. Today the time between breakfast and lunch is shorter, so a smaller breakfast should be consumed. A typical small breakfast consists of fruit or juice, cereal or an egg, a bread, and tea or coffee.

OATMEAL-PINEAPPLE PUDDING— BUDIN DE AVENA CON PINA

¼   cup oatmeal
1⅓ cups fat-free powdered milk
2   egg yolks
5   egg whites
½   teaspoon ground cinnamon
1   teaspoon margarine
¼   cup packed dark-brown sugar
8   pineapple slices, canned, unsweetened, drained
      (save liquid)
1   teaspoon baking powder
4   packets sugar substitute

1. In a medium bowl, combine oatmeal, powdered milk, egg yolks, egg whites, cinnamon and ½ cup reserved pineapple liquid; beat well.

2. Over medium heat, melt margarine in an 8-inch non-stick skillet; add sugar and stir well; add pineapple slices and caramelize on both sides.

3. Add baking powder and sugar substitute to oatmeal mixture; pour the batter over pineapple slices.

4. Cover tightly; cook for 20 to 30 minutes over very low heat until an inserted toothpick comes out clean.

5. Cool and remove from pan with pineapple slices on top.

Serves 4.

Each Latina Lite serving contains: 55 calories
Total Fats: 1 gm
Saturated Fats: 0 gm   Protein: 3 gm
Unsaturated Fats: 1 gm   Sodium: 53 mg
Carbohydrates: 10 gm

FRIED EGG—*HUEVO ESTRELLADO*

The advantage of this Latina Lite fried egg is that it contains less fat and the yolk seldom breaks.

½   *teaspoon margarine*
1   *egg, plus one egg white*
1   *teaspoon chicken broth or tomato juice or* salsa *or water*

1. Over medium heat, melt margarine in a small nonstick skillet.

2. Break egg into skillet and add egg white.

3. When whites begin to set, add broth or substitute and cover tightly.

4. Continue cooking over medium heat for 1 minute more.

5. Serve a perfect *huevo estrellado*.

Serves 1.

Each Latina Lite serving contains: 108 calories
Total Fats: 7 gm
Saturated Fats: 2 gm   Protein: 10 gm
Unsaturated Fats: 5 gm   Sodium 162 mg
Carbohydrates: 1 gm

Havana-Style Egg— *Huevo Habanero*

2   tablespoons **SOFRITO** *(page 66)*
4   *eggs*
Salt and freshly ground black pepper to taste

1. Preheat the oven to 350°F.

2. Spread *Sofrito* in bottom of an 8-inch glass pie pan. Break eggs on top of *Sofrito*, being careful not to break yolks.

3. Bake until whites are set and yolks are still soft, about 10 minutes.

4. Season with pepper and half salt, half salt-substitute mixture from your shaker.

Serves 4.

Each Latina Lite serving contains: 83 calories
Total Fats: 6 gm
Saturated Fats: 2 gm   Protein: 7 gm
Unsaturated Fats: 4 gm   Sodium: 69 mg
Carbohydrates: 1 gm

Egg with Tomato-*Chile* Sauce— *Huevo Ranchero*

¼   cup finely diced onion
1   garlic clove, minced
1   teaspoon margarine
½   cup canned tomatoes
½   chile serrano, minced (optional)
3   sprigs fresh cilantro, chopped
1   egg
1   corn tortilla
Salt and freshly ground black pepper to taste

1. In a small skillet, over medium heat, sauté onion and garlic in ½ teaspoon margarine until translucent; add tomatoes, *chile*, and 2 sprigs chopped cilantro.

2. Cover; cook over medium-low heat for 3 minutes. Set aside.

3. Melt remaining ½ teaspoon margarine in a small skillet; add egg.

4. When white begins to set, add just-prepared sauce; cover tightly; cook over low heat for 1 minute more.

5. Serve on *tortilla*; garnish with remaining sprig of chopped cilantro.

6. Add pepper and half salt and half salt-substitute mixture from your shaker.

Serves 1.

Each Latina Lite serving contains: 228 calories
Total Fats: 11 gm
Saturated Fats: 3 gm   Protein: 10 gm
Unsaturated Fats: 8 gm   Sodium: 355 mg
Carbohydrates: 27 gm

MEXICAN SCRAMBLED EGGS—
HUEVOS MEXICANOS

1 tablespoon vegetable oil
½ medium onion, chopped
2 fresh chiles serranos, cored, seeded, and minced
1 cup diced lean turkey ham
3 egg yolks
6 egg whites
2 tablespoons milk
1 tomato, chopped
½ teaspoon half salt, half salt-substitute mixture
Freshly ground black pepper to taste

   1. Heat oil in a large nonstick skillet; over medium heat, sauté onion and *chiles* until translucent; add turkey ham; sauté 2 minutes more.
   2. In a small bowl, beat egg yolks, whites, and milk until frothy.
   3. Add egg mixture and tomato to skillet.
   4. Scramble with a fork until set.
   5. Remove from burner.
   6. Add salt and pepper and serve.

Serves 4.

Each Latina Lite serving contains: 202 calories
Total Fats: 11 gm
Saturated Fats: 3 gm   Protein: 20 gm
Unsaturated Fats: 8 gm   Sodium: 800 mg
Carbohydrates: 8 gm

POACHED EGGS WITH BEANS IN SAUCE— HUEVOS MOTULENOS

2 teaspoons vegetable oil
2 fresh chiles serranos, cored, seeded, and cut into strips
1 cup tomato sauce
½ teaspoon half salt, half salt-substitute mixture
4 corn tortillas
1 cup FRIJOLES REFRITOS (page 194)
4 eggs
½ cup green peas
¼ cup thinly sliced red onion
¼ cup crumbled part-skim milk cheese

1. In a small skillet, heat 1 teaspoon oil over medium heat; sauté *chile*; add tomato sauce and salt; lower heat and simmer for 5 minutes.

2. Set aside.

3. Wrap *tortillas* in a cloth; microwave on High for 1 minute.

4. Spread *Frijoles Refritos* on each *tortilla*. Heat remaining 1 teaspoon oil in a large nonstick skillet over medium heat; add eggs.

5. When eggs begin to set pour sauce into skillet; cover tightly, reduce heat, and simmer for 2 to 3 minutes until eggs are poached.

6. Carefully place 1 egg on each bean-covered *tortilla*; cover with sauce left in pan.

7. Serve with peas, onion slices, and cheese on top.

Serves 4.

Each Latina Lite serving contains: 316 calories
Total Fats: 13 gm
Saturated Fats: 4 gm   Protein: 18 gm
Unsaturated Fats: 9 gm   Sodium: 81 mg
Carbohydrates: 35 gm

SCRAMBLED EGGS WITH SALTED COD—
HUEVOS REVUELTOS CON BACALAO

1   *tablespoon vegetable oil*
1   *medium onion, thinly sliced*
1   *green bell pepper, cored, seeded, and finely chopped*
2   *cups cooked and shredded* **BACALAO—***Salted Cod*
       (page 99)
3   *egg yolks*
6   *egg whites*
2   *tablespoons milk*
Salt and freshly ground black pepper to taste

1. Heat oil in a large nonstick skillet over medium heat; sauté onion until translucent; add green pepper and shredded cod; sauté for 3 minutes.

2. In a small bowl, beat egg yolks, whites, and milk until frothy.

3. Pour into skillet; scramble with a fork until set.

4. Remove from burner and serve.

5. Add pepper and half salt, half salt-substitute mixture from your shaker.

Serves 4.

Each Latina Lite serving contains: 239 calories
Total Fats: 9 gm
Saturated Fats: 2 gm   Protein: 34 gm
Unsaturated Fats: 7 gm   Sodium: 162 mg
Carbohydrates: 6 gm

Eggs in a *TORTILLA*, YUCATECAN STYLE—*HUEVOS YUCATECOS*

4   corn tortillas
2   tablespoons *vegetable oil*
4   *eggs*
½   *cup diced onion*
2   *fresh* chiles poblanos *or* Californias, *cut into strips
        (you may substitute any available fresh, large,
        long green* chiles*)*
1   *cup tomato sauce*
½   *teaspoon half salt, half salt-substitute mixture*
½   *cup fat-free plain yogurt*
½   *cup fat-free sour cream*

1. With the tips of your fingers rub water on each *tortilla* until you can separate it into 2 layers; carefully remove top layer from each one.

2. Heat 1 tablespoon oil in a nonstick skillet over medium heat; gently sauté *tortillas* until soft.

3. Break egg over each *tortilla*, lower heat; cover; cook for about 2 minutes or until yolk begins to firm.

4. Carefully remove each *tortilla* with egg on top to a large platter.

5. Cover each egg with remaining *tortilla* layer. In the same skillet, heat remaining 1 tablespoon of oil over medium heat; sauté onions until translucent; add *chile* strips, tomato sauce, and salt.

6. Lower heat and simmer for 5 minutes.

7. In a small bowl, combine yogurt and sour cream.

8. Pour tomato sauce over egg-*tortilla* "sandwiches"; top with cream mixture.

Serves 4.

Each Latina Lite serving contains: 254 calories
Total Fats: 13 gm
Saturated Fats: 2 gm   Protein: 12 gm
Unsaturated Fats: 11 gm   Sodium: 294 mg
Carbohydrates: 24 gm

EGGS WITH DRIED SHREDDED MEAT— MACHACA CON HUEVOS

1   cup machaca, *packaged dried shredded beef*
2   *tablespoons finely diced onion*
1   *tablespoon vegetable oil*
2   *tomatoes, diced*
1   *fresh* chile serrano, *cored, seeded, and minced*
3   *egg yolks*
6   *egg whites*

1. Soak *machaca* in 2 cups warm water 10 minutes.
2. Discard water; add 2 cups fresh water and soak 10 minutes more; then drain and cut beef into ⅓-inch pieces.
3. Set aside.
4. In a medium skillet, sauté onion in oil over medium heat until translucent; add meat, tomatoes, and *chile*; sauté for 5 minutes.
5. In a small bowl, whisk egg yolks and whites together; add to pan; scramble with a fork until set.

Serves 4.

Each Latina Lite serving contains: 218 calories
Total Fats: 10 gm
Saturated Fats: 3 gm   Protein: 25 gm
Unsaturated Fats: 7 gm   Sodium: 1934 mg
Carbohydrates: 8 gm

SWEET BREAD—*PAN DULCE*

This *pan dulce* satisfies your sweet tooth without stuffing extra fat calories into your fat cells.

1   *slice whole-wheat bread*
1   *teaspoon margarine*
1   *apple, peeled, cored, and cut into 8 wedges*
2   *egg whites*
¼   *cup nonfat cottage cheese*
2–3 *packets sugar substitute*
¼   *teaspoon ground cinnamon*
1   *teaspoon sugar*

1. Preheat the oven to 375°F.
2. Toast the bread lightly, and while still hot, butterfly it into 2 thinner slices with a sharp knife.
3. Spread ½ teaspoon margarine on the toast.
4. Simmer apple wedges in a small covered saucepan in ¼ cup of water for 2 minutes; set aside.
5. In a small bowl, combine egg whites, cottage cheese, and sugar substitute and mix until creamy.
6. Spread the mixture on toast, add partially cooked apple wedges; top with small flecks of the remaining ½ teaspoon of margarine.
7. Mix cinnamon and sugar, and sprinkle on top.
8. Bake for 5 to 10 minutes.

Serves 1.

Each Latina Lite serving contains: 320 calories
Total Fats: 7 gm
Saturated Fats: 2 gm   Protein: 17 gm
Unsaturated Fats: 5 gm   Sodium: 532 mg
Carbohydrates: 52 gm

*Ö*MELET WITH TURKEY HAM—
TORTILLA CALAFIA

3   egg yolks
6   egg whites
½   cup finely diced onion
½   cup lean turkey ham, cut into bite-size pieces
1   tablespoon chopped fresh Italian parsley
1   tablespoon margarine

1. In a medium bowl, beat egg yolks with egg whites; add onion, turkey ham, and parsley.

2. Melt margarine over medium heat in a large nonstick skillet and add egg mixture.

3. When eggs have browned but are not completely set, fold one side over the other.

4. Brown both sides, but keep omelet soft inside.

5. Serve with *SALSA ROJA MEXICANA* (page 64).

Serves 4.

Each Latina Lite serving contains: 139 calories
Total Fats: 8 gm
Saturated Fats: 2 gm   Protein: 13 gm
Unsaturated Fats: 6 gm   Sodium: 405 mg
Carbohydrates: 3 gm

℧MELET WITH ZUCCHINI AND CACTUS LEAVES—*TORTILLA DE CALABACITA Y NOPALES*

4   egg yolks
¼   cup milk
2   tablespoons chopped fresh Italian parsley
1   cup diced and cooked zucchini
1   cup diced and cooked NOPALES *(page 164)*
2   slices yellow cheese, chopped
8   egg whites
1   tablespoon vegetable oil
½   teaspoon half salt, half salt-substitute mixture
¼   teaspoon freshly ground black pepper

1. Beat egg yolks and milk in a medium bowl.
2. Add parsley, zucchini, *Nopales*, and cheese to the beaten yolks.
3. Set aside.
4. In medium bowl, whip egg whites until they peak; gently fold beaten egg whites into yolk mixture.
5. Heat oil in a nonstick large skillet over medium heat; pour egg mixture into skillet; lower heat; cover tightly; cook for 20 minutes or until eggs are set; sprinkle with salt and pepper.
6. Serve hot accompanied by a *SALSA* of your choice (pages 63–65).

Serves 4.

Each Latina Lite serving contains: 169 calories
Total Fats: 10 gm
Saturated Fats: 3 gm   Protein: 13 gm
Unsaturated Fats: 7 gm   Sodium: 292 mg
Carbohydrates: 8 gm

SPANISH-STYLE OMELET WITH POTATOES AND ONIONS— *TORTILLA ESPAÑOLA*

1   tablespoon olive oil
½   cup thinly sliced onion
1   cup potatoes, peeled and sliced very thinly
3   egg yolks
6   egg whites
½   teaspoon half salt, half salt-substitute mixture

1. In a large skillet, sauté onion in oil over low heat until translucent; add potato slices and cook slightly; do not over-cook.

2. In a medium bowl, whisk egg yolks, egg whites, and salt together until frothy.

3. Raise heat to medium and pour eggs over potato mixture.

4. Lift bottom of omelet with spatula to allow uncooked eggs to contact hot skillet.

5. When omelet looks set place plate larger than *tortilla* over skillet; carefully flip omelet onto it, then slide omelet back into the skillet.

6. Over low heat, cook for 1 minute more.

Serves 4.

Each Latina Lite serving contains: 156 calories
Total Fats: 7 gm
Saturated Fats: 2 gm   Protein: 9 gm
Unsaturated Fats: 5 gm   Sodium: 225 mg
Carbohydrates: 14 gm

Appetizers— Antojitos

To me, the English word *Appetizers* means dainty portions designed to open my appetite without really filling it. On the other hand, I envision Spanish *Antojitos* as yearned for, completely satisfying foods. Eating should be pleasurable even when you're slimming down and staying that way. So go ahead and enjoy these Latina Lite *antojitos* either for regular meals or as special party fare.

Plantain and Meat Fritter— Alcapurria

2   cups peeled yautía *(taro root)*
3   *green plantains, peeled*
½   *teaspoon half salt, half salt-substitute mixture*
1   *tablespoon CUBAN* ACHIOTE OIL *(page 50)*
1   *cup CUBAN* PICADILLO *(page 144)*
2   *tablespoons vegetable oil*

1. Grate *yautía* and plantains separately using grating disc of food processor or handheld grater.
2. In a medium bowl, combine grated vegetables with salt and Cuban *Achiote* oil; mash with a fork to form dough.

3. Wet your hands; divide dough into 8 balls; flatten ½ of each dough ball with the palm of your hand; form a small depression in the middle; fill with *picadillo*; cover with other half of dough.

4. Repeat.

5. Make 8 *alcapurrias*.

6. In a large skillet, heat oil over medium heat; fry fritters until golden brown on both sides; blot excess oil on paper towels.

Serves 4.

Each Latina Lite serving contains: 503 calories
Total Fats: 16 gm
Saturated Fats: 3 gm   Protein: 13 gm
Unsaturated Fats: 13 gm   Sodium: 347 mg
Carbohydrates: 85 gm

ßURRITO—FLOUR TORTILLA TACO

1   teaspoon *vegetable oil*
1   cup *CUBAN* PICADILLO *(page 144)*
1   cup *diced and cooked potato*
4   *flour* tortillas
½   cup *fat-free yogurt*
½   cup *fat-free sour cream*
1   tablespoon *Japanese seasoned rice vinegar*[*]
PICO DE GALLO *(page 61)*

1. In a medium skillet, heat oil over medium heat; lightly sauté *picadillo* with the potato.

[*]Japanese seasoned rice vinegar can be found in the Asian food section of your supermarket.

2. Wrap flour *tortillas* in a cloth and microwave on High for 1 minute 20 seconds.

3. Place 2 tablespoons meat mixture in middle of each *tortilla*; fold both ends toward middle, then the ends over each other to form a compact square.

4. In a small bowl, whisk yogurt, sour cream, and vinegar together.

5. Serve with yogurt topping and *Pico de Gallo* sauce.

Serves 4.

Each Latina Lite serving contains: 342 calories
Total Fats: 9 gm
Saturated Fats: 2 gm   Protein: 20 gm
Unsaturated Fats: 7 gm   Sodium: 417 mg
Carbohydrates: 47 gm

FISH, PICKLED IN LEMON JUICE WITH AVOCADO—*CEVICHE ACAPULQUENO*

Ceviche, a delectable seafood dish, is most popular in Mexico and Peru. Preparation of *ceviche* is not time consuming and when piled high on a *TOSTADA* (page 203) it makes a delicious lunch or great party fare.

1   pound mackerel (or other firm fish)
Juice of 6 to 8 lemons
¼   cup fresh orange juice
2   large tomatoes, peeled* and chopped

---

*To peel tomatoes, gently scorch tomato skin over stove burner until it blisters; then immediately wrap tomatoes in a cool damp cloth for a few minutes. The peel will separate easily.

1   medium white onion, chopped
1   tablespoon olive oil
1   tablespoon cider or pineapple vinegar
4   chiles serranos, cored, peeled, and finely chopped
1   teaspoon fresh oregano
½   teaspoon half salt, half salt-substitute mixture
Freshly ground black pepper to taste
1   large ripe avocado, peeled and sliced

    1. Wash fish, discard skin and bones.
    2. Cut fish into ½-inch squares.
    3. Place fish in a square glass pan and cover with lemon and orange juices.
    4. Marinate the fish in the refrigerator for at least 4 hours; the fish should appear "cooked" on all sides.
    5. Stir in remaining ingredients, except avocado.
    6. Garnish with avocado slices to serve.

Serves 4.

Each Latina Lite serving contains: 316 calories
Total Fats: 13 gm
Saturated Fats: 2 gm   Protein: 33 gm
Unsaturated Fats: 11 gm   Sodium: 218 mg
Carbohydrates: 18 gm

NOTE: Make just the amount of *ceviche* necessary. The fish is raw within and should not be eaten after 24 hours.

TUNA IN LEMON—*CEVICHE DE ATUN*

Juice of 3 to 4 lemons
3   *tablespoons fresh orange juice*
1   *6⅛-ounce can water-packed tuna, rinsed, drained,*
        and crumbled
1   *teaspoon olive oil*
1   *tablespoon tomato sauce*
¼   *cup finely diced onion*
1   *large tomato, peeled* and finely chopped*
8   *green olives stuffed with pimiento, sliced*
1–2 *small green fresh* chiles serranos, *seeded and finely*
        chopped
Fresh cilantro to taste, chopped
½   *teaspoon half salt, half salt-substitute mixture*

1. In a square glass dish, combine lemon and orange
juices.
2. Marinate tuna in juice for 1 hour.
3. Add remaining ingredients; mix well and chill.
4. Serve in small bowls over lettuce leaves, or on
TOSTADAS (page 203), accompanied by grated lettuce and
SALSA ROJA (page 64) or Tabasco sauce.

Serves 2 dinners or 4 appetizers.

Each Latina Lite appetizer serving contains: 101 calories
Total Fats: 3 gm
Saturated Fats: 0 gm   Protein: 13 gm
Unsaturated Fats: 3 gm   Sodium: 475 mg
Carbohydrates: 8 gm

*To peel tomato, gently scorch tomato skin over stove burner until it blisters.
Wrap tomato in a cool damp cloth for a few minutes. The peel will separate easily.

*T*ORTILLA STRIPS IN *CHILE SAUCE*— *CHILAQUILES*

Freshly grilled *tortillas* are delicious. Day-old *tortillas* taste wonderful in *chilaquiles*. Generally, *chilaquiles* is a breakfast or supper dish but can be dressed up for an elegant party. Here are three versions.

8   corn tortillas, cut into strips
2   teaspoons vegetable oil
4   tablespoons diced onion
1   garlic clove, minced
2   cups tomato sauce
1–3 chiles serranos, fresh or canned, cored, seeded, and
       minced
½   chicken bouillon cube or ½ teaspoon consommé
       granules
½   cup grated part-skim milk cheese
1   tablespoon minced onion

1. Dry *tortilla* strips in the sun, in a toaster oven, or on a dry griddle until crunchy.
2. In a large skillet, heat oil over medium heat; sauté onion and garlic until onion becomes translucent; set aside.
3. Purée onion, garlic, tomato sauce, and *chiles* in blender; add sauce to skillet; add bouillon; bring to a boil; simmer for 5 minutes.
4. Add dried *tortilla* strips.
5. Simmer for 1 minute more.
6. Sprinkle cheese and minced onion on top.

Serves 4.

Each Latina Lite serving contains: 286 calories
Total Fats: 9 gm
Saturated Fats: 4 gm   Protein: 14 gm
Unsaturated Fats: 5 gm   Sodium: 831 mg
Carbohydrates: 41 gm

TORTILLA STRIPS AND FISH IN CHILE SAUCE—CHILAQUILES CON PESCADO

8   corn tortillas, cut into strips
½   pound green tomatoes (tomatillos), skinned, washed, and quartered
1–3 fresh chiles serranos, cored, seeded, and halved
2   tablespoons chopped onion
1   garlic clove, minced
½   chicken bouillon cube or ½ teaspoon consommé granules
1   teaspoon vegetable oil
2   cups cooked red snapper, sole, or catfish, cut into bite-size pieces
½   cup part-skim milk cheese
¼   cup chopped fresh cilantro
1   tablespoon minced onion

1. Preheat the oven to 375°F.

2. Dry *tortilla* strips in the sun, in a toaster oven, or on a dry griddle until crunchy.

3. Purée green tomatoes, *chiles*, onion, garlic, and bouillon cube or consommé granules in blender.

4. Rub oil on a rectangular glass baking pan.

5. Place ⅓ of green sauce in pan; cover with half of dried *tortilla* strips; place fish over *tortilla* strips; add ⅓ more sauce, a final layer of *tortilla* strips, and top with last ⅓ of the green sauce.

6. Bake for 8 to 12 minutes, or until thoroughly heated but not cooked dry.

7. Sprinkle cheese, cilantro, and minced onion over top just before serving.

Serves 4.

Each Latina Lite serving contains: 401 calories
Total Fats: 10 gm
Saturated Fats: 4 gm   Protein: 42 gm
Unsaturated Fats: 6 gm   Sodium: 441 mg
Carbohydrates: 36 gm

*T*ORTILLA STRIPS AND CHICKEN IN CHILE SAUCE—*CHILAQUILES CON POLLO*

1. Follow basic *chilaquiles* recipe (page 22).

2. When the dried *tortilla* strips are added to sauce, add 2 cups of cooked and shredded chicken breast.

Serves 4.

Each Latina Lite serving contains: 426 calories
Total Fats: 12 gm
Saturated Fats: 4 gm   Protein: 40 gm
Unsaturated Fats: 8 gm   Sodium: 643 mg
Carbohydrates: 41 gm

SOY SAUSAGE PATTIES—
CHORIZO DE SOYA

1   pound prepared soy dough (follow package
        directions)
½   cup pineapple or cider vinegar
3   garlic cloves, minced
1   tablespoon ground cumin
½–1 teaspoon ground cayenne pepper
1   teaspoon half salt, half salt-substitute mixture
2   tablespoons vegetable oil

1. Mix all ingredients together in a medium bowl.
2. Cover and refrigerate overnight.
3. Shape soy dough into patties. In a large skillet, heat oil over medium heat and fry patties until crispy brown on both sides.
4. Blot excess oil on paper towels.
5. May be frozen for future use.

Serves 4.

Each Latina Lite serving contains: 215 calories
Total Fats: 15 gm
Saturated Fats: 2 gm   Protein: 14 gm
Unsaturated Fats: 13 gm   Sodium: 268 mg
Carbohydrates: 11 gm

MEAT TURNOVERS—*EMPANADAS*

One of the most popular *antojitos* in Latin America. Originally from Argentina, *empanadas*—meat turnovers—are enjoyed in Uruguay, Chile, Colombia, Cuba, Mexico, etc. You'll need extra time to prepare this special dish, but for a party or extraordinary dinner the results are well worth the time.

Step I:

½   *pound lean ground pork loin*
½   *pound ground turkey breast*
2   *tablespoons diced onion*
2   *tablespoons diced scallions*
1   *teaspoon ground cumin*
½   *teaspoon half salt, half salt-substitute mixture*
¼   *teaspoon freshly ground black pepper*

   1. The night before, mix meat thoroughly with onion, scallions, cumin, salt, and pepper.
   2. Cover and refrigerate.

Step II:

1   *tablespoon olive oil*
½   *cup chopped white onion*
½   *cup chopped scallions*
Meat mixture from Step I
1   *cup chopped canned tomatoes*
4   *small potatoes, boiled and mashed*
1   *teaspoon ground cumin*
¼   *teaspoon freshly ground black pepper*
½   *teaspoon half salt, half salt-substitute mixture*

1. In a large skillet, heat oil over medium heat; sauté onion and scallions until translucent; remove and set aside.

2. Brown meat mixture in same oil over medium heat.

3. Add 1 cup water; lower heat and simmer.

4. Stir occasionally for 25 minutes until meat is cooked; add sautéed onion and scallions, chopped tomatoes, mashed potatoes, and seasonings.

5. Simmer over low heat 3 to 4 minutes.

6. Allow mixture to cool.

7. You can freeze the meat filling and defrost it when you are ready to make the *empanadas*.

Makes 20 small *empanadas*.

Dough:

1   *pound freshly ground* tortilla masa,* or
3   cups Maseca *(packaged* tortilla *mix)*
1   *tablespoon light-brown sugar*
1   *tablespoon cornstarch*
½   *cup fat-free sour cream*
½   *cup water*
2   *tablespoons vegetable oil*

1. If you are using a brand of *tortilla* mix other than *Maseca*, follow directions on package for ½ pound of dough substituting ½ cup sour cream for ½ cup water.

2. Fresh dough ferments easily even under refrigeration and must be used within 24 hours.

3. Knead sugar, cornstarch, sour cream, and water into dough; divide into 20 little balls; flatten each ball into a patty about ⅛-inch thick; place a spoonful of meat mixture in middle; fold over and seal edges.

4. On a nonstick *comal*—griddle—brown *empanaditas* in oil over medium heat on all sides.

*Masa is usually sold where *tortillas* are made.

5. Remove and blot excess oil on paper towels; serve immediately.

6. You may prepare them a few hours ahead for a party and reheat in a brown paper bag in a 150°F oven. THEY CANNOT BE FROZEN.

7. Always accompany *empanadas* with *CHIMICHURRI* (page 54).

Serves 4 dinners, or 8 appetizers.

Each Latina Lite appetizer serving contains: 426 calories
Total Fats: 12 gm
Saturated Fats: 2 gm   Protein: 22 gm
Unsaturated Fats: 10 gm   Sodium: 309 mg
Carbohydrates: 55 gm

CHEESE ENCHILADAS— ENCHILADAS DE QUESO

*E*nchiladas are folded *tacos*, *tortillas* doubled over with filling inside covered by *salsa*. The filling may vary although cheese and chicken are perennial favorites.

2   chiles poblanos *or* Californias *(you may substitute any available fresh, large, long green* chiles*), cored and seeded*
2   *teaspoons vegetable oil*
½   *cup diced onion*
1   *cup tomato sauce*
½   *teaspoon half salt, half salt-substitute mixture*
½   *cup fat-free yogurt*
½   *cup fat-free sour cream*
8   corn *tortillas*
1   *cup grated white cheese*

1. Prepare *chiles* according to instructions for PREPARING FRESH *CHILES* (page 148).

2. If you prefer milder *chiles* soak them in 2 cups warm water with 1 teaspoon vinegar and ½ teaspoon salt for at least 1 hour to reduce level of *picante*.

3. Rinse and drain *chiles*, then chop.

4. In a medium skillet, heat oil over low heat; sauté onion until translucent; add *chiles* and continue to sauté.

5. Add tomato sauce and salt.

6. In a small bowl, whisk yogurt and sour cream together, blend into tomato sauce mixture.

7. Meanwhile, wrap *tortillas* in a damp cloth and microwave on High for 1 minute 20 seconds to make them pliable.

8. Place cheese on each *tortilla* and fold over.

9. Cover with heated sauce.

Serves 4.

Each Latina Lite serving contains: 310 calories
Total Fats: 7 gm
Saturated Fats: 2 gm   Protein: 24 gm
Unsaturated Fats: 5 gm   Sodium: 453 mg
Carbohydrates: 40 gm

COTTAGE CHEESE ENCHILADAS—
ENCHILADAS DE QUESO COTTAGE

8   corn tortillas
1   cup fat-free cottage cheese
½   cup fat-free sour cream
2   tablespoons chopped Italian parsley
2   tablespoons minced scallions
½   teaspoon half salt, half salt-substitute mixture

2   chiles chipotles, *canned, rinsed and dried, cored and*
      seeded
½   *cup water*
1   *tablespoon cornstarch*
½   *cup tomato sauce*
1   *chicken bouillon cube or 1 teaspoon consommé*
      granules
1   *cup fat-free yogurt*
Few sprigs fresh parsley
4   *onion rings, raw*

1. Wrap the *tortillas* in a damp cloth; microwave on High for 1 minute 20 seconds.

2. In small bowl, combine cottage cheese with sour cream, parsley, scallions, and salt; mix well; put 1 tablespoon cottage cheese mixture in each *tortilla*; fold over.

3. Arrange *enchiladas* on serving platter.

4. Purée *chiles chipotles* with ½ cup water in blender.

5. Dissolve cornstarch in puréed *chiles*.

6. Transfer purée to medium saucepan and simmer over low heat; stir constantly; add tomato sauce and bouillon.

7. When mixture begins to thicken add yogurt gradually.

8. Continue stirring until thoroughly blended.

9. Pour heated sauce over *enchiladas*.

10. Decorate with a sprig of parsley and onion ring.

Serves 4.

Each Latina Lite serving contains: 254 calories
Total Fats: 3 gm
Saturated Fats: 1 gm   Protein: 16 gm
Unsaturated Fats: 2 gm   Sodium: 933 mg
Carbohydrates: 44 gm

*T*ORTILLA, FOLDED WITH CHICKEN AND GREEN SAUCE—*ENCHILADAS SUIZAS*

8   *corn* tortillas
1½ *cups shredded cooked chicken*
½   *teaspoon half salt, half salt-substitute mixture*
½   *teaspoon freshly ground black pepper*
SALSA VERDE MEXICANA *(page 65)*

Topping:

¼   *cup fat-free plain yogurt*
¼   *cup fat-free sour cream*
1   *tablespoon Japanese seasoned rice vinegar**
¼   *cup chopped fresh cilantro*
¼   *cup crumbled part-skim milk white cheese*

1. Wrap the *tortillas* in a damp cloth; microwave on High for 1 minute 20 seconds.
2. Season chicken with salt and pepper.
3. Put chicken on each *tortilla* and fold over.
4. Place *enchiladas* on bottom of serving dish.
5. Heat the *Salsa Verde Mexicana* until very hot.
6. Combine yogurt, sour cream, and vinegar.
7. Pour heated sauce over *enchiladas*. Top with yogurt mixture and cilantro; sprinkle with cheese.

Serves 4.

Each Latina Lite serving contains: 370 calories
Total Fats: 8 gm
Saturated Fats: 3 gm   Protein: 37 gm
Unsaturated Fats: 5 gm   Sodium: 424 mg
Carbohydrates: 39 gm

*Japanese seasoned rice vinegar can be found in the Asian food section of your supermarket.

YUCA FRITTERS—FRITURAS DE YUCA

2   cups cooked yuca, *frozen or fresh*
2   *egg yolks*
1   *garlic clove, minced*
1   *tablespoon fresh lemon juice*
½   *teaspoon half salt, half salt-substitute mixture*
4   *egg whites*
2   *tablespoons vegetable oil*

1. Immediately after *yuca* is cooked, and still hot, grind in a food processor. (Hot *yuca* is tender and easy to grind.)

2. Add egg yolks, garlic, lemon juice, and salt to *yuca*.

3. In a medium bowl, beat egg whites until they peak; carefully fold into mixture.

4. Heat oil over medium heat in a large skillet; drop in teaspoons of batter; fry until golden brown on both sides; blot excess oil on paper towels; keep warm in a brown paper bag in a 150°F oven.

Serves 4.

Each Latina Lite serving contains: 211 calories
Total Fats: 10 gm
Saturated Fats: 2 gm   Protein: 8 gm
Unsaturated Fats: 8 gm   Sodium: 440 mg
Carbohydrates: 24 gm

PLANTAINS PICKLED IN *AJILIMOJILI*— *GUINEOS VERDES EN AJILIMOJILI*

4   green plantains
4   cups water
1   teaspoon half salt, half salt-substitute mixture
AJILIMOJILI *sauce, double recipe (page 54)*

1. Slit peel lengthwise on green plantains.
2. In a medium saucepan, bring water and salt to a boil, add plantains; cover; lower heat and simmer for 15 minutes; drain and peel.
3. When cool cut plantains into ½-inch rounds.
4. Place in a rectangular glass dish in layers, covering each layer with *Ajilimójili* sauce.
5. Top with sauce; cover with plastic wrap and refrigerate for 24 hours.

Serves 12 appetizers.

Each Latina Lite appetizer serving contains: 87 calories
Total Fats: 2 gm
Saturated Fats: 0 gm   Protein: 1 gm
Unsaturated Fats: 2 gm   Sodium: 129 mg
Carbohydrates: 17 gm

Cooked cheese, tamaulipas-style— GUISADO DE QUESO TAMAULIPECO

2   teaspoons vegetable oil
½   cup diced white onion
4   fresh chiles poblanos or Californias, cored, seeded, cut into strips (you may substitute any available fresh, large, long green chiles)
1½ cups tomato juice
1   chicken bouillon cube or 1 teaspoon consommé granules
2   cups cubed part-skim milk white cheese
8   corn tortillas TOSTADAS (page 203), broken into chips

   1. In a large skillet, heat oil over medium heat; lightly brown onion; add *chile* strips, tomato juice, and bouillon; mix well.
   2. Lower heat and simmer for 10 to 12 minutes.
   3. Add cheese and continue to simmer for another 2 minutes.
   4. Serve hot with toasted *tortilla* chips.

Serves 4 dinners or 8 appetizers

Each Latina Lite appetizer serving contains: 183 calories
Total Fats: 7 gm
Saturated Fats: 3 gm   Protein: 11 gm
Unsaturated Fats: 4 gm   Sodium: 332 mg
Carbohydrates: 21 gm

CHEESE TURNOVERS IN BEANS— INDITOS

4   chiles pasillas, *packaged dried*
2   *cups cooked black beans*
1   *cup chicken stock or 1 bouillon cube or 1 teaspoon*
        consommé granules with 1 cup water
4   corn *tortillas, cut in half*
1   *egg yolk*
2   *egg whites*
1   *cup grated part-skim milk cheese*
2   *tablespoons vegetable oil*
½   *cup fat-free plain yogurt*
½   *cup fat-free sour cream*
1   *tablespoon Japanese seasoned rice vinegar*[*]
4   *tablespoons crumbled part-skim milk white cheese*

1. Soak *chiles* in warm water until pliable; core and seed.
2. Purée *chiles*, beans, and stock in the blender.
3. Transfer bean mixture to a large saucepan; simmer at low heat.
4. Wrap *tortillas* in a damp cloth and microwave on High for 1 minute to make them pliable.
5. In a small bowl, beat egg yolk and whites together.
6. Place 1 level tablespoon of cheese in middle of each half *tortilla*, fold like a turnover, pin with a toothpick, and dip into the egg mixture.
7. In a large skillet, heat oil over medium heat; brown the *tortilla* turnovers on all sides.
8. Blot excess oil on paper towels.
9. In a small bowl, whisk yogurt, sour cream, and vinegar together.
10. Place *tortilla* turnovers into hot bean sauce and simmer for 3 minutes.

[*]Japanese seasoned rice vinegar can be found in the Asian food section of your supermarket.

11. Serve hot with cheese sprinkled on top, accompanied by the yogurt mixture.

Serves 4.

Each Latina Lite serving contains: 470 calories
Total Fats: 17 gm
Saturated Fats: 6 gm   Protein: 29 gm
Unsaturated Fats: 11 gm   Sodium: 533 mg
Carbohydrates: 53 gm

PLANTAIN BALLS—*MOFONGO*

2   *green plantains, peeled and cut into ½-inch diagonals*
1   *quart water*
1   *teaspoon half salt, half salt-substitute mixture*
3   *tablespoons olive oil*
1   *cup diced lean smoked turkey ham*
2   *large garlic cloves, halved*

1. Soak green plantain diagonals in water and ½ teaspoon salt for 15 minutes.
2. Meanwhile, in a large skillet, heat 2 tablespoons olive oil over medium heat; fry turkey ham until well browned.
3. Remove turkey ham with a slotted spoon; save oil.
4. Blot excess oil from turkey ham with paper towels.
5. Drain and dry plantain slices; fry on both sides (DO NOT BROWN) in same oil used for turkey ham.
6. In a mortar, crush garlic cloves, remaining ½ teaspoon salt, and remaining 1 tablespoon of olive oil.
7. Set mixture aside.
8. In same mortar, crush part of fried plantain slices with the browned turkey ham; add part of garlic mixture.
9. Repeat process until all is ground.

10. Form 4 2-inch balls.
11. Keep warm in 150°F oven.
12. Serve hot with your favorite sauce or with soup.

Serves 4.

Each Latina Lite serving contains: 263 calories
Total Fats: 13 gm
Saturated Fats: 2 gm   Protein: 12 gm
Unsaturated Fats: 11 gm   Sodium: 1020 mg
Carbohydrates: 27 gm

Puerto Rican-Style Dumplings— *Pasteles*

Filling:

½   *pound ground turkey breast*
1   *cup chickpeas (garbanzos), cooked or canned and drained*
10 *pimiento-stuffed olives, finely chopped*
2   *teaspoons capers*
2   *teaspoons raisins*
1   *tablespoon SOFRITO (page 66)*

1. In a medium bowl, mix all ingredients for the filling together.
2. Set aside.

Dough:

2   *cups peeled yautía*
2   *cups green plantains*
½   *cup warm milk*

1   tablespoon Cuban **ACHIOTE** oil *(page 50)*
8   *plantain leaves for cooking or green corn husks or
        cooking papers*

1. Grate *yautía* and plantains into a large bowl; mash together with lukewarm milk to form a smooth paste; divide dough into 8 balls.

2. Brush *Achiote* oil on each leaf or paper.

3. Place 1 ball of dough in middle of each leaf; form a depression and insert ⅛ of filling.

4. Fold leaf or paper and tie with kitchen string.

5. In a large saucepan, bring 3 quarts of water with 1 tea-spoon salt to a boil.

6. Add the 8 *pasteles*; boil, covered, for ½ hour; turn *pasteles*; boil, covered, for 30 minutes more.

7. Remove from the water with a slotted spoon.

Serves 4 dinners or 8 appetizers.

Each Latina Lite appetizer serving contains: 240 calories
Total Fats: 6 gm
Saturated Fats: 1 gm   Protein: 11 gm
Unsaturated Fats: 5 gm   Sodium: 193 mg
Carbohydrates: 35 gm

Q̃UESADILLAS

Traditional melted cheese-*tortilla* fold-overs, *quesadillas* can be prepared with vegetables, lowfat cheese, or lowfat meat filling. They are best eaten hot accompanied by GREEN SAUCE or RED SAUCE and *GUACAMOLE* (pages 65, 64, and 182).

Dough:

½ *pound freshly ground* tortilla masa,* or
2 *cups* Maseca *(packaged* tortilla *mix)*
½ *cup fat-free sour cream*
¼ *cup water*
½ *teaspoon baking powder*
2 *tablespoons vegetable oil*

Cheese Filling:

1 *cup grated part-skim milk white cheese*

1. If you are using freshly ground corn for dough, add ¼ cup fat-free sour cream and baking powder.
2. With *Maseca* knead with sour cream and water until a smooth dough is formed; mix in baking powder.
3. Divide into 8 parts.
4. Cut 2 thin plastic film rounds for both sides of a *tortilla* press; place dough inside and press.
5. Repeat 8 times. (You may form *tortillas* by hand.)
6. Place cheese inside dough; fold and seal ends.
7. In a large nonstick skillet, heat oil over medium heat; lightly fry both sides until golden brown.
8. Blot excess oil on paper towels.

Serves 4 dinners or 8 appetizers.

Each Latina Lite appetizer serving contains: 181 calories
Total Fats: 9 gm
Saturated Fats: 3 gm   Protein: 10 gm
Unsaturated Fats: 6 gm   Sodium: 226 mg
Carbohydrates: 16 gm

*Masa is usually sold where *tortillas* are made.

VARIATIONS:
Instead of cheese, fill the *quesadilla* with REFRIED BEANS (page 194), *CHILE* STRIPS AND ONION (page 155), CUBAN *PICADILLO* (page 144), or *CHAMPINONES TAPATIOS* (page 158).

$\mathcal{S}$EAFOOD COMBINATION COCKTAIL— *VUELVE A LA VIDA*

A hearty elegant delight whose taste lingers on the palate. Whether served on special occasions or every day, the comments will be, "This is ambrosia—food fit for the gods."

16 *large cooked shrimp, cleaned and peeled*
16 *oysters*
1   *cup cooked octopus, cleaned and chopped*
Juice of 6 lemons
1   *cup tomato sauce*
1   *teaspoon mustard*
2   *tablespoons Japanese seasoned rice vinegar**
1   *tablespoon sugar*
1   *tablespoon Worcestershire sauce*
1   *medium onion, finely diced*
4   *tablespoons chopped fresh cilantro*
1   *avocado, peeled and sliced*
SALSA ROJA MEXICANA *(page 64)*

   1. In a medium bowl, combine shrimp, oysters, and octopus.
   2. Pour lemon juice over seafood.
   3. Refrigerate for 1 hour.
   4. Meanwhile, in a small bowl, combine tomato sauce, mustard, vinegar, sugar, and Worcestershire.

---

*Japanese seasoned rice vinegar can be found in the Asian food section of your supermarket.

5. Just before serving, remove seafood from refrigerator; add sauce, onion, and cilantro; mix thoroughly.

6. Divide into 8 portions.

7. Top with sliced avocado.

8. Serve with fresh *Salsa Roja Mexicana*.

Serves 8.

Each Latina Lite serving contains: 200 calories

Total Fats:	7 gm
Saturated Fats:	1 gm
Unsaturated Fats:	6 gm
Carbohydrates:	17 gm

Protein: 18 gm
Sodium: 430 mg

TACOS

Most Americans consider *tacos* the *haute cuisine* of Mexico. The truth is *tacos* are seldom served as a main dish. Traditionally, *taquerías*—*taco* stands—open in early evening and sell their *tacos* for *cenas*—suppers, or evening snacks. Although a *taco* is nothing more than a rolled or folded filled corn *tortilla*, there is an art to making a good one. The *tortillas* must be fresh and hot and the ingredients well combined and fresh. *Tacos* from the northern states are usually fried and crispy while central and southern varieties are apt to be soft. I've included five of the most popular *tacos*, but invent your own by serving your favorite *platillos* in a rolled or folded, crisp or soft *tortilla*.

TACOS WITH CHICKEN, GOLDEN FRIED— FLAUTAS DORADAS DE PANCHO VILLA

12 small corn tortillas *(3-inch diameter)* or
    8 ordinary-size tortillas
2 *chicken breasts, skinned, cooked, and shredded*
SALSA ROJA MEXICANA *(page 64)*
2 *tablespoons vegetable oil*
2 *cups grated lettuce*

1. Wrap *tortillas* in a damp cloth and microwave on High for 1½ minutes to make them pliable.

2. Place ½₂ of shredded chicken on each small *tortilla* with ½ teaspoon *Salsa Roja Mexicana* or ⅛ of shredded chicken with ¾ teaspoon *Salsa* on a large one.

3. Fasten with a toothpick if necessary.

4. In a large skillet, heat oil over high heat; brown on all sides; remove with slotted spoon; blot excess oil on paper towels.

5. Remove toothpicks; keep warm in 150°F oven.

6. Serve covered with grated lettuce accompanied by remaining *Salsa Roja Mexicana*.

Serves 4.

Each Latina Lite serving contains: 346 calories
Total Fats: 12 gm
Saturated Fats: 2 gm   Protein: 27 gm
Unsaturated Fats: 10 gm   Sodium: 494 mg
Carbohydrates: 34 gm

*T*ACOS WITH CHARCOAL-GRILLED STEAK— *TACOS AL CARBON*

1   *pound top sirloin, trimmed*
8   *corn* tortillas
2   *teaspoons vegetable oil*
PICO DE GALLO *(page 61)*
2   *lemons, quartered*

1. Grill steak over charcoal.

2. In a large skillet, heat *tortillas* in oil over low heat; DO NOT BROWN *TORTILLAS.*

3. Cut cooked steak into bite-size pieces hot off the grill; place on *tortillas*; roll and eat.

4. Serve with *Pico de Gallo* and lemon garnish.

Serves 4.

Each Latina Lite serving contains: 413 calories
Total Fats: 13 gm
Saturated Fats: 4 gm   Protein: 39 gm
Unsaturated Fats: 9 gm   Sodium: 180 mg
Carbohydrates: 36 gm

 # TACOS WITH GRILLED PORK—
TACOS AL PASTOR

½   cup fresh orange juice
2   tablespoons fresh lemon juice
2   garlic cloves, minced
½   teaspoon half salt, half salt-substitute mixture
1   pound pork loin, trimmed of all fat
8   corn tortillas
1   tablespoon vegetable oil
1   cup canned, unsweetened pineapple cubes, drained
½   cup chopped fresh cilantro
PICO DE GALLO *(page 61)*

1. In a medium bowl, combine orange and lemon juices, garlic, and salt; marinate pork in mixture for at least 2 hours; remove pork; discard marinade.

2. Grill meat over charcoal on a spit or turning frequently until well cooked; DO NOT CHAR MEAT.

3. Cut pork into thin, bite-size slices.

4. In a large skillet, heat *tortillas* in hot oil; DO NOT BROWN.

5. Roll meat in hot *tortillas*.

6. Serve with pineapple cubes, cilantro, and *Pico de Gallo*.

Serves 4.

Each Latina Lite serving contains: 473 calories

Total Fats: 15 gm	
Saturated Fats: 4 gm	Protein: 40 gm
Unsaturated Fats: 11 gm	Sodium: 314 mg
Carbohydrates: 48 gm	

ISH *TACOS—TACOS DE PESCADO*

Topping:

2   *tablespoons mayonnaise*
2   *tablespoons fat-free yogurt*
1   *tablespoon pickle relish*

3   *tablespoons all-purpose flour*
¼   *cup corn flake crumbs*
2   *tablespoons oat bran*
½   *teaspoon half salt, half salt-substitute mixture*
2   *egg whites*
1   *pound fish fillets*
2   *tablespoons vegetable oil*
8   tortillas
1   *cup grated lettuce*
PICO DE GALLO *(page 61)*

1. In a small bowl, mix mayonnaise, yogurt, and pickle relish together for Topping; set aside.

2. On a sheet of wax paper, combine flour, corn flake crumbs, oat bran, and salt.

3. In a shallow bowl, beat egg whites.

4. Dip each fish fillet in egg whites, then bread with crumbs.

5. In a large skillet, heat oil over high heat; fry fish 2 minutes until crispy on both sides; blot excess oil on paper towels.

6. While frying fish, wrap *tortillas* in a damp cloth and microwave on High for 1½ minutes.

7. Place fish on the 8 *tortillas*; cover with grated lettuce, add Topping and serve with *Pico de Gallo*.

Serves 4.

Each Latina Lite serving contains: 450 calories

Total Fats:	16 gm	
Saturated Fats:	2 gm	Protein: 36 gm
Unsaturated Fats:	14 gm	Sodium: 495 mg
Carbohydrates:	43 gm	

STEAMED *TACOS—TACOS SUDADOS*

2   chiles anchos, *packaged dried, cored and seeded*
1   chile pasilla, *packaged dried, cored and seeded*
¼   *onion, cut into chunks*
1   *small garlic clove, halved*
1   *tablespoon peanut butter*
½   *teaspoon half salt, half salt-substitute mixture*
½   *pound pork loin, cooked and shredded (reserve broth)*
8   corn tortillas

1. Soak *chiles* in ¼ cup of reserved fat-free pork broth until soft.

2. Purée *chiles*, onion, and garlic in the blender; pour into a large skillet over medium heat.

3. Add peanut butter and salt; stir until smooth; add pork.

4. Lower heat and simmer, uncovered, for 10 minutes.

5. Wrap *tortillas* in a damp cloth and microwave on High for 1½ minutes to make them pliable.

6. Fill each *tortilla* with ⅛ of pork mixture, fold, and place on a steamer rack.

7. Steam for 15 minutes. (If you do not have a steamer, wrap *tacos* in a damp cloth and bake inside a straw basket at 150°F for 5 minutes.)

Serves 4.

Each Latina Lite serving contains: 641 calories
Total Fats: 38 gm
Saturated Fats: 8 gm   Protein: 37 gm
Unsaturated Fats: 30 gm   Sodium: 575 mg
Carbohydrates: 45 gm

*T*ACOS WITH PLANTAIN— *TACOS TABASQUENOS*

1   *tablespoon vegetable oil*
1   *plantain, ripe (black-brown skin), peeled and cut into ⅛-inch diagonals*
8   *corn* tortillas
CHIRMOLE *(page 154)*

1. In a large skillet, heat oil over high heat; brown plantain slices; remove with slotted spoon; blot excess oil on paper towels.

2. Lower flame; heat *tortillas* in the same oil; DO NOT BROWN.

3. Roll 2 plantain slices in each *tortilla*; if necessary, fasten with a toothpick.

4. Serve hot; top with *Chirmole*.

Serves 4.

Each Latina Lite serving contains: 270 calories
Total Fats: 7 gm
Saturated Fats: 1 gm   Protein: 6 gm
Unsaturated Fats: 6 gm   Sodium: 342 mg
Carbohydrates: 52 gm

MEXICAN TURKEY HAM SANDWICH— TORTA DE JAMON

Once you've eaten a *torta* you'll never be satisfied with an ordinary sandwich again. Everybody likes them. One of the most famous *torta* shops in all Mexico is located on the *Zocalo* (principal plaza) of Toluca, capital of the state of Mexico. People from all over the Republic crowd in to buy freshly prepared hot *tortas*. The contents may vary, but *tortas* are always prepared on Mexican *bolillos*—French-style rolls.

1   birote *or* bolillo *(Mexican roll) or 1 3- to 4-inch slice of French bread*
1   *teaspoon mayonnaise*
1   *teaspoon fat-free plain yogurt*
2   *slices lean turkey ham*
1   *slice white cheese*
Grated lettuce
½   *tomato, sliced*
3   *thin red onion slices*
¼   *ripe avocado, sliced*
2–4 *strips canned* jalapeño chile

1. Heat bread in a toaster oven, and while still hot, cut it in half lengthwise.

2. Mix mayonnaise and yogurt; spread on one side of bread; place turkey ham and cheese on the bread; top with other half of roll; grill both sides.

3. While still hot, add lettuce, tomato, onion slices, and avocado; top with *chile*.

4. Cut sandwich in half.

Serves 1.

Each Latina Lite serving contains: 400 calories
Total Fats: 20 gm
Saturated Fats: 6 gm   Protein: 25 gm
Unsaturated Fats: 14 gm   Sodium: 975 mg
Carbohydrates: 32 gm

$\mathcal{S}$ANDWICHES, DROWNED IN SAUCE— *TORTAS AHOGADAS*

2   *cups tomato sauce*
3   *garlic cloves, minced*
½   *teaspoon dried oregano*
3   *whole cloves*
½   *teaspoon half salt, half salt-substitute mixture*
4   bolillos *(Mexican French-style rolls)*
1   *cup* REFRIED BEANS LATINA LITE *(page 195)*
½   *pound chicken, cooked and shredded*
Canned chile, *to taste*

1. In a small saucepan, simmer tomato sauce with garlic, oregano, cloves, and salt for 5 minutes; remove and discard cloves; transfer to a serving bowl.

2. Cut *bolillos* in half lengthwise.

3. Spread ¼ of beans on the roll.

4. Arrange shredded chicken over beans; put *chile* on sandwich and submerge in tomato sauce for a "dripping good" *torta*.

5. If you prefer "half drowned," submerge half of the sandwich in the sauce.

Serves 4.

 Each Latina Lite serving contains: 239 calories
Total Fats: 5 gm
Saturated Fats: 1 gm   Protein: 24 gm
Unsaturated Fats: 4 gm   Sodium: 998 mg
Carbohydrates: 27 gm

Sauces and Seasonings—Salsas y Sazonadores

To a Latina, *salsa* is more than just a dance—it is the foundation of Latina cooking. Most dishes derive their flavors from special *salsas* and seasonings. Some are Puerto Rican, others Cuban or Mexican. Try them all! Basic sauces include *recaito*, *achiote* oil, *sofrito*, Mexican *achiote*, *ajilimójili*, *mojito de ajo*, *salsa verde* (green sauce), *salsa roja* (red sauce), *mole*, Cuban and Mexican *adobo*, and a pickling sauce called *escabeche*. Remember, *chiles* vary in their degree of *picante*. Reduce or increase the number of *chiles* in these lowfat *salsas* according to your taste.

Annato and Oil—Achiote Cubano

Achiote oil, also called *axiote* and *annato*, is widely used in Cuban *SOFRITO*. It adds a distinctive flavor to Cuban cooking. This bright orange-red seasoned oil is made from *achiote* seeds, which are also used to flavor Mexican dishes from the Caribbean states. The Cuban seeds are sold by weight, and are usually available in Latino markets. Mexican *axiote* seeds are sold precrushed and seasoned in block form.

2   *cups olive oil*
½   *cup* achiote *seeds or* ½ *block Mexican* axiote
       (If using Mexican axiote, *dissolve in* ¼ *cup hot water)*

1. In a small saucepan, heat oil over medium heat; when hot, add seeds or half the *axiote* block dissolved in warm water; lower heat and simmer for 5 minutes until oil acquires a rich orange-red color.
2. Remove from heat; cool.
3. Strain oil, discard seeds, and store in a jar in refrigerator for later use.
4. The oil will keep for several months.

Makes 2 cups.

This Latina Lite recipe contains: 3820 calories;
one teaspoon contains 38 calories

Total Fats:	432 gm	
Saturated Fats:	58 gm	Protein: 0 gm
Unsaturated Fats:	374 gm	Sodium: 0 mg
Carbohydrates:	0 gm	

ANNATO AND LEMON— *ACHIOTE MEXICANO*

½   *block* achiote *(also spelled* axiote*)*
2   *tablespoons olive oil*
½   *cup fresh lemon juice or vinegar*

1. Dissolve the *achiote* with the oil and lemon juice in a small bowl. *Achiote* sauce may be used for fish, chicken, or pork.
2. Cover meat, fowl, or fish with sauce and marinate in a covered glass dish overnight in refrigerator.

3. To prepare, wrap small amounts of fish, chicken, or pork in a corn husk or banana leaf; include a small strip of canned *jalapeño chile*; steam.

4. To prepare a dried corn husk, soak until pliable, place contents inside, and tie at both ends. A banana leaf may be folded into a square without tying.

5. *Achiote* imparts a marvelous taste without adding excessive fat.

Makes ¾ cup.

This Latina Lite recipe contains: 287 calories
Total Fats:	28 gm		
Saturated Fats:	4 gm	Protein:	1 gm
Unsaturated Fats:	24 gm	Sodium:	2 mg
Carbohydrates:	14 gm		

SPICY SEASONING—ADOBO

Adobo can be used for fish, meat, or poultry. This version, a common seasoning in Puerto Rico, is enough to flavor 1½ pounds of raw fish, poultry, or meat. Because *adobos* are commonly thought to preserve food, some of us neglect to chill them. Bacteria can thrive in all fish, meat, and poultry, so be sure to refrigerate *adobos*.

2   *garlic cloves, minced*
¼   *medium onion, finely chopped*
1   *teaspoon dried oregano*
¼   *teaspoon half salt, half salt-substitute mixture*
½   *teaspoon freshly ground black pepper*

1. In a small bowl, combine all ingredients; rub on skinless chicken, fish, or meat.

2. Refrigerate for 2 to 3 hours to season well.

Makes 2 ounces.

This Latina Lite recipe contains: 30 calories
Total Fats: 0 gm
Saturated Fats: 0 gm   Protein: 1 gm
Unsaturated Fats: 0 gm   Sodium: 535 mg
Carbohydrates: 7 gm

GARLIC, *CHILE,* AND VINEGAR SAUCE— *ADOBO MEXICANO*

Mexican *adobo* is hotter—*más picante*—than Cuban or Puerto Rican *adobo.* Try it for a different taste treat.

3   chiles anchos, *packaged dried*
3   *garlic cloves, peeled*
2   *tablespoons cider or pineapple vinegar*
¼   *teaspoon half salt, half salt-substitute mixture*
¼   *teaspoon freshly ground black pepper*

   1. Remove seeds and core from *chiles.*
   2. In a covered saucepan over low heat, cook *chiles* in ½ cup water for 8 minutes.
   3. Empty cooked *chiles* and liquid into blender, add garlic, vinegar, salt, and pepper.
   4. Spread *adobo* over 1½ pounds raw fish, meat, or poultry and refrigerate for 2 to 3 hours before cooking.

Makes ¾ cup.

This Latina Lite recipe contains: 46 calories
Total Fats: 1 gm
Saturated Fats: 0 gm   Protein: 2 gm
Unsaturated Fats: 1 gm   Sodium: 1934 mg
Carbohydrates: 11 gm

Sauce, GARLIC, PEPPER, AND LEMON— *AJILIMOJILI* SAUCE

A traditional Puerto Rican sauce served as an accompaniment to fish and chicken. Also makes *TOSTONES* (page 170) or vegetables tastier.

2   *garlic cloves, minced*
5   *sweet* chile *peppers or Italian peppers, peeled*
¼   *teaspoon half salt, half salt-substitute mixture*
¼   *teaspoon freshly ground black pepper*
2   *tablespoons fresh lemon juice*
2   *tablespoons olive oil*

1. Grind garlic and *chiles* in a food processor; add salt, pepper, lemon juice, and oil; mix thoroughly.

Serves 4.

Each Latina Lite serving contains: 80 calories
Total Fats: 7 gm
Saturated Fats: 1 gm   Protein: 1 gm
Unsaturated Fats: 6 gm   Sodium: 102 mg
Carbohydrates: 5 gm

Sauce WITH PARSLEY FROM ARGENTINA—*CHIMICHURRI*

Salsa Picante—hot sauce—found at almost every Mexican meal, has its counterpart in *chimichurri*, the ubiquitous sauce of Argentina, Uruguay, and Chile. A blending of Italian and Latin flavors, it enhances grilled meat and poultry. Rave reviews will be yours when you serve it with *EMPANADAS* (page 25) at a special *comida*—dinner.

½   cup olive oil
4   garlic cloves, halved
2   tablespoons balsamic vinegar
2   tablespoons cider vinegar
1   teaspoon fresh lemon juice
½   teaspoon fresh oregano
½   teaspoon fresh basil
1   cup finely chopped fresh Italian parsley
½   teaspoon half salt, half salt-substitute mixture
Freshly ground black pepper to taste

1. Purée all ingredients except parsley, salt, and pepper in the blender.

2. Place parsley in a glass jar with a tight lid. (Do not use plastic!)

3. Pour purée into jar.

4. Season with salt and pepper and shake vigorously.

5. Refrigerate for at least 2 days before using.

6. *Chimichurri* will last about 2 weeks refrigerated.

Serves 8.

Each Latina Lite serving contains: 245 calories
Total Fats: 27 gm
Saturated Fats: 4 gm   Protein: 0 gm
Unsaturated Fats: 23 gm   Sodium: 72 mg
Carbohydrates: 2 gm

$\mathcal{S}$AUCE WITH PARSLEY AND *CHILE—CHIMICHURRI MEXICANO*

1. Use the above recipe and add 1 to 2 small red very hot *chiles de arbol*, seeded and cored, to ingredients in blender. Substitute 1 cup fresh chopped cilantro for the parsley.
2. Store refrigerated in a glass jar.
3. This version has zing!

Serves 8.

Each Latina Lite serving contains: 248 calories
Total Fats: 27 gm
Saturated Fats: 4 gm   Protein: 0 gm
Unsaturated Fats: 23 gm   Sodium: 261 mg
Carbohydrates: 2 gm

$\mathcal{P}$ICKLING SAUCE, CUBAN OR PUERTO RICAN—*ESCABECHE*

Escabeche, a pickling sauce originally from Spain, historically dates from the time when refrigeration was unavailable to preserve food. Its ingredients vary from place to place. Traditionally, white vinegar was used since it was readily available, but for a different flavor in the two versions of Latina Lite *Escabeches*, try substituting balsamic, pineapple, apple, or Japanese seasoned rice vinegar.

4 tablespoons olive oil
3 large onions, sliced
1 green bell pepper, cored, seeded, and sliced
4 bay leaves
1 tablespoon black peppercorns
4 garlic cloves, minced
¼ cup pitted and chopped green olives
¼ cup capers (alcaparras)
¾ cup cider vinegar

1. In a medium skillet, heat oil over medium heat.

2. Add onions, green pepper, and bay leaves; sauté about 3 minutes or until onions are translucent.

3. Add remaining ingredients, lower heat, and simmer 2 minutes more; blend well.

4. Transfer into a glass-covered container with either poached fish, chicken, or boiled vegetables, such as carrots, *yuca*, mushrooms, or whole lightly steamed garlic. The pickling brine, *escabeche*, must cover the contents.

5. Seal the container with a tight-fitting lid and refrigerate for 3 days or more.

Makes 3½ cups *escabeche*.

This Latina Lite recipe contains: 722 calories
Total Fats: 60 gm
Saturated Fats: 8 gm   Protein: 9 gm
Unsaturated Fats: 52 gm   Sodium: 2216 mg
Carbohydrates: 51 gm

MEXICAN PICKLING SAUCE— *ESCABECHE MEXICANO*

4   *tablespoons olive oil*
5   *garlic cloves, minced*
4   *bay leaves*
3   *large onions, sliced*
6   chiles jalapeños, *washed and cut at both ends*
½   *cup cider vinegar*
½   *teaspoon half salt, half salt-substitute mixture*
1   *teaspoon black peppercorns*
1   *cup water*
3   *cloves*
1   *tablespoon fresh thyme* (tomillo)
½   *teaspoon fresh marjoram* (mejorana)

1. In a medium skillet, heat oil over medium heat; add garlic, bay leaves, onions, and *chiles*; sauté over low heat until skin on *chiles* begins to blister.

2. Add vinegar, salt, peppercorns, water, cloves, thyme, and marjoram; bring mixture to a boil; lower heat, cover, and simmer for 5 minutes.

3. Pour over vegetables, poached fish, or chicken in a container with a tight-fitting lid.

4. Chill in refrigerator for 48 hours; it will pickle perfectly.

Makes 4 cups *escabeche.*

This Latina Lite recipe contains: 700 calories
Total Fats: 56 gm
Saturated Fats: 5 gm   Protein: 7 gm
Unsaturated Fats: 51 gm   Sodium: 38 mg
Carbohydrates: 52 gm

SAUCE WITH GARLIC—
MOJITO DE AJO

Traditional Spanish garlic sauce. In Cuba and Puerto Rico, commonly used with *tostones* and vegetables. In Mexico, usually served with fish. Easy to make and delicious, this lowfat version may become habit-forming.

4   garlic cloves, minced
3   tablespoons olive oil
¼   teaspoon half salt, half salt-substitute mixture

1. In a small skillet, heat oil over low heat; sauté garlic until it is lightly toasted; add salt.
2. Serve hot.
3. If you wish, refrigerate this garlic sauce and serve cold.

Serves 4.

Each Latina Lite serving contains: 95 calories
Total Fats: 10 gm
Saturated Fats: 1 gm   Protein: 0 gm
Unsaturated Fats: 9 gm   Sodium: 126 mg
Carbohydrates: 1 gm

SAUCE WITH GARLIC AND *CHILE—* *MOJITO DE AJO LAS BUGAMBILIAS*

3   tablespoons olive oil
2   chiles pasillas, *packaged dried, cored and seeded,* *cut into strips*
6   *garlic cloves, minced*
¼   *teaspoon half salt, half salt-substitute mixture*

1. In a small skillet, heat oil over medium heat; sauté *chiles pasillas* until oil takes on color of the *chiles*; add garlic and lightly sauté; add salt.
2. Serve hot.

Serves 4.

Each Latina Lite serving contains: 98 calories
Total Fats: 10 gm
Saturated Fats: 1 gm   Protein: 0 gm
Unsaturated Fats: 9 gm   Sodium: 308 mg
Carbohydrates: 2 gm

CUBAN-STYLE GARLIC SAUCE— *MOJITO CRIOLLO*

3   *tablespoons vegetable oil*
4   *garlic cloves, minced*
1   *tablespoon fresh orange juice*
1   *tablespoon fresh lime or lemon juice*
¼   *teaspoon half salt, half salt-substitute mixture*

1. In a small skillet, heat oil over low heat; sauté garlic until lightly toasted; add orange and lime juices, and salt.

2. Serve hot.

Serves 4.

Each Latina Lite serving contains: 97 calories
Total Fats: 10 gm	
Saturated Fats: 1 gm	Protein: 0 gm
Unsaturated Fats: 9 gm	Sodium: 101 mg
Carbohydrates: 2 gm	

SAUCE WITH *CHILE*, SHARP AS A ROOSTER'S BEAK—*PICO DE GALLO*

A sauce for the brave at heart. More *picante* than its *primo hermano*—first cousin, red sauce, which is described later in this section—it probably will *enchilar*—burn your tongue. If this happens, do not drink water; put a few grains of soothing salt on your tongue.

2 large tomatoes, skinned and chopped
3 tablespoons finely diced onion
3 scallions, chopped
2 garlic cloves, minced
½ cup chopped fresh cilantro
½ teaspoon fresh lime or lemon juice
4–6 fresh serrano chiles (small green), seeded, cored, and
        minced

1. In a small bowl, combine all ingredients just before serving.

Serves 4.

Each Latina Lite serving contains: 46 calories
Total Fats: 0 gm
Saturated Fats: 0 gm   Protein: 2 gm
Unsaturated Fats: 0 gm   Sodium: 16 mg
Carbohydrates: 10 gm

BASIC CARIBBEAN SAUCE—*RECAITO*

Many Latin dishes from the Caribbean utilize *SOFRITO* (page 66). To make *Sofrito*, you must begin with *Recaíto*, which blends the best native Carib Indian, Spanish, and African seasoning.

½   *medium yellow onion, diced*
3   *mild* **chiles,** *seeded and diced*
2   *garlic cloves, quartered*
1   *green bell pepper, seeded and diced*
3   **recao** *leaves or 4 sprigs fresh cilantro, chopped*

1. Combine all ingredients in a blender. (It may be necessary to add 1 to 2 tablespoons of water before blending.)
2. You may want to prepare double or triple this recipe, and store ½-cup portions of sauce in zippered plastic bags.
3. Refrigerated, *Recaíto* will last about 10 days; frozen, it will last for 6 months.

Makes 1½ cups.

This Latina Lite recipe contains: 115 calories
Total Fats: 0 gm
Saturated Fats: 0 gm   Protein: 5 gm
Unsaturated Fats: 0 gm   Sodium: 16 mg
Carbohydrates: 27 gm

$\mathscr{C}$OOKED RED SAUCE—
SALSA RANCHERA

2   teaspoons vegetable oil
1   red tomato, canned and finely diced
1   cup tomato sauce
2   green chiles serranos, cored, seeded, and finely
       minced
1   medium onion, finely diced
¼   teaspoon half salt, half salt-substitute mixture
2   tablespoons chopped fresh cilantro

1. In a small skillet, heat oil over low heat; combine all ingredients except cilantro; simmer for 5 minutes; add cilantro.

Serves 4.

Each Latina Lite serving contains: 61 calories
Total Fats: 3 gm
Saturated Fats: 0 gm   Protein: 2 gm
Unsaturated Fats: 3 gm   Sodium: 770 mg
Carbohydrates: 9 gm

RAW RED SAUCE—*SALSA ROJA MEXICANA*

We use *Salsa Roja* daily in our home. It converts a simple *tortilla* into a *taco sabroso* and enhances the flavor of fish, poultry, eggs, *quesadillas*, soups, meat, and vegetables. Easy to prepare and flavorful, *Salsa Roja*, with its low fat and salt content, changes an ordinary dish into fun eating.

2   *red tomatoes, peeled* and finely diced
       (Fresh tomatoes are better; in emergencies 4
       canned tomatoes may be used)*

2   *green* **chiles serranos,** *cored, seeded, and finely
       minced*

1   *tablespoon chopped fresh cilantro*

1   *medium onion, finely diced*

2   *teaspoons vegetable oil*

¼   *teaspoon half salt, half salt-substitute mixture*

1. In a serving bowl, mix all ingredients well.

Serves 4.

Each Latina Lite serving contains: 63 calories
Total Fats: 3 gm
Saturated Fats: 0 gm   Protein: 2 gm
Unsaturated Fats: 3 gm   Sodium: 112 mg
Carbohydrates: 10 gm

*To peel tomatoes, gently scorch tomato skin over stove burner until it blisters; wrap tomatoes in a cool damp cloth for a few minutes. The peel will separate easily.

GREEN SAUCE—*SALSA VERDE MEXICANA*

Salsa Verde takes the place of Red Sauce in many dishes. The pungent taste of small green Indian tomatoes is pleasing to the palate. Eggs, *enchiladas*, *tamales*, and many other traditional *platillos* can be prepared with either green or red sauce. The firm *tomates verdes*, also called *tomatillos*, still encased in their paperlike skin, which must be discarded before using, are readily found in Latin markets.

16 *green tomatoes, quartered*
2 *green chiles serranos, seeded and minced*
2 *garlic cloves, minced*
4 *tablespoons chopped fresh cilantro*
1 *medium onion, finely diced*
¼ *teaspoon half salt, half salt-substitute mixture*

    1. In a large skillet, simmer green tomatoes with *chiles*, 1 garlic clove, and 2 tablespoons cilantro for 5 minutes; do not overcook *tomatillos*; they should remain firm.
    2. When sauce cools, add onion, remaining garlic clove, remaining 2 tablespoons cilantro, and salt.
    3. Purée in blender.

Serves 8.

Each Latina Lite serving contains: 41 calories
Total Fats: 1 gm
Saturated Fats: 0 gm   Protein: 1 gm
Unsaturated Fats: 1 gm   Sodium: 54 mg
Carbohydrates: 8 gm

VARIATION:
A variation of this sauce can be prepared by cooking only 8 green tomatoes and then adding 8 raw tomatillos to blender.

ANNATO SAUCE WITH VEGETABLES— *SOFRITO*

A spicy sauce that imparts a delicious flavor to many Cuban and Puerto Rican chicken, pork, and fish dishes. It takes minutes to prepare and is well worth the effort.

2   tablespoons ACHIOTE *OIL (page 50)*
4   tablespoons RECAITO *(page 62)*
2   tablespoons tomato paste
4   teaspoons chopped fresh oregano or 2 teaspoons dried
      oregano
1   slice turkey ham, finely chopped

    1. In a small skillet, heat oil over medium heat; combine ingredients; sauté lightly for 5 minutes.
    2. If you like your food spicy, add *chile* to taste.

Makes 1½ cups.

This Latina Lite recipe contains: 423 calories
Total Fats: 29 gm
Saturated Fats: 4 gm   Protein: 12 gm
Unsaturated Fats: 25 gm   Sodium: 320 mg
Carbohydrates: 34 gm

SOUPS— CALDOS, CREMAS Y SOPAS

Throughout Latin America, dinner usually begins with soup. It may be clear liquid *sopa*, or heartier *caldo*, broth or *una crema*, a delicate cream-based purée. Often, soup such as *pozole*, *birria*, *cocido*, or *asopao* is an entire meal. Rice and pasta dishes are also considered thick *sopas*. Traditionalists consider any meal incomplete without soup.

COLOMBIAN CHICKEN-POTATO SOUP— AJIACO

4   chicken breasts, skinned and quartered
1   medium onion, cut into chunks
2   garlic cloves, quartered
1   medium yam, cut into 8 pieces
4   cups chicken stock or 4 bouillon cubes or 4 teaspoons
       consommé granules dissolved in 4 cups water
6   scallions
10 sprigs fresh cilantro
2   medium potatoes, peeled and thinly sliced
2   ears corn, each cut into 4 pieces
3   tablespoons capers, drained
1   cup fat-free plain yogurt
1   avocado, peeled and sliced

1. Put chicken breasts, onion, garlic, yam, and stock in a casserole; cover and cook over low heat for 30 minutes; remove and save chicken pieces.

2. Strain stock through a sieve; return strained stock to casserole.

3. Add chicken, scallions, cilantro, potatoes, corn, and capers to stock; simmer, covered, for 10 minutes.

4. Remove from heat; discard scallions and cilantro sprigs.

5. Add yogurt, stir over low heat for 1 minute.

6. Serve in deep soup bowls accompanied by avocado.

Serves 6.

Each Latina Lite serving contains: 282 calories
Total Fats: 8 gm
Saturated Fats: 2 gm   Protein: 24 gm
Unsaturated Fats: 6 gm   Sodium: 921 mg
Carbohydrates: 31 gm

Puerto Rican Chicken Soup—*ASOPAO*

3   chicken breasts, skinned and cut into 8 pieces each
ADOBO *(page 52)*
½   cup lean smoked turkey ham, cut into small pieces
1   cup **SOFRITO** *(double recipe on page 66)*
1   cup short-grain white rice, rinsed and drained
5   cups boiling water
2   chicken bouillon cubes or 2 teaspoons consommé
       granules
1   cup tomato sauce
2   tablespoons capers
1   cup green peas, fresh or frozen
1   cup canned asparagus tips, drained
½   cup red pimientos, canned or jarred and drained

1. Three to 4 hours before you plan to cook this dish, season chicken with *Adobo*; refrigerate.

2. In a large saucepan, heat turkey ham over medium heat until it begins to brown; lower heat, add *Sofrito*; simmer, covered, for 2 minutes; add rice, boiling water, chicken, bouillon, tomato sauce, and capers; cover and cook over low heat for 35 minutes until chicken and rice are cooked.

3. In a small saucepan, steam peas in ¼ cup water for 2 minutes and drain.

4. Adorn with peas, asparagus tips, and red pimiento.

Serves 6.

Each Latina Lite serving contains: 324 calories
Total Fats: 6 gm
Saturated Fats: 1 gm   Protein: 24 gm
Unsaturated Fats: 5 gm   Sodium: 1087 mg
Carbohydrates: 44 gm

CREAMED CORN AND CHILE SOUP— CALDO DE ELOTE Y CHILE

2   teaspoons margarine
½   medium onion, finely diced
2   cups corn kernels, fresh or canned and drained
2   cups water
2   chicken bouillon cubes or 2 teaspoons consommé
        granules
¼   teaspoon freshly ground black pepper
1   teaspoon vegetable oil
8   chiles pasillas, packaged dried, cored, seeded, and cut
        into strips
2   cups fat-free evaporated milk

1. In a large saucepan, melt margarine over medium heat; sauté onion until translucent; add corn; sauté for 3 minutes; add water, bouillon, and pepper; boil for 5 minutes until corn softens; lower heat; simmer, covered.

2. Meanwhile, heat oil in a small skillet; toast *chile* strips but do not burn.

3. Add *chile* and milk to soup; simmer for 5 minutes.

4. Serve hot.

Serves 4.

Each Latina Lite serving contains: 234 calories
Total Fats: 4 gm
Saturated Fats: 1 gm   Protein: 13 gm
Unsaturated Fats: 3 gm   Sodium: 1375 mg
Carbohydrates: 40 gm

FISH SOUP—*CALDO DE PESCADO*

This easy-to-make, marvelous fish soup formerly took all day to prepare. Before blenders and food processors, all ingredients were ground in a stone *molcajete*—mortar. Today, you can purée in minutes.

1   tablespoon olive oil
1   large white onion, quartered
5   garlic cloves, chopped
1   12-ounce can tomatoes
5   black peppercorns
2   bay leaves
6   sprigs fresh parsley
½   teaspoon ground cumin
½   teaspoon half salt, half salt-substitute mixture
2   medium potatoes, peeled and cubed

1–3 chiles jalapeños, serranos, *or* pasillas *(optional)*
4   cups tomato-clam juice
Juice of 1 large lemon
1   pound firm fish (cod, red snapper, etc.), cut into
bite-size pieces

1. In a medium casserole, heat oil over medium heat; sauté onion until translucent; add garlic; stir for 1 minute; add tomatoes, peppercorns, bay leaves, parsley, cumin, salt, potatoes, *chiles*, tomato-clam juice, and lemon juice.
2. Bring to a boil; lower heat, cover and simmer for 20 minutes or until potatoes are tender.
3. Remove from heat.
4. Discard bay leaves.
5. Cool and purée in blender.
6. Transfer purée to the casserole; taste and add cumin or ground pepper, if needed.
7. Heat soup; add fish; simmer for 10 minutes, or until fish is cooked.
8. Serve with the following garnish.

Garnish:

Lemon quarters
½   cup chopped fresh cilantro
½   cup chopped onion
½   cup chopped avocado

Serves 6.

Each Latina Lite serving contains: 253 calories
Total Fats: 7 gm
Saturated Fats: 1 gm   Protein: 24 gm
Unsaturated Fats: 6 gm   Sodium: 455 mg
Carbohydrates: 26 gm

$\mathcal{S}$EAFOOD SOUP—*CALDO SANTO DE PESCADO*

Special foods are eaten during *cuaresma*—Lent. "Holy Fish Soup," with its blending of African and Latin flavors, is a Puerto Rican treat that you can serve at Easter time or enjoy throughout the year.

1   *cup* BACALAO (see page 99)
4   *cups fat-free milk*
2   *teaspoons coconut extract*
¼   *cup annato seeds or* ¼ achiote *block*
½   *cup* RECAITO *(page 62)*
Broth from bacalao *(add enough water to fill 1 quart)*
2   *tablespoons capers*
15   *pimiento-stuffed green olives, sliced*
2   *cups* yuca, *peeled and cut into small cubes*
2   *cups* batata, *peeled and cut into small cubes*
2   *cups* yautía, *peeled and cut into small cubes*
2   *cups* calabaza, *peeled and cut into small cubes*
½   *green plantain, peeled, shredded, and rolled into*
        small balls
1   *cup large cooked shrimp, peeled, cleaned,*
        and cut in half
1   *cup shredded imitation crabmeat*

1. The night before you plan to cook the *bacalao*, cover it with water in a large container for at least 2 hours. (You need not refrigerate.)
2. Drain fish.
3. Cover with fresh water and soak overnight.
4. The next day, drain well; remove any skin or bones; cover fish with cold water in a large pot; bring to a boil; lower heat and simmer, uncovered, for 15 minutes.

5. Drain; reserve cooking liquid.

6. Cool fish and shred.

1. To prepare soup, in a small bowl mix 3 cups milk with coconut extract; set aside.

2. Heat remaining 1 cup of milk with annato seeds in a small saucepan, or if you are using *achiote* in block form, dissolve in milk; simmer at low heat; stir until milk turns red.

3. Remove from heat.

4. Strain.

5. Discard seeds.

6. Set strained milk aside.

7. In a large pot, combine red milk, 3 cups milk with coconut, and *recaíto*; stir well; simmer for 5 minutes and add broth from the *bacalao*, capers, olives, *yuca, batata, yautía, calabaza*, and plantain; bring to a boil; lower heat; simmer, covered, for 30 minutes until vegetables are cooked.

8. Just before serving, add seafood.

9. Allow to cool before serving.

Serves 8.

Each Latina Lite serving contains: 260 calories
Total Fats: 2 gm
Saturated Fats: 1 gm   Protein: 20 gm
Unsaturated Fats: 1 gm   Sodium: 596 mg
Carbohydrates: 40 gm

Costa Rican Black Bean Soup— CALDO TICO DE FRIJOL NEGRO

2   cups black beans
8   cups water
½   onion, cut into chunks
2   bay leaves
2   beef bouillon cubes or 2 teaspoons consommé
       granules
½   cup diced onion
2   garlic cloves, minced
2   green bell peppers, chopped
1   cup chopped celery
½   cup chopped fresh cilantro
8   egg whites

Garnish:

½   cup fat-free sour cream
½   cup fat-free plain yogurt
½   cup fresh cilantro
1   lemon, quartered
Tabasco sauce, to taste
½   cup chopped scallions
8   corn tortillas

1. Rinse beans, cover with water in a large bowl, and soak in refrigerator overnight.

2. After soaking, drain water; replace with 8 cups fresh water; add onion chunks, bay leaves, and bouillon.

3. Boil beans in a large covered saucepan over medium heat for 3 hours.

4. When beans are tender, add diced onion, garlic, green pepper, celery, and cilantro; continue cooking over low heat for another 20 minutes.

5. Add egg whites; simmer for 5 minutes more.
6. In a small bowl, mix sour cream and yogurt.
7. Serve with cilantro, lemon quarters, Tabasco, scallions, sour cream mixture, and corn *tortillas*.

Serves 10.

Each Latina Lite serving contains: 142 calories
Total Fats: 2 gm
Saturated Fats: 0 gm   Protein: 9 gm
Unsaturated Fats: 2 gm   Sodium: 316 mg
Carbohydrates: 25 gm

CHICKEN, *CHILE*, AND AVOCADO SOUP— *CALDO TLALPENO*

¾ cup chickpeas (garbanzos)
2 cups chicken stock or 2 bouillon cubes or 2 teaspoons
       consommé granules
1 medium onion, cut into chunks
2 garlic cloves, minced
2 teaspoons fresh oregano or 1 teaspoon dried oregano
2 chicken breasts, skinned and cut into 8 parts
3 chiles chipotles, canned, rinsed and dried, cored and
       seeded
4 carrots, peeled and sliced
4 zucchini, cut into 6 strips each
½ cup green beans, cut into 1-inch pieces
1 avocado, peeled and sliced
½ medium onion, chopped
3 lemons, quartered

1. The night before you plan to prepare the soup, cover chickpeas with water in a medium bowl and soak in refrigerator.

2. The following day, drain chickpeas; add 2 cups fresh water or stock, or consommé with 2 cups water, onion, garlic, and oregano; simmer for 2 hours.

3. Add chicken and *chiles chipotles*; if necessary, add water; simmer for ½ hour more.

4. Add vegetables; simmer, covered, for 20 minutes until vegetables are tender.

5. Serve with avocado, chopped onion, and lemon quarters.

Serves 6.

Each Latina Lite serving contains: 170 calories
Total Fats: 7 gm
Saturated Fats: 2 gm   Protein: 12 gm
Unsaturated Fats: 5 gm   Sodium: 393 mg
Carbohydrates: 18 gm

CRAB SOUP—*CHILPACHOLE DE JAIBA*

1   *pound fresh crabmeat or imitation crabmeat, cooked and shredded*

2   *teaspoons vegetable oil*

2   *medium onions, finely diced*

2   *garlic cloves, finely diced*

2   *large tomatoes, diced*

1   *cup tomato sauce*

3   *cups water*

2   *cups chicken stock or 2 bouillon cubes or 2 teaspoons consommé granules*

2   *tablespoons fresh oregano or 1 tablespoon dried oregano*

2   *sprigs fresh Italian parsley*

4   *lemons, sliced*

2   *fresh green chiles serranos, minced*

1. If you are using imitation crabmeat, cover with water in a small bowl, refrigerate for at least 1 hour; drain.

2. In a large saucepan, heat oil over medium-low heat; sauté onion and garlic until onion turns translucent; add tomatoes; sauté for 3 minutes.

3. Add crabmeat; sauté for 3 minutes more.

4. Add tomato sauce, water, stock, oregano, and parsley; bring to boil and cook no more than 5 minutes.

5. Remove parsley sprigs with a slotted spoon.

6. Serve hot with lemon slices and *chile*.

Serves 6.

Each Latina Lite serving contains: 158 calories

Total Fats:	4 gm		
Saturated Fats:	1 gm	Protein:	12 gm
Unsaturated Fats:	3 gm	Sodium:	1143 mg
Carbohydrates:	24 gm		

CREAM OF WATERCRESS SOUP— CREMA DE BERRO

2   bunches watercress, rinsed thoroughly
2   potatoes, peeled and boiled
4   cups chicken broth or 4 bouillon cubes or 4 teaspoons
        consommé granules with 4 cups water
1   leek, rinsed thoroughly and chopped
1   cup fat-free plain yogurt
Freshly ground black pepper to taste

1. Set aside a few sprigs of watercress to decorate the soup.

2. Purée watercress, potatoes, and 1 cup broth in blender.

3. Set aside.

4. Simmer leek in a large covered saucepan with the remaining 3 cups broth over low heat for 8 minutes.

5. Add puréed watercress-potato mixture, simmer for 5 minutes more.

6. Add yogurt; stir well.

7. Garnish each bowl with a reserved sprig of watercress; serve hot or cold. Season each serving with pepper.

Serves 6.

Each Latina Lite serving contains: 78 calories
Total Fats: 1 gm
Saturated Fats: 0 gm   Protein: 4 gm
Unsaturated Fats: 1 gm   Sodium: 721 mg
Carbohydrates: 15 gm

CREAMED GREEN PLANTAIN SOUP— CREMA DE PLATANOS VERDES

A rich, creamy Cuban soup, made from the island's abundant economical food staple, green plantains.

2   *medium-large green plantains*
¼   *cup fresh lime or lemon juice*
4   *cups chicken broth or 4 teaspoons consommé*
         granules or 4 bouillon cubes with 4 cups water
4   *tablespoons cornstarch*

1. Slash skin of plantain; cut fruit into 1-inch pieces; discard skin.

2. Sprinkle plantain with lime juice.

3. In a large saucepan, bring broth to a boil; add plantains; cover and simmer over low heat for 20 minutes until plantain is tender; remove from heat and cool.

4. In a food processor or blender, pulse just enough to achieve a uniform smooth consistency.

5. Mix cornstarch with 1 cup cooled plantain-broth mixture in a small saucepan; stir over low heat until cornstarch turns translucent and mixture is smooth.

6. Add rest of broth with plantain to cornstarch mixture gradually; stir; simmer over low heat; stir briskly with a whisk until soup is hot, thick, and creamy.

7. If necessary, season with half salt, half salt-substitute mixture from your shaker.

Serves 6.

Each Latina Lite serving contains: 92 calories
Total Fats: 0 gm
Saturated Fats: 0 gm   Protein: 1 gm
Unsaturated Fats: 0 gm   Sodium: 682 mg
Carbohydrates: 23 gm

CREAM OF VEGETABLE SOUP— CREMA DE VERDURA

You may substitute carrots in this recipe for any cooked vegetable. *Chayotes, calabazas* (all squashes), green peas, or spinach are especially good replacements.

1   *cup cooked carrots*
½   *cup liquid from cooked carrots or water*
1   *teaspoon chicken consommé granules or*
        1 bouillon cube
¾   *cup water*
1   *cup fat-free milk*
1   *teaspoon margarine*
Freshly ground black pepper to taste

1. Purée carrots with their liquid in blender.
2. Transfer purée to a small saucepan and stir consommé and water into mixture; heat over medium-low heat; add milk gradually, stir frequently.
3. Pour soup into 2 bowls with margarine on top.
4. Season with pepper.

Serves 2.

Each Latina Lite serving contains: 102 calories
Total Fats: 3 gm
Saturated Fats: 1 gm　　　Protein: 6 gm
Unsaturated Fats: 2 gm　　Sodium: 646 mg
Carbohydrates: 15 gm

CHILLED VEGETABLE SOUP— GAZPACHO

Gazpacho would not exist if the Spanish explorers had not introduced tomatoes to the Spaniards. The secret of good gazpacho rests in the tomatoes. Prepare this dish only in tomato season and choose the reddest, juiciest, ripest tomatoes.

4　large red ripe tomatoes, peeled* and seeded
1　medium cucumber, peeled
2　cups tomato juice
½　medium red onion, cut into chunks
½　yellow or green bell pepper, cored and seeded, cut into chunks

*To peel tomatoes, gently scorch tomato skin over stove burner until it blisters; then immediately wrap tomatoes in a cool damp cloth for a few minutes. The peel will separate easily.

3–4 garlic cloves, halved
2   tablespoons olive oil
2   tablespoons balsamic vinegar or red wine vinegar
¼   teaspoon ground cumin
½   teaspoon half salt, half salt-substitute mixture
Few dashes of Tabasco sauce
1   medium ripe avocado, peeled and cubed
2   lemons, quartered
½   cup diced red onion
½   cup chopped fresh Italian parsley
8   slices French bread

1. Purée tomatoes, cucumber, tomato juice, onion, bell pepper, and garlic in blender.

2. Strain in a fine sieve forcing liquid into a medium bowl; discard seeds and peel left in strainer.

3. Stir in olive oil, vinegar, cumin, salt, and Tabasco.

4. Chill for 2 to 3 hours.

5. Garnish with side bowls of avocado, lemon wedges, onion, and parsley.

6. Serve with 8 slices toasted French bread.

Serves 8.

Each Latina Lite serving contains: 162 calories
Total Fats: 8 gm
Saturated Fats: 1 gm   Protein: 4 gm
Unsaturated Fats: 7 gm   Sodium: 223 mg
Carbohydrates: 21 gm

COLD GREEN VEGETABLE SOUP—
GAZPACHO VERDE

3   cucumbers, peeled and cut into chunks
12   green tomatoes (tomatillos), skinned and halved
½   medium red onion, cut into chunks
½   yellow or green bell pepper, seeded, cut into chunks
1   cup chopped fresh cilantro
1   chile habanero, cored, seeded, and cut into pieces
½   avocado, peeled, cut into chunks
3–4 garlic cloves, halved
2   tablespoons olive oil
2   tablespoons Japanese seasoned rice vinegar*
2   cups defatted chicken broth
1   teaspoon half salt, half salt-substitute mixture
2   lemons, quartered
1   cup grated iceberg lettuce
½   cup diced red onion

1. Purée all ingredients in blender except lemons, lettuce, and red onion.
2. Strain through a sieve.
3. Refrigerate for 1 hour.
4. Accompany with lemon, lettuce, and red onion.

Serves 6.

Each Latina Lite serving contains: 115 calories
Total Fats: 8 gm
Saturated Fats: 1 gm   Protein: 3 gm
Unsaturated Fats: 7 gm   Sodium: 453 mg
Carbohydrates: 12 gm

*Japanese seasoned rice vinegar can be found in the Asian food section of your supermarket.

LARGE-KERNEL HOMINY CORN SOUP (WHITE)—*POZOLE BLANCO*

Pozole, a one-dish meal, is perfect on Super Bowl Sunday, or as a special *cena*, supper. Eaten with grated lettuce, chopped scallions, and radish slices, it is really soup and salad in a single bowl. When prepared ahead of time it is even tastier.

2 cups liquid from cooked large kernel corn or canned
2 cups chicken stock or 2 teaspoons consommé granules
    or 2 bouillon cubes dissolved in 2 cups water
2 cups cooked or canned large-kernel hominy corn
1 head garlic, each clove cut in half
1 large white onion, cut into chunks
4 tablespoons fresh oregano or 2 tablespoons dried
        oregano
3 medium chicken breasts, skinless, cut into bite-size
        pieces
½ cup lean turkey ham, cut into bite-size pieces

GARNISH:

3 lemons, sliced
1 cup grated lettuce
1 cup sliced red radishes
3 tablespoons finely diced onion
2 tablespoons crushed fresh oregano
2 tablespoons crushed red cayenne pepper
1 teaspoon salt

1. In a large saucepan, over high heat, bring corn liquid and stock to a boil; add hominy corn, garlic, onion, and oregano.

2. Lower heat, cover, and simmer for 45 minutes until corn kernels explode.

3. Add chicken and turkey ham; cover and simmer for 10 to 20 minutes more.

4. Serve garnish with soup.

Serves 6.

Each Latina Lite serving contains: 207 calories
Total Fats: 4 gm
Saturated Fats: 1 gm   Protein: 21 gm
Unsaturated Fats: 3 gm   Sodium: 751 mg
Carbohydrates: 26 gm

LARGE-KERNEL HOMINY CORN SOUP (RED)—*POZOLE ROJO*

6   chiles pasillas, *dried, soaked, cored, and seeded*
4   *large garlic cloves, cut in half*
1   *large white onion, cut into chunks*
4   *medium chicken breasts, skinless, cut into bite-size pieces*
2   *cups liquid from cooked large kernel corn or canned*
2   *cups chicken stock or 2 teaspoons consommé granules or 2 bouillon cubes dissolved in 2 cups water*
2   *tablespoons fresh oregano or 1 tablespoon dried oregano*
1½ *cups large-kernel hominy corn, cooked or canned*

GARNISH:

2   cups grated lettuce
½   cup chopped scallions
8–12   red radishes, sliced
8   tablespoons fresh oregano or 4 tablespoons dried
         oregano
2   lemons, in wedges
Tabasco sauce

1. In a small saucepan, cook *chiles* in 1 cup water for 5 minutes over medium heat.

2. Purée *chiles* and cooking liquid in blender with garlic and onion.

3. In the same saucepan, simmer chicken in *chile* broth for 15 to 20 minutes. Set aside.

4. In a large casserole with a tight-fitting lid, combine hominy corn liquid with 2 cups stock (if you are using consommé or bouillon cubes, add 2 cups water) and oregano; add corn; cover and simmer for 25 minutes until corn kernels explode.

5. Add chicken in chile broth; simmer covered for 5 to 10 minutes more.

6. If necessary, add water.

7. Serve garnish with soup.

Serves 8.

Each Latina Lite serving contains: 144 calories

Total Fats:	3 gm	
Saturated Fats:	0 gm	Protein: 16 gm
Unsaturated Fats:	3 gm	Sodium: 453 mg
Carbohydrates:	17 gm	

NOTE: Fresh large-kernel hominy corn may be used, when available. The corn should be precooked for 1 hour, until tender. Broth from corn may be used in place of liquid from canned corn.

LARGE-KERNEL HOMINY CORN SOUP (GREEN)—*POZOLE VERDE*

16   green tomatoes (tomatillos)
½   medium onion, cut into chunks
2   garlic cloves, halved
3   chiles serranos, canned, cored and seeded
2   cups broth from cooked corn or canned
2   cups water
2   teaspoons chicken consommé granules or 2 bouillon
      cubes
2   cups large-kernel hominy corn, cooked or canned
2   teaspoons fresh oregano or 1 teaspoon dried oregano
12 ounces cooked lean pork, cut into chunks

GARNISH:

½   cup chopped onion
1   cup grated lettuce
1   cup sliced red radishes
2   lemons, quartered
½   cup chopped fresh cilantro

    1. Purée tomatoes, onion, garlic, and *chiles* in 1 cup corn broth in blender.
    2. Transfer purée to a large saucepan; add rest of corn broth, water, consommé, corn, and oregano; bring to a boil; lower heat; cover and simmer for 25 minutes.
    3. Add cooked pork; simmer for 7 minutes more.
    4. Serve hot with garnish.

Serves 8.

Each Latina Lite serving contains: 179 calories
Total Fats: 4 gm
Saturated Fats: 1 gm   Protein: 16 gm
Unsaturated Fats: 3 gm   Sodium: 292 mg
Carbohydrates: 21 gm

CHICKEN-*TORTILLA* SOUP— *SOPA AZTECA*

4   corn tortillas, *dried and cut into strips*
3   tablespoons *vegetable oil (divided)*
1   *medium onion, chopped*
1   *garlic clove, minced*
½   *cup tomato sauce*
3   cups *chicken broth or 3 bouillon cubes or 3 teaspoons
        consommé granules with 3 cups water*
1   *teaspoon fresh oregano*

GARNISH:

½   *cup fat-free plain yogurt*
½   *cup fat-free sour cream*
1   *tablespoon Japanese seasoned rice vinegar*[*]
4   **chiles pasillas,** *cored, seeded, and cut into strips*
½   *cup grated white cheese*
½   *avocado, sliced*

1. Dry *tortilla* strips on a baking sheet in the oven or in the sun.
2. Heat 1 tablespoon oil on a nonstick griddle over low heat; fry dried *tortilla* strips until lightly browned; remove from pan and blot excess oil on paper towels.
3. Set aside.
4. Sauté onion and garlic in 1 tablespoon oil over low heat in a casserole until onion becomes translucent; add tomato sauce, broth, and oregano; tightly cover casserole; simmer for 30 minutes.
5. Whisk yogurt, sour cream, and vinegar together; refrigerate.
6. Heat remaining 1 tablespoon of oil in a small skillet, over low heat; toast strips of *chile pasilla*; remove and blot *chile* on paper towels.

[*]Japanese seasoned rice vinegar can be found in the Asian food section of your supermarket.

7. Just before serving, float browned *tortilla* strips on top of hot soup.

8. Garnish with yogurt-sour cream, toasted *chile* strips, cheese, and avocado.

Serves 8.

Each Latina Lite serving contains: 163 calories
Total Fats: 9 gm
Saturated Fats: 2 gm   Protein: 6 gm
Unsaturated Fats: 7 gm   Sodium: 576 mg
Carbohydrates: 14 gm

CREAM OF PUMPKIN FLOWER SOUP— *SOPA DE FLOR DE CALABAZA*

2   cups rinsed and chopped pumpkin flowers, discard
        stems
½   cup chopped onion
2   tablespoons margarine
4   cups milk or 2 cups fat-free evaporated milk
2   tablespoons all-purpose flour
3   teaspoons chicken consommé granules or 3 bouillon
        cubes
1   cup finely chopped zucchini
½   cup corn kernels, fresh, frozen, or canned
Freshly ground black pepper to taste

1. In a large saucepan, over medium heat, sauté pumpkin flowers and onion in 1 tablespoon margarine; when onion is translucent add 2 cups milk; lower heat and simmer for 3 minutes.

2. Purée onion, flowers, and milk mixture in blender.

3. In the same saucepan, melt the remaining 1 tablespoon margarine; stir flour into margarine until a thick paste is formed; continue stirring; gradually add flower mixture.

4. When soup thickens stir in consommé, zucchini, corn, and remaining 2 cups milk; simmer for 10 minutes over low heat; stir occasionally.

5. Season with pepper.

Serves 6.

Each Latina Lite serving contains: 136 calories
Total Fats: 5 gm
Saturated Fats: 1 gm   Protein: 7 gm
Unsaturated Fats: 4 gm   Sodium: 640 mg
Carbohydrates: 18 gm

TROPICAL LENTIL SOUP—
SOPA TROPICAL DE LENTEJAS

1   cup lentil beans
4   cups water
½   teaspoon half salt, half salt-substitute mixture
1   bay leaf
1   tablespoon vegetable oil
½   medium onion, chopped
1   garlic clove, minced
1   cup tomato sauce
2   chicken bouillon cubes or 2 teaspoons consommé
        granules
1   cup cored and cubed fresh pineapple
1   cup peeled and cubed green plantain
1   cup cooked and cubed boniato or yams
Freshly ground black pepper to taste

1. Rinse and soak lentils in 4 cups water in a medium bowl the night before you plan to cook this soup.

2. Change water the next day.

3. Cook covered in a medium saucepan with salt and bay leaf for 2½ hours until lentils are soft; discard bay leaf.

4. In a large skillet, heat oil over low heat; sauté onion and garlic; when onions are translucent, add tomato sauce, bouillon, lentils with their liquid; simmer for 10 minutes.

5. Add pineapple and plantain, simmer for 1 hour more.

6. Add *boniato*, heat for 5 minutes.

7. If necessary, add water.

8. Season with pepper.

Serves 6.

Each Latina Lite serving contains: 163 calories
Total Fats: 3 gm
Saturated Fats: 0 gm   Protein: 5 gm
Unsaturated Fats: 3 gm   Sodium: 772 mg
Carbohydrates: 32 gm

ᵀARO ROOT-*CHAYOTE*-LEEK SOUP—
SOPA DE YAUTIA-CHAYOTE-PORO

During March, April, and May, the warmest months in Mexico, a bowl of chilled refreshing *Sopa de Papa, Chayote y Poro*—Potato, *Chayote*, Leek Soup—was most welcome. This adaptation substitutes *yautía*, taro root, for the potato. *Yautía* is available in most Latino markets selling Puerto Rican products. If unavailable, use potato.

2   cups peeled and diced yautía
2   chayote squashes, peeled and diced
1   large leek, rinsed thoroughly and cut into bite-size
      pieces
3   cups chicken stock or 3 teaspoons consommé
      granules or 3 bouillon cubes dissolved in
      3 cups water
1   cup fat-free evaporated milk
1   teaspoon ground white pepper

1. In a large casserole, over medium heat, cook *yautía*, *chayote*, and leek in stock, covered, for 30 minutes or until tender; cool.
2. Purée in blender and strain.
3. Transfer to a large bowl; stir in milk, add pepper.
4. Refrigerate for 2 hours.
5. Serve in chilled small bowls.

Serves 4.

Each Latina Lite serving contains: 102 calories
Total Fats: 0 gm
Saturated Fats: 0 gm   Protein: 4 gm
Unsaturated Fats: 0 gm   Sodium: 804 mg
Carbohydrates: 21 gm

COLD CUCUMBER SOUP—
SOPA FRIA DE PEPINO

4   tomatoes, peeled and diced
1   chile serrano, *minced*
2   garlic cloves, minced
1   medium onion, finely diced
1   tablespoon fresh lemon juice or ½ tablespoon white
      wine vinegar
3   cups chicken broth or 3 teaspoons consommé
      granules or 3 bouillon cubes with 3 cups water
2   cucumbers, peeled and grated
½   cup tomato juice
2   teaspoons sugar
Freshly ground black pepper to taste

1. In a medium bowl, combine all ingredients in the order given.
2. Refrigerate for at least 2 to 3 hours.
3. Serve cold.

Serves 6.

Each Latina Lite serving contains: 52 calories
Total Fats: 1 gm
Saturated Fats: 0 gm   Protein: 2 gm
Unsaturated Fats: 1 gm   Sodium: 519 mg
Carbohydrates: 11 gm

MAIN DISHES—PLATOS FUERTES

A main dish is served at the principal meal of the day. Usually the *plato fuerte* is fish, seafood, poultry, or meat. Occasionally, eggs, vegetables, salads, soups, or *antojitos*—appetizers—fill in as main dishes. We look forward to the *plato fuerte* and want it to be tasty and satisfying. All of the Latina Lite main dishes will inspire your family to *chupar sus dedos* because they are "finger-lickin' good!"

FISH AND SEAFOOD— PESCADO Y MARISCOS

SHRIMP BALLS—ALBONDIGAS DE CAMARON

1   egg yolk
2   egg whites
1   pound medium shrimp, peeled and cleaned
1   tablespoon vegetable oil
2   garlic cloves, crushed
1   teaspoon ground coriander (cilantro seed)
2   teaspoons fresh oregano or 1 teaspoon dried oregano
½   cup Maseca (packaged corn tortilla mix)
2   tablespoons warm water
1   teaspoon half salt, half salt-substitute mixture
¼   teaspoon freshly ground black pepper
2   cups green beans, cut on the diagonal
1   cup sliced carrots
1   cup tomato sauce
½   medium onion, thinly sliced
1–2 chiles chipotles, canned, rinsed and drained, cored
     and seeded
3   cups boiling water
¼   cup chopped fresh cilantro

1. In a small bowl, mix egg yolk and whites; set aside.

2. Finely chop shrimp; mix eggs with shrimp; add oil, garlic, coriander, oregano, *Maseca*, water, ½ teaspoon salt, and pepper; mix well to form dough.

3. With wet palms form 1-inch balls.

4. Refrigerate for 1 hour.

5. Meanwhile, steam beans, carrots, and onion in 1 cup water in a covered casserole; add tomato sauce, *chiles*, and remaining ½ teaspoon salt; pour boiling water over all; lower heat; simmer for 5 minutes.

6. Add shrimp balls; simmer for 5 minutes more.

7. Garnish with fresh cilantro.

Serves 6.

Each Latina Lite serving contains: 210 calories
Total Fats: 5 gm
Saturated Fats: 1 gm   Protein: 21 gm
Unsaturated Fats: 4 gm   Sodium: 666 mg
Carbohydrates: 22 gm

FISH BALLS—*ALBONDIGAS DE PESCADO*

2   cups tomato sauce
½   medium onion, cut into chunks
2   garlic cloves, 1 peeled, 1 minced
1   chile pasilla, packaged dried, cored, seeded, and cut
        into strips
1   chicken bouillon cube or 1 teaspoon consommé
        granules
½   cup water
½   teaspoon ground cumin
1   bay leaf
1   cup peeled and sliced carrots
1   cup celery, cut into 1-inch pieces
2   cups cooked and crumbled fish

¼   cup bread crumbs
3   tablespoons white wine vinegar
3   egg whites, beaten
½   teaspoon half salt, half salt-substitute mixture
¼   teaspoon freshly ground black pepper

1. Purée tomato sauce, onion, and peeled garlic clove in blender.

2. Transfer purée to a large saucepan; add *chile*, bouillon, water, cumin, and bay leaf; simmer, covered, for 3 minutes; add carrots and celery; simmer for 8 minutes; remove from heat; cool.

3. Discard bay leaf.

4. In a medium bowl, combine fish, minced garlic, bread crumbs, vinegar, egg whites, salt, and pepper.

5. Wet the palms of your hands; form 1-inch fish balls.

6. Place fish balls in heated sauce and simmer, covered, for 8 minutes more.

Serves 4.

Each Latina Lite serving contains: 248 calories
Total Fats: 3 gm
Saturated Fats: 1 gm   Protein: 34 gm
Unsaturated Fats: 2 gm   Sodium: 1179 mg
Carbohydrates: 23 gm

CRAB AND RICE—
ARROZ CON JUEYES (JAIBA)

1   cup imitation crabmeat
2   slices lowfat turkey ham, chopped
2   garlic cloves, minced
2   tablespoons chopped fresh cilantro

½   teaspoon half salt, half salt-substitute mixture
¾   cup long-grain white rice, rinsed and drained
1   cup tomato sauce
1   cup hot water
1   cup fat-free evaporated milk
1½   teaspoons coconut extract
1   6-ounce jar red pimiento, cut into strips, drained

1. In a small bowl, soak crabmeat in water for at least 2 hours; drain and set aside.

2. In a large skillet, over low heat, sauté turkey ham with garlic, cilantro, and salt; stir constantly.

3. Add crabmeat, rice, tomato sauce, water, milk, and coconut extract; mix well; simmer until rice is cooked (about 35 minutes).

4. Decorate with red pimiento strips.

Serves 4.

Each Latina Lite serving contains: 180 calories
Total Fats: 2 gm
Saturated Fats: 1 gm   Protein: 14 gm
Unsaturated Fats: 1 gm   Sodium: 1189 mg
Carbohydrates: 27 gm

Tuna Marinated in *RECAITO*— *ATUN EN RECAITO*

2   teaspoons olive oil
¼   cup fresh orange juice
¼   cup fresh lemon juice
¼   cup tomato sauce
¼   cup RECAITO (page 62)
1¼   pounds fresh tuna

Sauce:

1 cup papaya, cut into chunks
1 tablespoon dark-brown sugar
¼ cup fresh lemon juice
¼ cup fresh orange juice
2 scallions, chopped
1 garlic clove, minced
¼ teaspoon red cayenne pepper
¼ teaspoon half salt, half salt-substitute mixture

1. In a small bowl, combine olive oil, orange and lemon juices, tomato sauce, and *Recaíto*; mix well.

2. In a glass dish, cover fish with marinade.

3. Refrigerate for 2 hours, turning fish at least once.

4. While fish is marinating, combine papaya, sugar, and lemon and orange juices in blender.

5. Empty sauce into a jar; add scallions, garlic, red cayenne pepper, and salt; shake well.

6. Refrigerate.

7. When fish is seasoned, drain and discard marinade.

8. Grill fish over hot coals until done outside and pink inside; DO NOT OVERCOOK.

9. Accompany with prepared chilled sauce.

Serves 4.

Each Latina Lite serving contains: 285 calories
Total Fats: 9 gm
Saturated Fats: 2 gm   Protein: 34 gm
Unsaturated Fats: 7 gm   Sodium: 252 mg
Carbohydrates: 16 gm

$\mathcal{S}$ALTED CODFISH—*BACALAO*

If you are unaccustomed to dried salted codfish, its appearance may seem repellent and unappetizing. But cooked *bacalao*, with its flaky, lively flavor, is considered a delicacy and turns people who avoid fish into fish lovers. The preparation is certainly worth the results. *Bacalao*—salted cod—is available in most Latin and many Italian markets.

Preparing *Bacalao*:

1. The night before you plan to cook this fish, cover the *bacalao* with water and soak for at least 2 hours. (You need not refrigerate.)
2. Drain water; change water; soak overnight.
3. The following day, drain well; remove skin and bones; cut fish into smaller pieces.
4. Cover fish with cold water in a large saucepan and bring to a boil. Lower heat and simmer, uncovered, for 15 minutes.
5. Drain fish again; reserve cooking liquid.

$\mathcal{B}$ASQUE-STYLE COD— *BACALAO A LA VIZCAINA*

1   *tablespoon olive oil*
4   *medium potatoes, peeled and thinly sliced*
1   *pound dried salted codfish fillets, cooked and cubed*
2   *large onions, peeled and thinly sliced*
1   *green bell pepper, cored, seeded, and sliced into thin rings*
¼   *cup sliced pimiento-stuffed olives*
1   *tablespoon capers* (alcaparras)

¼   cup seeded raisins
3   garlic cloves, peeled and minced
1   cup tomato sauce
1¼ cups fish broth from cooked bacalao
½   cup water
1   tablespoon white vinegar
2   bay leaves

1. Coat bottom of a large skillet with oil; arrange alternate layers of potatoes, codfish, onions, and bell pepper; form at least 2 layers.

2. Top with olives, capers, raisins, garlic, tomato sauce, fish broth, water, vinegar, and bay leaves.

3. Bring to a boil; simmer, partially covered, for 30 minutes until potatoes are fork-tender.

4. Discard bay leaves.

Serves 6.

Each Latina Lite serving contains: 256 calories
Total Fats: 9 gm
Saturated Fats: 2 gm   Protein: 30 gm
Unsaturated Fats: 7 gm   Sodium: 605 mg
Carbohydrates: 46 gm

SARDINE CASSEROLE—
CACEROLA DE SARDINAS

2   tablespoons olive oil
8   corn tortillas, cut into strips
1   fresh chile California (or other long green chile),
    cored, seeded, and cut into strips
2   tablespoons finely diced onion
1   cup tomato sauce
2   garlic cloves, quartered

¼   teaspoon half salt, half salt-substitute mixture
½   cup fat-free evaporated milk
1½ cups sardines, canned, rinsed, drained, and mashed
½   cup grated white cheese

1. Preheat the oven to 400°F.

2. In a large skillet, heat 1 tablespoon oil over medium heat; fry *tortilla* strips until golden but not hard; blot excess oil on paper towels; set aside.

3. In same skillet, sauté *chile* strips in remaining 1 tablespoon of oil for 5 minutes until soft; remove with slotted spoon and blot excess oil on paper towels; save remaining oil; set aside.

4. Purée onion, tomato sauce, garlic, and salt in blender.

5. Empty into same skillet; simmer sauce for 5 minutes.

6. In a baking dish, layer *tortilla* strips, chile strips, tomato sauce, ¼ cup milk, and ½ of the mashed sardines.

7. Repeat, ending with tomato sauce and remaining ¼ cup milk.

8. Sprinkle cheese over top and bake for 15 minutes.

Serves 4.

Each Latina Lite serving contains: 487 calories
Total Fats: 23 gm
Saturated Fats: 5 gm   Protein: 34 gm
Unsaturated Fats: 18 gm   Sodium: 1033 mg
Carbohydrates: 37 gm

SQUID—CALAMARES

Fresh squid has more flavor than frozen squid, but frozen squid is more convenient, since it is precleaned and has its ink sacs placed inside the body.

Preparing *Calamares:*

1. To prepare fresh squid, firmly grasp the body; pull tentacles; discard head, eyes, and innards attached to tentacles.

2. Carefully remove the ink sacs located behind each tentacle; place ink sacs in a small bowl.

3. Cut off the thin membrane covering the body of the squid; remove the 2 flat pieces of cartilage inside body.

4. Discard membrane and bones.

5. Rinse squid tentacles and body under cold running water until clean.

6. The squid is now pan-ready.

Squid in its ink—*CALAMARES EN SU TINTA*

2   *tablespoons olive oil*
1   *medium onion, diced*
2   *garlic cloves, minced*
1½ *cups tomato sauce*
½   *cup chopped fresh Italian parsley*
2   *fresh mint leaves*
2   *tablespoons bread crumbs*
¼   *cup red wine*
1½ *pounds squid, fresh or frozen, cleaned*
Squid ink
2   *cups cooked long-grain white rice*
1   *teaspoon half salt, half salt-substitute mixture*
¼   *teaspoon freshly ground black pepper*

1. In a nonstick skillet, heat oil over medium heat; sauté onion and garlic until translucent; add tomato sauce, parsley, mint leaves, and bread crumbs.

2. Lower heat and simmer for 4 minutes; add wine and squid; simmer, covered, for 1 to 2 hours until squid is almost cooked.

3. Strain the ink dissolved in ½ cup hot water and add to skillet; simmer for 15 minutes more.

4. Serve hot over rice.

5. Add salt and pepper at table.

Serves 4.

Each Latina Lite serving contains: 336 calories
Total Fats: 9 gm
Saturated Fats: 1 gm
Unsaturated Fats: 8 gm
Carbohydrates: 32 gm
Protein: 29 gm
Sodium: 1437 mg

NOTE: In case you break ink sacs, packets of squid ink, called *chipirón*, are sold in Latin food stores.

FISH STICKS, PUERTO RICAN-STYLE— PALITOS DE PESCADO

ADOBO (page 52)
¼   *cup bread crumbs*
2   *tablespoons oat bran*
¼   *cup all-purpose flour*
1½ *pounds fish fillet, cut into strips, ½-inch wide and*
      2 inches long
2   *egg whites, beaten*
2   *tablespoons vegetable oil*

1. On a sheet of wax paper, combine *Adobo*, bread crumbs, oat bran, and flour.

2. Dip each fish strip into beaten egg whites and coat in crumbs mixture.

3. In a large skillet, fry strips in hot oil until golden brown; blot excess oil on paper towels.

4. They may be kept warm in a 275°F degree oven.

Serves 4.

Each Latina Lite serving contains: 333 calories
Total Fats: 10 gm
Saturated Fats: 1 gm   Protein: 45 gm
Unsaturated Fats: 9 gm   Sodium: 361 mg
Carbohydrates: 14 gm

FISH IN ADOBO—*PESCADO ADOBADO*

1½ pounds fish fillets

Marinade:

½   *cup fresh lime or lemon juice*
2   *garlic cloves, minced*
¼   *cup minced onion*
½   *teaspoon half salt, half salt-substitute mixture*

Adobo:

4   **chiles pasillas,** *packaged dried, cored and seeded*
2   **garlic cloves,** *halved*
½   **cup fresh orange juice**

1. Wash and dry fish; place in a square glass baking dish.

2. Combine lime juice, garlic, onion, and salt; bathe fish in marinade; cover and refrigerate for at least 1 hour.

3. Preheat the oven to 350°F.

4. Purée *chiles*, garlic, and orange juice in blender; add *Adobo* to marinade.

5. Cover tightly with a lid or aluminum foil; bake for 20 to 25 minutes.

Serves 4.

Each Latina Lite serving contains: 194 calories
Total Fats: 2 gm
Saturated Fats: 1 gm   Protein: 32 gm
Unsaturated Fats: 1 gm   Sodium: 337 mg
Carbohydrates: 12 gm

FISH WITH AVOCADO—*PESCADO BANADO CON AGUACATE*

1½ pounds whole fish or fish steaks
2   cups water
¼   cup cider vinegar
6   peppercorns
1   bay leaf
1   tablespoon fresh lemon juice

1. Clean, rinse, and dry fish; place in a large skillet with a tight-fitting lid.

2. Add water, vinegar, peppercorns, bay leaf, and lemon juice.

3. Bring to a boil; cover; lower heat, and steam 10 to 15 minutes until fish is cooked.

4. Remove and drain fish; discard liquid and bay leaf.

Sauce:

1   ripe avocado
1   tablespoon fresh lemon juice
2   tablespoons capers, drained
½   teaspoon half salt, half salt-substitute mixture
½   cup chopped fresh Italian parsley

1. In a small bowl, mash avocado.
2. Add lemon juice, capers, and salt.
3. Place avocado pit in sauce to prevent it from blackening.
4. Serve fish hot or cold sprinkled with parsley accompanied by the sauce.

Serves 4.

Each Latina Lite serving contains: 301 calories
Total Fats: 11 gm
Saturated Fats: 2 gm   Protein: 42 gm
Unsaturated Fats: 9 gm   Sodium: 491 mg
Carbohydrates: 5 gm

FISH, BRAZILIAN-STYLE— PESCADO BRASILIERO

Brazilians as well as their Portuguese ancestors are known worldwide to be great fishermen. This is a popular easy-to-prepare Brazilian fish dish perfected over the last five hundred years.

Marinade:

½   large white onion, diced
1–2 chiles serranos, *fresh or canned, cored and seeded*
1   cup tomato sauce
1   garlic clove, halved
1½ tablespoons fresh lime or lemon juice
½   teaspoon half salt, half salt-substitute mixture

1½ pounds fish fillet (sea bass, halibut, salmon, red
        snapper, etc.)
1   tablespoon olive oil
¼   cup water
½   cup chopped fresh cilantro

1. Liquefy onion, *chiles*, tomato sauce, garlic, lime juice, and salt in blender.
2. Put fish in a flat container; saturate with marinade.
3. Cover, refrigerate, and marinate for 2 hours.
4. Place fish and sauce in a large skillet; add oil and water; cover tightly; simmer for 7 to 10 minutes.
5. Serve over rice; sprinkle with fresh cilantro.

Serves 4.

Each Latina Lite serving contains: 283 calories
Total Fats: 6 gm
Saturated Fats: 1 gm   Protein: 46 gm
Unsaturated Fats: 5 gm   Sodium: 538 mg
Carbohydrates: 8 gm

FISH IN A BAG—*PESCADO EMBOLSADO*

1½ pounds fish fillet
Aluminum foil
Freshly ground black pepper to taste
4   *teaspoons margarine*
2   *cups sliced mushrooms*
2   *tomatoes, peeled and chopped*
1   *cup thinly sliced white onion*
1   *cup long green fresh chile, cored, seeded, and cut into*
      strips
4   *sprigs fresh parsley*
4   *teaspoons Worcestershire sauce*

1. On a large square of aluminum foil, grind pepper on fish, and dot with margarine.

2. Add mushrooms, tomatoes, onion, *chile*, parsley, and Worcestershire.

3. Close foil, forming a bag.

4. Grill on both sides for about 5 minutes.

Serves 4.

Each Latina Lite serving contains: 296 calories
Total Fats: 7 gm
Saturated Fats: 1 gm   Protein: 45 gm
Unsaturated Fats: 6 gm   Sodium: 463 mg
Carbohydrates: 14 gm

PICKLED FISH—*PESCADO EN ESCABECHE*

4   *fresh fish fillets (6½ ounces each)*
2   *lemons*
2   *teaspoons vegetable oil*
1   *cup* **ESCABECHE** *(page 56)*
1   *cup grated lettuce*
4   *red onion rings, raw*

1. Rinse and dry fish.
2. Squeeze lemons over fish; allow to stand for 1 hour.
3. Heat oil in a large nonstick skillet over medium heat; lightly fry fish for 1½ minutes on each side.
4. Blot excess oil on paper towels.
5. Place in rectangular glass dish; add *Escabeche*; cover with plastic wrap.
6. Refrigerate for 24 to 48 hours.
7. When ready to serve, remove with slotted spoon; allow all excess oil to drip off.
8. Serve hot or cold.
9. Adorn with grated lettuce and onion rings.

Serves 4.

Each Latina Lite serving contains: 275 calories
Total Fats: 9 gm
Saturated Fats: 1 gm   Protein: 39 gm
Unsaturated Fats: 8 gm   Sodium: 346 mg
Carbohydrates: 8 gm

FISH WITH GARLIC SAUCE— PESCADO CON MOJITO DE AJO

2 whole fish, 1 pound each, split lengthwise
1 tablespoon ADOBO (page 52)
2 tablespoons all-purpose flour
1 tablespoon vegetable oil
1 recipe MOJITO DE AJO (page 59)
1 lemon, quartered

1. One hour before cooking, season fish with *ADOBO* and lightly dust with flour.
2. Heat oil in a large nonstick skillet over medium heat; fry fish on both sides until golden brown. DO NOT OVERCOOK.
3. Serve with hot or cold *Mojito de Ajo* and lemon.

Serves 4.

Each Latina Lite serving contains: 404 calories
Total Fats: 14 gm
Saturated Fats: 1 gm   Protein: 61 gm
Unsaturated Fats: 13 gm   Sodium: 257 mg
Carbohydrates: 6 gm

FISH IN NOPALES— PESCADO EN NOPALES

1 pound fish fillet, 4 fillets, 4 ounces each
8 whole NOPALES (cactus leaves), palm-size, cleaned
      and cooked (page 164)
4 slices part-skim milk white cheese, cut into bite-size
      pieces
12 strips chile jalapeño, canned, rinsed and dried

2   tablespoons all-purpose flour
3   egg whites
2   tablespoons vegetable oil
1   cup thinly sliced white onion
2   cups tomato sauce
1   teaspoon half salt, half salt-substitute mixture
1   cup water
2   teaspoons fresh oregano or ½ teaspoon dried
      oregano
1   teaspoon fresh cilantro

GARNISH:

1   cup sliced red radishes
½   cup chopped fresh cilantro

1. For each serving, arrange fish on a *nopal*; put 1 slice cheese and 3 *chile* strips on top; cover with another leaf.

2. Secure with toothpicks.

3. Lightly dust outside of *nopales* with flour.

4. Meanwhile, in a medium bowl, beat egg whites until they peak.

5. Coat each "sandwich" with beaten egg whites. In a large skillet, brown both sides in hot oil

6. Remove; do not wash skillet; blot excess oil on paper towels; set aside.

7. In same skillet, sauté onion over medium heat until translucent; add tomato sauce, salt, water, and herbs.

8. When sauce is hot, add browned *Nopales* sandwiches; cover; lower heat and simmer for 5 minutes.

9. Adorn with radishes and cilantro.

Serves 4.

Each Latina Lite serving contains: 407 calories
Total Fats: 15 gm
Saturated Fats: 4 gm   Protein: 41 gm
Unsaturated Fats: 11 gm   Sodium: 1775 mg
Carbohydrates: 29 gm

FISH, VERACRUZ-STYLE—
PESCADO VERACRUZANO

1   *tablespoon olive oil*
1   *large white onion, thinly sliced*
1   *cup tomato sauce*
1   *teaspoon half salt, half salt-substitute mixture*
2   *tablespoons capers*
15 *green olives stuffed with pimiento, sliced*
2   *tablespoons fresh oregano or 1 teaspoon dried oregano*
3–5 *whole long yellow chiles, canned (if unavailable, substitute 3–5 whole canned jalapeños)*
4   *fish steaks or fillets, 5 ounces each (sea bass, red snapper, etc.)*

1. In a medium casserole, heat oil over low heat; add onion; sauté until translucent; add tomato sauce and salt; simmer for 5 minutes.

2. Add capers, olives, oregano, and *chiles*; simmer for another 5 minutes.

3. Add fish; continue to simmer until fish is cooked and still firm.

Serves 4.

Each Latina Lite serving contains: 275 calories
Total Fats: 8 gm
Saturated Fats: 1 gm   Protein: 40 gm
Unsaturated Fats: 7 gm   Sodium: 1216 mg
Carbohydrates: 11 gm

FISH POTPIE—
TAMBOR DE PESCADO

2   cups cooked fish, cut into chunks
1   cup diced and cooked carrots
1   cup diced and cooked chayotes
1   cup chopped and cooked yuca
1   medium onion, coarsely chopped
2   garlic cloves, minced
2   tablespoons chopped fresh cilantro
½   teaspoon ground cumin
2   tablespoons all-purpose flour
1   teaspoon half salt, half salt-substitute
        mixture
½   cup hot water
2   egg whites
¼   cup fat-free evaporated milk
½   teaspoon half salt, half salt-substitute
        mixture
¼   teaspoon freshly ground black pepper
2   cups mashed potatoes
Paprika
1   tablespoon margarine

1. Preheat the oven to 400°F.
2. Put fish, carrots, *chayotes, yuca,* and onion on bottom of a baking dish; sprinkle with garlic, cilantro, and cumin.
3. Dissolve flour and salt in hot water; stir until smooth; add to contents in baking dish.
4. In a small bowl, whisk egg whites with milk, salt, and pepper; stir into mashed potatoes.

5. Top pie with potato mixture; sprinkle with paprika; dot with margarine.

6. Bake for 25 minutes or until top browns.

Serves 4.

Each Latina Lite serving contains: 355 calories
Total Fats: 5 gm
Saturated Fats: 1 gm   Protein: 34 gm
Unsaturated Fats: 4 gm   Sodium: 907 mg
Carbohydrates: 43 gm

Poultry—Aves

Turkey Meatballs in Tamarind Sauce—Albondigas de Pavo con Salsa de Tamarindo

The versatile tamarind fruit is especially liked in most Latin countries. Young children grow up adoring the flavor of tamarind pulp with sugar, salt, and *chile*. In this old Puerto Rican recipe, the tamarind makes a tangy sauce that may be used over all poultry dishes. You may choose to omit the *Tabasco*.

1½ pounds ground turkey
½   cup cooked short-grain white rice or ½ cup
        uncooked couscous*
1   medium onion, finely diced
2   garlic cloves, minced
1   teaspoon half salt, half salt-substitute mixture
2   egg whites, beaten
1   tablespoon oil
1   cup chicken stock

*Couscous may be found in the Middle Eastern food section of your supermarket.

1. In a large bowl, combine ground turkey with cooked rice or *couscous* to ensure tender meatballs.

2. Add onion, garlic, salt, and egg whites; form 12 turkey meatballs.

3. In a large skillet, heat oil over medium heat; brown meatballs on all sides; add stock; cover tightly; bring to a boil; lower heat, simmer for 25 minutes until meatballs are thoroughly cooked.

4. If necessary, add water.

5. Remove meatballs from pot; set aside.

6. Reserve broth left in pan, refrigerate; when cool, remove fat.

7. Use defatted broth in the tamarind sauce, a future soup, or another recipe.

Tamarind Sauce

½ *pound tamarinds*
1 *cup chicken broth*
1 *tablespoon sugar*
1 *tablespoon cornstarch*
¼ *teaspoon half salt, half salt-substitute mixture*
Tabasco sauce to taste (optional)
4 *scallions, chopped (optional)*

1. Use your fingers to shell tamarinds; remove pulp and soak in warm water; discard seeds and thick vinelike strings.

2. Purée pulp, broth, and sugar in blender.

3. Dissolve cornstarch in ½ cup of puréed tamarind; transfer to large saucepan; stir constantly over low heat until sauce thickens.

4. Add remaining purée; stir until smooth.

5. Heat turkey balls in sauce.

6. If you wish, add salt and Tabasco immediately before serving.

7. Garnish with chopped scallions.

Serves 4.

Each Latina Lite serving contains: 523 calories
Total Fats: 26 gm
Saturated Fats: 5 gm   Protein: 50 gm
Unsaturated Fats: 21 gm   Sodium: 1223 mg
Carbohydrates: 20 gm

CUBAN CHICKEN AND RICE— ARROZ CON POLLO

4   medium chicken breasts, skinned and cut into
        bite-size pieces
3   garlic cloves, minced
¼   cup sweet fresh orange juice
¼   cup fresh lime or lemon juice
2   tablespoons Cuban **ACHIOTE** oil (page 50)
1   large onion, finely diced
1   green bell pepper, cored, seeded, and finely diced
¼   teaspoon freshly ground black pepper
1   bay leaf
¼   teaspoon ground cayenne pepper
¼   teaspoon ground saffron or turmeric
2   tablespoons tomato sauce
1   cup defatted chicken broth
1   cup long-grain white rice, rinsed and drained
1   cup beer
1   10-ounce package frozen green peas
1   6-ounce jar red pimientos, cut into strips

1. Place chicken pieces in a glass container.
2. To prepare marinade, in a small bowl combine garlic, orange and lime juices.
3. Pour over chicken.
4. Cover and refrigerate for at least 1 hour (added time permits the chicken to absorb more flavor).

5. Remove chicken pieces; reserve marinade.

6. Heat *Achiote* oil in a large skillet over medium heat; sauté chicken until lightly browned; remove chicken pieces; blot excess oil on paper towels.

7. Lightly fry onion and green pepper in same oil used for chicken until onion becomes translucent, about 3 minutes.

8. Add black pepper, bay leaf, cayenne pepper, saffron, tomato sauce, broth, and the reserved marinade; simmer over medium heat for five minutes.

9. Add rice and 1 cup beer or enough to fully cover rice; stir lightly; simmer, uncovered, over medium-low heat until liquid has been absorbed, about 30 minutes.

10. Add chicken pieces and peas; simmer for 6 minutes more.

11. Discard bay leaf.

12. Transfer to a large serving platter; garnish with red pimiento strips.

13. Season with half salt, half salt-substitute mixture from your shaker at table.

14. If you like *picante*, add a little *chile*.

Serves 4.

Each Latina Lite serving contains: 400 calories
Total Fats: 11 gm
Saturated Fats: 2 gm   Protein: 34 gm
Unsaturated Fats: 9 gm   Sodium: 433 mg
Carbohydrates: 40 gm

CHICKEN AND VEGETABLES FOR THE "STOUT OF TONGUE"—*CLEMOLE*

4   chicken breasts, skinned and cut into 4 pieces each
2   cups water
1   onion, cut into chunks
3   garlic cloves, cut into 4 pieces each
2   chicken bouillon cubes or 2 teaspoons consommé
      granules
½   teaspoon ground cloves
½   teaspoon freshly ground black pepper
1   cup green beans, cut into 1-inch pieces
1   cup sliced zucchini
2   ears corn, each cob cut into 6 slices
8   chiles cascabeles or habaneros, packaged dried,
      cored and seeded
3   chiles anchos, packaged dried, cored and seeded

1. In a large covered pot, cook chicken over low heat, in water; add onion, 2 garlic cloves, bouillon, cloves, and pepper; simmer for 25 minutes.

2. Add green beans, zucchini, and corn.

3. Meanwhile, soak *chiles* in warm water until pliable; grind *chiles* in a mortar with the remaining 1 garlic clove.

4. Stir into chicken and vegetables; simmer for 8 minutes more.

Serves 4.

Each Latina Lite serving contains: 264 calories
Total Fats: 4 gm
Saturated Fats: 1 gm   Protein: 32 gm
Unsaturated Fats: 3 gm   Sodium: 586 mg
Carbohydrates: 28 gm

STUFFED CORNISH GAME HEN— *CODORNIZ RELLENO*

½   cup finely diced onion
½   tablespoon vegetable oil
2   slices lean smoked turkey ham, cut into bite-size
      pieces
4   cups fresh spinach or 1 10-ounce package chopped
      frozen spinach
½   teaspoon half salt, half salt-substitute mixture
2   bolillos or French rolls or 4 slices bread, toasted and
      cubed
1   egg
1   egg white
1   teaspoon baking powder
4   Cornish game hens, skinned and cleaned
2   oven-roasting bags for chicken
1   teaspoon margarine

   1. Preheat the oven to 375°F.
   2. In a large skillet, heat oil over medium heat; sauté onion until translucent; add turkey ham, spinach, and salt; sauté for 3 minutes more. (If you are using frozen spinach, steam for 1 minute in a separate pot and drain.)
   3. Add bread cubes; sauté for 3 minutes.
   4. Transfer turkey mixture to a medium bowl.
   5. In a small bowl, beat egg with egg white.
   6. Combine beaten egg with filling; mix thoroughly.
   7. Gently fold baking powder into the mixture.
   8. Stuff each bird.
   9. Place 2 birds in each cooking bag; be sure to prick each bag in several places for ventilation.
   10. Place bagged birds on a roasting pan rack and bake at 375°F for 30 minutes.
   11. Cut and fold bags back.
   12. Spread a little margarine on each breast.

13. Raise oven temperature to 425°F and brown the birds for 5 to 10 minutes.

14. Check often to avoid scorching.

Serves 4.

Each Latina Lite serving contains: 208 calories
Total Fats: 7 gm
Saturated Fats: 2 gm   Protein: 22 gm
Unsaturated Fats: 5 gm   Sodium: 686 mg
Carbohydrates: 14 gm

CHICKEN FRICASSEE, SPANISH-STYLE— FRICASE ESPAÑOL DE POLLO

So many wonderful dishes are adapted from Spanish cooking. This recipe dates from the days of Benito Juárez and Abraham Lincoln. I have added the Cuban touch of an orange-lemon juice marinade to give it a special tang.

Marinade:

¼   cup fresh orange juice
¼   cup fresh lemon juice
3   garlic cloves, minced
½   teaspoon half salt, half salt-substitute mixture
½   teaspoon freshly ground black pepper
4   medium chicken breasts, skinned and quartered
1   tablespoon vegetable oil
1   large white onion, finely diced
1   green bell pepper, cored, seeded, and finely diced
1   cup tomato sauce
2   tablespoons capers
15 stuffed green olives, sliced
4   medium potatoes, peeled and cubed

1. In a small bowl, combine orange and lemon juices, garlic, salt, and pepper.

2. In a glass baking dish, cover chicken with mixture; marinate for 2 to 6 hours.

3. Remove chicken; reserve marinade. Heat oil in a casserole over low heat; sauté onion until translucent.

4. Add pepper and chicken; sauté over low heat until chicken is lightly browned.

5. Add reserved marinade, tomato sauce, capers, olives, and potatoes; cover casserole; simmer for 30 minutes until chicken is tender.

Serves 4.

Each Latina Lite serving contains: 358 calories
Total Fats: 9 gm
Saturated Fats: 1 gm   Protein: 31 gm
Unsaturated Fats: 8 gm   Sodium: 917 mg
Carbohydrates: 40 gm

CHICKEN AND FRUIT (THE TABLECLOTH SPOTTER DISH)—*MANCHAMANTELES*

4   chiles anchos, *packaged dried, cored and seeded*
6   chicken breasts, *skinned, boned, and cut into bite-size
        pieces*
1½ cups water
1   chicken bouillon cube or 1 teaspoon consommé
        granules
1   medium onion, cut into chunks
2   garlic cloves, halved
½   cup bread crumbs
1   cup tomato sauce

1   *loin pork chop, boned and trimmed (no fat),*
       cooked and cubed
2   *tablespoons sugar*
1   *tablespoon cider vinegar*
1   *cup plantain, cut into half slices*
1   *cup pineapple chunks*
2   *apples, peeled, cut, and sliced*
1   *cup boniato or yam, cooked and cut into quarter*
       slices
1   *cup green peas, fresh or frozen*

1. The day before you plan to cook this dish, prepare *CHILES* (page 148), cut them into strips; soak overnight in 1 cup hot water, ½ teaspoon salt, and 1 tablespoon cider vinegar.

2. The following day, in a large saucepan, over medium heat cook chicken pieces with water and bouillon for 15 minutes.

3. When tender, remove chicken; reserve broth.

4. Drain *chiles*; purée them with onion, garlic, bread crumbs, and reserved broth in blender.

5. In a casserole or skillet, simmer *chile* mixture for 5 minutes; add tomato sauce; simmer for 3 minutes more.

6. Add chicken, pork, sugar, vinegar, plantain, and pineapple; simmer, uncovered, just under boiling point until sauce reduces and thickens.

7. Add apple, *boniato*, and green peas; simmer for 3 minutes.

8. Serve with white rice.

Serves 6.

Each Latina Lite serving contains: 381 calories
Total Fats: 5 gm
Saturated Fats: 2 gm   Protein: 36 gm
Unsaturated Fats: 3 gm   Sodium: 514 mg
Carbohydrates: 48 gm

CHICKEN OR TURKEY IN CHOCOLATE-CHILE SAUCE—*MOLE POBLANO*

All *moles* are prepared from ingredients *molidos*, that are ground together. The most popular is *Mole Poblano*, from the state of Puebla, Mexico. Chicken or turkey in *mole*, served with rice and beans, is a gourmet treat often reserved for special occasions. The Latina Lite presentation is as flavorful as those prepared with lard and nuts.

4   chiles pasillas, *packaged dried, rinsed, cored, and seeded*
4   chiles anchos, *packaged dried, rinsed, cored, and seeded*
1   tablespoon *vegetable oil*
2   chiles chipotles, *canned, rinsed, cored, seeded, and dried*
¼   cup raisins
2   corn tortillas, *cut into strips*
2   cups chicken stock
3   tablespoons unsweetened cocoa or 2 squares unsweetened Baker's chocolate
2   tablespoons creamy peanut butter
1   cup diced green plantain
4   cloves
3   whole black peppercorns
1   teaspoon ground cinnamon
2   medium onions, chopped
4   garlic cloves
2   cups tomato sauce
¼   cup sugar
4   chicken breasts, skinned, quartered, and cooked, or 2 cups cooked turkey pieces

1. Soak the *chiles pasillas* and *anchos* in 1 to 2 cups of tepid water, until pliable.

2. In a medium skillet, heat oil over low heat; lightly fry the softened *chiles* with the *chiles chipotles*.

3. Add raisins and *tortilla* strips, and continue frying until the *tortilla* strips are saturated.

4. Dissolve the unsweetened cocoa or Baker's chocolate in the stock, add the *chile* mixture, and all other ingredients except the cooked chicken, and purée in blender.

5. Transfer to a large saucepan; bring to a boil; simmer for 15 minutes.

6. Add chicken or turkey pieces and continue simmering for 20 minutes more.

7. Serve hot over rice.

Serves 6.

Each Latina Lite serving contains: 367 calories
Total Fats:	13 gm	
Saturated Fats:	4 gm	Protein: 24 gm
Unsaturated Fats:	9 gm	Sodium: 734 mg
Carbohydrates:	46 gm	

CHICKEN IN RED *MOLE—MOLE ROJO*

6   chiles anchos
1   *cup tomato sauce*
1   *medium onion, cut into chunks*
2   *garlic cloves, peeled*
½ *cup dried sesame seeds*
Pinch of ground cinnamon
Pinch of ground cloves
½ *teaspoon half salt, half salt-substitute mixture*
1½ *cups defatted broth from cooked chicken*
4   *chicken breasts, skinned, cooked, and cut into pieces*
      (on the bones)

1. Cover *chiles* with warm water; soak at least 1 hour; core and seed.

2. Purée *chiles* with tomato sauce, onion, garlic, and sesame seeds in blender; stir in cinnamon, cloves, and salt.

3. Transfer to a large saucepan; simmer over low heat, covered, for 8 minutes.

4. Add broth and chicken pieces; simmer, covered, for 8 minutes more.

Serves 4.

 Each Latina Lite serving contains: 301 calories
Total Fats: 14 gm
Saturated Fats: 3 gm   Protein: 34 gm
Unsaturated Fats: 11 gm   Sodium: 770 mg
Carbohydrates: 13 gm

CHICKEN IN GREEN *MOLE*— *MOLE VERDE, PIPIAN*

½ cup shelled pumpkin seeds
12 green tomatoes (tomatillos), *skinned, washed, and quartered*
½ medium onion, cut into chunks
1 garlic clove, halved
1 chile serrano, *rinsed and drained, cored and seeded*
½ cup chicken broth or ½ bouillon cube or ½ teaspoon consommé granules with ½ cup water
¼ teaspoon freshly ground black pepper
4 chicken breasts, skinned, cooked, and cut into pieces (on the bones)

1. Purée pumpkin seeds, tomato, onion, garlic, *chile*, and broth in blender.

2. Transfer to a large saucepan; add pepper; simmer, covered, over low heat for 15 minutes.

3. Add chicken; simmer for 15 minutes more.

Serves 4.

Each Latina Lite serving contains: 282 calories
Total Fats: 13 gm
Saturated Fats: 3 gm   Protein: 33 gm
Unsaturated Fats: 10 gm   Sodium: 196 mg
Carbohydrates: 9 gm

CHICKEN, SEAFOOD, RICE EXTRAVAGANZA—*PAELLA*

No group of Latin recipes would be complete without a recipe for *paella*. Every household has a recipe for this classic *platillo* from Catalonia, the northeast region of Spain bordering on France. In the ancient language of Catalán a *paella* is a large stove-to-table pan ideal for preparing and serving this dish. If you don't have this utensil, don't worry—a Chinese wok or a large skillet will do.

3   chicken bouillon cubes or 3 teaspoons consommé
        granules
6   cups water
1   pound large frozen shrimp
1   10-ounce jar or can of clams, drained, reserve liquid
4   tablespoons Cuban ACHIOTE oil (page 50)
1   pound chicken thighs and breasts, skinless, cut into
        bite-size pieces
2   cups diced yellow onion
4   garlic cloves, minced

¼   pound lowfat turkey ham, cut into bite-size pieces
1   green bell pepper, cored, seeded, and chopped
1   cup tomato sauce
9   cups liquid (shrimp and clam liquid plus 2 cups
        water)
1   teaspoon half salt, half salt-substitute mixture
1   tablespoon paprika
1   bay leaf
½   teaspoon fresh oregano
½   teaspoon fresh thyme
4   threads saffron
3   cups short-grain white rice, rinsed and drained
2   cups chickpeas (garbanzos), cooked or canned,
        drained
1   10-ounce package frozen artichoke hearts (optional)
1   10-ounce package frozen green peas
1   6-ounce jar red pimiento strips, drained
½   cup chopped fresh Italian parsley
4   limes, cut into wedges

1. In a large saucepan, add bouillon cubes or consommé to 6 cups of water; bring to a boil; add shrimp; cook for 3 minutes; add drained clams; reserve clam juice; lower heat and cook for 1 minute more.

2. Remove shrimp and clams; reserve cooking liquid; add reserved clam juice to seafood broth; set aside.

3. Heat *Achiote* oil over medium heat in a *paellera* or large skillet; brown chicken on all sides; remove chicken, set aside; reserve oil

4. In the same skillet, sauté onion until translucent in remaining *Achiote* oil.

5. Add garlic and turkey ham; mix thoroughly with a wooden spoon.

6. Add green bell pepper, tomato sauce, 9 cups seafood broth (if there is less than 9 cups of broth, add additional water to total 9 cups), salt, paprika, bay leaf, oregano, thyme.

7. Toast saffron in a small skillet over low heat and crumble it into the *paella* pan.

8. Add chicken pieces and rice.

9. Cover and simmer until rice is tender and has consumed all of the liquid.

10. Add chickpeas, artichoke hearts, shrimp, and clams; simmer for 8 minutes more.

11. Add peas; cook for 3 minutes more.

12. Discard bay leaf.

13. Garnish with red pimiento strips, parsley, and lime wedges.

Serves 12.

Each Latina Lite serving contains: 413 calories

Total Fats:	8 gm	
Saturated Fats:	1 gm	Protein: 33 gm
Unsaturated Fats:	7 gm	Sodium: 730 mg
Carbohydrates:	52 gm	

NOTE: If available, last, add saffron seeds or yellow food coloring for more attractive color.

DRUNKEN CHICKEN—*POLLO BORRACHO*

1   *tablespoon oil*
3   *chicken breasts, skinned, each cut into quarters*
4   *slices lean turkey ham, cut into strips*
½   *cup tomato sauce*
½   *cup dry sherry wine*
1   *garlic clove, minced*
1   *teaspoon fresh Italian parsley or ½ teaspoon dried*
        parsley
½   *teaspoon almond extract*
2   *tablespoons raisins*
¼   *teaspoon ground cinnamon*
¼   *teaspoon ground cloves*
Pinch of ground nutmeg
½   *teaspoon half salt, half salt-substitute mixture*

1. In a large skillet, heat oil over medium heat; brown chicken and turkey ham; add tomato sauce, sherry, garlic, parsley, almond extract, raisins, cinnamon, cloves, nutmeg, and salt.

2. Cover tightly; cook over medium-low heat for 45 minutes.

Serves 4.

> Each Latina Lite serving contains: 218 calories
> Total Fats: 7 gm
> Saturated Fats: 1 gm   Protein: 26 gm
> Unsaturated Fats: 6 gm   Sodium: 720 mg
> Carbohydrates: 7 gm

CHICKEN BREADED IN CORNMEAL— POLLO CON MASECA

⅓   cup cornmeal (Maseca, *flour used to make* tortillas)
2   tablespoons all-purpose flour
2   tablespoons oat bran
2   teaspoons dried oregano, crumbled without stems
¼   teaspoon garlic powder
1   teaspoon powdered red chile
4   medium chicken breasts, skinless and boneless
3   egg whites
2   tablespoons water
2   tablespoons olive oil

1. Preheat oven to 375°F.
2. On a large piece of wax paper, combine cornmeal, flour, oat bran, oregano, garlic powder and *chile.*
3. Wash chicken.
4. In a shallow bowl, beat egg whites and 2 tablespoons water.
5. Dip chicken pieces into egg whites and coat with dry mixture.

6. Arrange breasts on a nonstick cookie sheet; dribble oil on top.

7. Bake for 35 minutes until chicken is tender.

Serves 4.

> Each Latina Lite serving contains: 283 calories
> Total Fats: 11 gm
> Saturated Fats: 2 gm   Protein: 32 gm
> Unsaturated Fats: 9 gm   Sodium: 106 mg
> Carbohydrates: 15 gm

SHREDDED CHICKEN—
ROPA VIEJA DE POLLO

The Cuban version of this traditional Spanish dish is usually prepared with beef. Latina Lite *Ropa Vieja* substitutes chicken for beef, but retains the flavor of Spain, enhanced by the spices and *picante* of Cuba.

4   *medium chicken breasts, skinless and boneless*
2   *cups water*
1   *chicken bouillon cube or 1 teaspoon consommé*
        granules
2   *tablespoons white onion, cut into chunks*
2–4 *garlic cloves, minced*
1   *tablespoon vegetable oil*
4   *tablespoons diced white onion*
1   *green bell pepper, seeded and diced*
1   *cup tomato sauce*
1½ *cups broth from cooked chicken*
½   *cup capers, drained*
½   *teaspoon ground cayenne pepper*
½   *teaspoon ground cumin*

6 chiles *in* escabeche, *canned*
Fresh minced parsley to taste
Freshly ground black pepper to taste
2 cups cooked long-grain white rice

1. Remove all fat from chicken.
2. In a large saucepan, over medium heat, cook breasts in water with bouillon, onion, and garlic.
3. When cooked, cool and shred chicken by pulling it apart, strand by strand.
4. Purée chicken broth with onion and garlic in blender; set aside.
5. In a large saucepan, heat oil over medium heat; sauté diced onion and bell pepper until onion becomes translucent; add tomato sauce, 1½ cups puréed chicken broth; add shredded chicken, capers, cayenne pepper, cumin, and *chiles.*
6. Lower heat and simmer, uncovered, until most liquid is absorbed.
7. Sprinkle with parsley and pepper; serve over cooked rice.
8. If necessary, season with half salt, half salt-substitute mixture from your shaker.

Serves 4.

Each Latina Lite serving contains: 356 calories
Total Fats: 7 gm
Saturated Fats: 1 gm   Protein: 33 gm
Unsaturated Fats: 6 gm   Sodium: 1197 mg
Carbohydrates: 41 gm

Meats—Carnes

Albaniles—Steak with Onions and Chile

Albaniles are skilled laborers in the construction industry. Masters in the art of building with concrete, they spend their days scampering up and down high scaffolding hauling heavy buckets of cement. For *comida*, they will often prepare this hearty dish over a makeshift fire pit constructed at the job site.

1   tablespoon vegetable oil
2   cups thinly sliced onions
2   tomatoes, peeled* and chopped
1   pound beef, thinly sliced
3   tablespoons chopped fresh cilantro
2   chiles serranos, cored, seeded, and chopped
½   teaspoon half salt, half salt-substitute mixture

1. In a large skillet, heat oil over low heat; sauté onions until browned; add tomatoes; simmer for 5 minutes.
2. Add beef, cilantro, *chiles*, and salt; simmer for 10 minutes until beef is cooked.

Serves 4.

*To peel tomatoes, gently scorch tomato skin over stove burner until it blisters; wrap tomatoes in a cool damp cloth for a few minutes. The peel will separate easily.

Each Latina Lite serving contains: 309 calories
Total Fats: 13 gm
Saturated Fats: 4 gm   Protein: 37 gm
Unsaturated Fats: 9 gm   Sodium: 288 mg
Carbohydrates: 11 gm

Meat loaf with *Chipotle—* *Albondigon con Chipotle*

2   egg whites
¾   pound ground turkey breast
8   ounces lean ground beef
½   cup cooked short-grain white rice
½   cup diced onion
1   teaspoon half salt, half salt-substitute mixture
1   tablespoon Worcestershire sauce
¼   teaspoon freshly ground black pepper
2   teaspoons vegetable oil
1   cup tomato sauce
2   garlic cloves, halved
2   chiles chipotles, canned, rinsed and dried, cored and
        seeded
1   cup fresh orange juice
1   cup carrots, peeled and cut into strips
4   apples, cored, peeled, and cubed

1. In a small bowl, beat the egg whites.

2. In a large bowl, combine turkey, beef, rice, onion, salt, Worcestershire, beaten egg whites, and pepper; form into a meat loaf.

3. In a large skillet, heat oil over medium heat; brown meat loaf on both sides; remove from heat.

4. Purée tomato sauce, garlic, and *chiles chipotles* in blender; stir in orange juice; pour over meat; simmer over low heat for 5 minutes.

5. Add carrots; cover tightly; cook over low heat for 50 minutes.

6. Add apple; simmer for 5 minutes more.

7. If necessary, season with half salt, half salt-substitute mixture from your shaker at table.

Serves 6.

Each Latina Lite serving contains: 389 calories
Total Fats: 13 gm
Saturated Fats: 3 gm   Protein: 31 gm
Unsaturated Fats: 10 gm   Sodium 649 mg
Carbohydrates: 40 gm

BREADED STEAK—
BISTEC EMPANIZADO

4   *5-ounce top sirloin steaks, trimmed*
¼   *cup fresh orange juice*
¼   *cup fresh lemon juice*
1   *garlic clove, minced*
¼   *cup all-purpose flour*
¼   *cup corn flake crumbs*
2   *tablespoons oat bran*
½   *teaspoon half salt, half salt-substitute mixture*
2   *egg whites*
2   *tablespoons vegetable oil*
AJILIMOJILI SAUCE *(page 54)*

1. Pound meat with a meat hammer or iron skillet between 2 pieces of wax paper until it is ¼-inch thick.

2. In a medium glass dish, combine orange and lemon juices and garlic; add meat and marinate for 1 hour; remove steaks; drain and dry.

3. On a sheet of wax paper, combine flour, corn flake crumbs, oat bran, and salt.

4. In a shallow bowl, beat egg whites.

5. Dip each steak in egg whites; coat with crumbs.

6. In a large skillet, heat oil until very hot; fry steak quickly on both sides; blot excess oil on paper towels.

7. Serve with *Ajilimójili*.

Serves 4.

Each Latina Lite serving contains: 485 calories
Total Fats: 25 gm	
Saturated Fats: 6 gm	Protein: 47 gm
Unsaturated Fats: 19 gm	Sodium: 456 mg
Carbohydrates: 17 gm	

STEAK AND ONIONS— BISTEC ENCEBOLLADO

Marinade:

2   tablespoons vegetable oil
1   medium onion, chopped
2   garlic cloves, minced
1   medium green bell pepper, cored, seeded, and cut into strips
1   cup tomato sauce
1   tablespoon red wine vinegar
2   tablespoons capers
2   teaspoons fresh oregano or 1 teaspoon dried oregano
½   teaspoon ground cumin
1   teaspoon half salt, half salt-substitute mixture
¼   teaspoon freshly ground black pepper

1½ pounds beef top round, thinly sliced
2   cups thinly sliced onion

1. To prepare marinade, in a small saucepan, heat 1 tablespoon oil over low heat; sauté chopped onion and garlic until onion becomes translucent; add green bell pepper; sauté for 3 minutes more.

2. Add tomato sauce, vinegar, capers, oregano, cumin, salt, and pepper.

3. In a glass dish, pour sauce over meat; marinate from 2 to 48 hours in refrigerator. The longer meat marinates the better the flavor.

4. In a nonstick skillet, heat remaining 1 tablespoon oil over medium heat; sauté onion rings until golden brown.

5. Add meat and sauce; cover partially; cook for 15 minutes.

Serves 4.

Each Latina Lite serving contains: 475 calories
Total Fats: 21 gm
Saturated Fats: 6 gm   Protein: 54 gm
Unsaturated Fats: 15 gm   Sodium: 892 mg
Carbohydrates: 17 gm

BEEF ROLL, CUBAN STYLE— BISTEC ENROLLADO CUBANO

Marinade:

¼   cup fresh orange juice
¼   cup fresh lemon juice
3   garlic cloves, minced
½   teaspoon ground cumin
½   teaspoon half salt, half salt-substitute mixture

1½ pounds flank steak
1   egg yolk

3   egg whites
1   tablespoon vegetable oil
4   slices lean turkey ham, chopped
2   carrots, peeled and grated
1   medium onion, chopped
¼   cup dry red wine
½   cup tomatoes, fresh or canned, chopped
1   bay leaf
½   teaspoon half salt, half salt-substitute mixture
¼   teaspoon freshly ground black pepper

1. To prepare marinade, combine orange and lemon juices, garlic, cumin, and salt in rectangular glass baking dish.

2. On large piece of wax paper, place flank steak; cover with another sheet of wax paper; pound with a meat hammer or heavy skillet until ¼-inch thick.

3. Cover meat with mixture; marinate in refrigerator for 6 hours.

4. Remove and drain meat; blot on paper towels; save marinade.

5. In a small bowl, beat egg yolk with whites; in large skillet, heat oil over medium heat; fry egg mixture until set; remove and lay over flank steak; reserve oil.

6. Arrange turkey ham, carrots, and half the onion evenly over egg; roll flank steak; tie each end with kitchen string.

7. Reheat remaining oil; brown beef roll over high heat on all sides.

8. Add reserve marinade, the remaining half onion, wine, tomatoes, bay leaf, salt and pepper; cover tightly; lower heat; simmer for 2½ hours.

9. Discard bay leaf.

10. Allow to cool for 10 minutes; cut into slices; pour pan juice over meat.

Serves 6.

Each Latina Lite serving contains: 345 calories
Total Fats: 15 gm
Saturated Fats: 4 gm   Protein: 42 gm
Unsaturated Fats: 11 gm   Sodium: 821 mg
Carbohydrates: 7 gm

ʙEEF POT ROAST CUBAN-STYLE— *BOLICHE ASADO*

1½ pounds lean beef
1   tablespoon fresh lemon juice
¼   teaspoon ground thyme
1   garlic clove, minced
1   tablespoon chopped fresh cilantro
3   cups water
2   beef bouillon cubes or 2 teaspoons consommé granules
1   medium onion, cut into chunks
4   potatoes, peeled and quartered
1   green bell pepper, cored, seeded, and chopped

1. Trim all fat from meat.

2. In a small bowl, mix lemon juice, thyme, garlic, and cilantro together; rub into meat.

3. In a covered casserole, over medium-high heat, sear meat on all sides.

4. Add water and bouillon; bring to a boil; cover; reduce heat and simmer for 2 hours.

5. Add onion, potatoes, and bell pepper; simmer for 40 minutes more.

6. Can be prepared ahead and saved for following day.

Serves 6.

Each Latina Lite serving contains: 323 calories
Total Fats: 10 gm
Saturated Fats: 4 gm   Protein: 37 gm
Unsaturated Fats: 6 gm   Sodium: 420 mg
Carbohydrates: 21 gm

PORK AND CHICKEN WITH ANNATO— COCHINITA PIBIL

2   cups fresh orange juice
4   ounces Mexican annato (achiote) in block form or 2
        tablespoons ground annato seeds
4–6 garlic cloves, minced
½   teaspoon ground cumin
1   tablespoon fresh chopped oregano
½   teaspoon freshly ground black pepper
1   teaspoon half salt, half salt-substitute mixture
4   chicken breasts, skinned, boned, and cut into
        2-inch by ½-inch strips
1½ pounds lean pork loin, trimmed and cut into
        2-inch by ½-inch strips
2   large banana leaves
2   oranges, thinly sliced

1. To prepare marinade, combine orange juice, annato, garlic, cumin, oregano, pepper, and salt in a rectangular glass baking dish.

2. Add chicken and pork to marinade; cover with a lid or aluminum foil; refrigerate for 24 hours.

3. The following day, preheat the oven to 350°F.

4. Place a banana leaf in a roasting pan, arrange chicken and meat over leaf.

5. Pour marinade over meat; arrange orange slices on top.

6. Cover with remaining banana leaf.

7. Bake for 1 hour or until well cooked.

8. Serve hot accompanied by PICKLED ONIONS (page 157).

Serves 8.

Each Latina Lite serving contains: 289 calories
Total Fats: 9 gm
Saturated Fats: 3 gm   Protein: 40 gm
Unsaturated Fats: 6 gm   Sodium: 278 mg
Carbohydrates: 11 gm

BEEF STRIPS WITH VEGETABLES— FAJITAS

Fajitas are not a conventional Latin dish, but a Cal-Tex-Mex way to make inexpensive meat palatable and stretch to feed everybody. Recently arrived Mexican immigrants struggled to feed their families and found skirt steak, or *falda*, an economical but tough cut of beef. Ingeniously, they cut the meat into small strips, or *fajitas*, sautéed it with onions, green bell peppers, and garlic and converted it into one of the most popular *Nuevo Latino* dishes. Unfortunately, along with the success and popularity of *fajitas* the price of skirt steak has risen. I prefer to use chicken breast instead of beef in this dish to keep the fat content low. However, this is a lowfat beef cut and could be chosen for your "once a week" beef meal.

Marinade:

½   *cup fresh lime or lemon juice*
½   *tablespoon freshly ground black pepper*
2–3 *garlic cloves, minced*
1   *tablespoon low-sodium soy sauce*

• • •

1½ *pounds skirt steak, or 4 medium chicken breasts,*
  skinned and boned
1½ *large white onions*
1   *tablespoon vegetable oil*
1½ *large green bell peppers, cut into strips*
1   *teaspoon beef consommé granules or 1 bouillon cube*

Topping:

⅓ *cup fat-free yogurt*
⅓ *cup fat-free sour cream*
1   *teaspoon Japanese seasoned rice vinegar**
½ *cup crumbled fat-free cheese*

Accompaniments:

8   *Corn tortillas*
PICO DE GALLO *(page 61)*
½ *recipe for* GUACAMOLE *(page 182)*

1. To prepare marinade, combine lime juice, pepper, garlic, and soy sauce in a shallow square dish.

2. If you use beef, peel the fatty membrane from skirt steak with a very sharp knife to ensure tenderness; for chicken, pound breasts flat between 2 pieces of wax paper on a hard flat surface.

3. Add meat or chicken to marinade; cover; marinate overnight in refrigerator.

4. The following day, slice onions into ¼-inch slices; quarter each slice.

5. Lightly grill meat to seal juices within; if using chicken, grill until almost cooked.

6. Cool; cut chicken or meat into ¼-inch-wide strips; for beef, be sure to cut it across the grain.

---

*Japanese seasoned rice vinegar can be found in the Asian food section of your supermarket.

7. Meanwhile, in a large skillet, heat oil over medium heat, sauté onion until translucent; add pepper strips, consommé, and beef or chicken; sauté for 2 minutes more.

8. In a small bowl, combine yogurt, sour cream, and vinegar while *Fajitas* are cooking. Serve hot with cheese, yogurt-sour cream topping, *Pico de Gallo, Guacamole,* and hot *tortillas.*

Serves 6.

Each Latina Lite serving contains: 446 calories
Total Fats: 15 gm
Saturated Fats: 4 gm   Protein: 45 gm
Unsaturated Fats: 11 gm   Sodium: 781 mg
Carbohydrates: 34 gm

BEEF IN CHOCOLATE SAUCE— *FILETE EN CHOCOLATE*

At first it's shocking to imagine chocolate as a meat sauce. But, are you a chocolate lover? Probably so. If you like the taste, try adding red wine for a different flavor. In *cacao* country the cocoa bean enhances meat, poultry, and vegetable dishes as well as rich sweet *dulces.*

2½ pounds fresh brisket
½   teaspoon half salt, half salt-substitute mixture
1   medium onion, cut into chunks
3   garlic cloves, minced
1   stick cinnamon
1   cup water
½   cup white wine
1   beef bouillon cube or 1 teaspoon consommé granules
2   squares unsweetened Baker's chocolate, grated
½   cup chopped fresh Italian parsley

1. Sprinkle salt over meat.

2. In a large skillet, over medium-high heat, sear meat on all sides; add onion, garlic, cinnamon, water, wine, and bouillon.

3. Cover tightly; lower heat and cook for 2 to 3 hours until meat is tender.

4. Remove meat from skillet and cool; reserve pan juice.

5. Put skillet with juice from cooked meat in the refrigerator for 1 to 2 hours.

6. Remove congealed fat from broth.

7. Slice meat across grain.

8. Heat broth over low heat; discard large pieces of onion; add grated chocolate and meat; simmer for 8 minutes.

9. Sprinkle with parsley just before serving.

Serves 8.

Each Latina Lite serving contains: 366 calories
Total Fats: 12 gm
Saturated Fats: 5 gm   Protein: 32 gm
Unsaturated Fats: 7 gm   Sodium: 331 mg
Carbohydrates: 6 gm

Hash, Cuban-Style—*Picadillo Cubano*

Versatile *Picadillo* can be covered with a browned crust of mashed potatoes that have been mixed with fat-free milk instead of butter, and lightly browned in the oven to become *Tambor de Picadillo*—Hash Drum or Pie. It may also be used as the filling for *empanadas*. Traditionally, *picadillo* is served with two fried eggs, adding another 184 calories and contributing to the 68 percent fat content of this *platillo* prepared in the old way. In this Latina Lite makeover, eggs are omitted.

1   *pound uncooked ground turkey breast*
½   *pound uncooked ground lean beef*
1   *tablespoon olive oil*
½   *cup diced onion*
½   *large green bell pepper, seeded, cored, and diced*
2   *garlic cloves, minced*
¼   *teaspoon ground cayenne pepper*
1   *cup tomato sauce*
¼   *teaspoon ground cumin*
¼   *cup capers, drained*
Freshly ground black pepper to taste
2   *cups cooked long-grain white rice*
BAKED PLANTAIN (page 167)

1. In a large bowl, thoroughly mix ground turkey with lean ground beef; set aside.

2. In a large skillet, heat oil over medium heat; sauté onion until translucent.

3. Add bell pepper, garlic, and cayenne pepper; simmer over medium heat for 3 to 5 minutes.

4. Add meat; stir constantly; keep ground meat separated into small pieces.

5. When meat is browned, add tomato sauce, cumin, and capers; lower heat and simmer for another 8 minutes; add pepper to taste.

6. Serve each portion over ½ cup of cooked rice with Baked Plantain.

7. If necessary, season with half salt, half salt-substitute mixture from your shaker at table.

Serves 6.

Each Latina Lite serving contains: 408 calories
Total Fats: 18 gm
Saturated Fats: 5 gm   Protein: 34 gm
Unsaturated Fats: 13 gm   Sodium: 477 mg
Carbohydrates: 27 gm

STEW, PUERTO RICAN-STYLE— *SANCOCHO*

1   tablespoon olive oil
1   medium onion, coarsely chopped
1   green bell pepper, cored, seeded, and chopped
2   garlic cloves, minced
2   slices smoked lean turkey ham, chopped
2   pounds lean beef round steak, trimmed and cut into
      chunks
3   chicken breasts, skinned and cut into 4 pieces each
4   cups water
½   cup RECAITO (page 62)
1   cup tomato sauce
4   chicken bouillon cubes or 4 teaspoons consommé
      granules
2   teaspoons fresh oregano or 1 teaspoon dried oregano
1   tablespoon chopped fresh cilantro
3   cups yuca, peeled and cut into 1-inch cubes
2   cups yautía, peeled and cut into 1-inch cubes
2   cups ñame, peeled and cut into 1-inch cubes
1   cup yams, peeled and cut into 1-inch cubes
2   cups pumpkin, peeled and cut into 1-inch cubes
2   green plantains, peeled and cut into 2-inch pieces
2   ears corn, cut into 1-inch slices

1. In a large pot, heat oil over medium heat; sauté onion until translucent; add bell pepper, garlic, turkey ham; sauté for 4 minutes.

2. Add beef and chicken; brown for 3 minutes.

3. Add water, *Recaíto*, tomato sauce, bouillon, oregano, cilantro, *yuca, yautía, ñame,* and yams; cover tightly and bring to boil; lower heat and simmer for 1½ hours.

4. Add pumpkin, plantain, and corn; simmer for 35 minutes more.

Serves 12.

Each Latina Lite serving contains: 471 calories
Total Fats: 22 gm
Saturated Fats: 8 gm   Protein: 31 gm
Unsaturated Fats: 14 gm   Sodium: 614 mg
Carbohydrates: 37 gm

PORK, POTATOES, AND AVOCADOS— TINGA

1¼ pounds lean pork loin
2   medium onions
1   tablespoon vegetable oil
4   canned tomatoes, diced
2   cups cubed and cooked potatoes
4   chiles chipotles (canned), rinsed and dried
½   tablespoon cider vinegar
½   teaspoon half salt, half salt-substitute mixture
1   large ripe avocado

1. In a large saucepan, cook pork covered in water with ½ onion cut into 3 chunks; when tender, remove meat and cool; discard onion chunks; shred pork and set aside.

2. Thinly slice remaining 1½ onions.

3. In a large skillet, heat oil over medium heat; sauté onion slices until translucent. Add pork, tomatoes, potatoes, *chiles chipotles*, vinegar, and salt; cook until almost all liquid is absorbed.

4. Peel and thinly slice avocado; gently mix in to avoid bruising.

Serves 4.

Each Latina Lite serving contains: 495 calories
Total Fats: 23 gm
Saturated Fats: 6 gm   Protein: 47 gm
Unsaturated Fats: 17 gm   Sodium: 258 mg
Carbohydrates: 27 gm

CHILES

Chiles, a part of Latin cuisine for over 6,000 years, are the most widely used seasoning in the world—there are over 200 different varieties. They transform ordinary dishes into culinary delights with colors ranging from clear to red, green, purple, and even black, sweet and pungent aromas, and stimulating spicy flavors. *Chiles* may be used raw, dried, frozen, powdered, canned, pickled, fried, baked, broiled, and barbecued. Their effect on the oral cavity ranges from a pleasant tingle to tongue-smarting, sweat-producing, palate-challenging torment. If you happen to bite into an extra hot one, put a little salt on your tongue to extinguish the fiery feeling. Since *chiles* affect delicate body areas in the same way as your mouth, be especially careful not to touch your eyes, nose, or lips immediately after preparing *chiles*. I have selected some of my favorite pepper preparations, including varieties of *chiles* easily available in supermarkets and grocery stores.

Preparing Fresh *Chiles*:

1. Roast fresh *chiles* on the *comal*—griddle—until skin blisters and blackens.
2. Wrap in a damp cloth until cool, then peel; they will peel easily.
3. Slit each *chile* on one side, discard core and seeds.

Using Canned *Chiles*

1. A 27-ounce can contains about 25 whole green *chiles*; carefully remove the *chiles* that are already peeled, cored, seeded, and slit.

2. Blot with paper towels to remove excess liquid.

*C*HILES, STUFFED WITH MEAT AND FRUIT—*CHILES EN NOGADA*

12 fresh California, pasilla, *or* poblano chiles
     or 12 canned whole green chiles

Filling:

1	*pound ground turkey breast*
¾	*pound lean ground beef*
1	*cup cooked short-grain white rice*
½	*cup raisins*
4	*tablespoons vegetable oil (divided)*
1	*cup diced onion*
3	*garlic cloves, minced*
1	*teaspoon half salt, half salt-substitute mixture*
1	*ripe plantain, diced*
4	*tablespoons chopped fresh Italian parsley*
6	*egg whites*
¼	*cup all-purpose flour*

Topping:

2	*tablespoons cornstarch*
2	*tablespoons cold water*
1½	*cups fat-free plain yogurt*
1	*tablespoon Japanese seasoned rice vinegar*[*]
1	*teaspoon almond extract*

[*]Japanese seasoned rice vinegar can be found in the Asian food section of your supermarket.

GARNISH:

Red pomegranate seeds
12 sprigs curly parsley

1. To prepare fresh *CHILES* (page 148), soak *chiles* in 1 quart warm water with ½ teaspoon salt for 2 to 4 hours to make them less *picante*.

1. To prepare filling, in a large bowl combine turkey, beef, and rice; set aside.
2. Plump raisins in hot water; set aside.
3. In a large skillet, heat 2 tablespoons oil over medium heat; sauté onion until translucent.
4. Add garlic, meat mixture, and salt; lower heat, sauté for 5 minutes; stir occasionally.
5. Add drained raisins, plantain, and parsley; sauté for 3 minutes more; set aside.
6. Remove *chiles* from water; drain and dry *chiles*.
7. Stuff each *chile* with filling; close with toothpicks.

1. To fry *chiles*, in a large bowl beat egg whites until they peak.
2. Lightly dust *chiles* with flour.
3. Coat each *chile* with beaten egg white.
4. In a large skillet, heat remaining 2 tablespoons oil over medium heat; brown stuffed *chiles* on all sides.
5. Remove *chiles*; blot excess oil on paper towels.
6. Arrange *chiles* in a rectangular glass baking dish; if you prefer warm *chiles*, heat in a 150°F oven.

1. To prepare sauce, in a small saucepan dissolve cornstarch in 2 tablespoons cold water; stir constantly over low heat until thick.
2. Add yogurt gradually, vinegar, and almond extract; continue stirring.
3. Remove *chiles* from oven; pour yogurt topping over *chiles*.
4. Do not reheat!

5. Sprinkle pomegranate seeds on top.
6. Decorate with curly parsley.

Serves 8.

Each Latina Lite serving contains: 461 calories
Total Fats: 21 gm
Saturated Fats: 5 gm   Protein: 36 gm
Unsaturated Fats: 16 gm   Sodium: 373 mg
Carbohydrates: 32 gm

CHILES STUFFED WITH BEANS— CHILES RELLENOS CON FRIJOLES

8 fresh chiles Californias, pasillas, or poblanos or 8 canned whole green chiles

Filling:

Cooking spray
½   cup finely diced onion
2   garlic cloves, minced
1   cup tomato sauce
1   cup cooked mashed beans
1   teaspoon half salt, half salt-substitute mixture

¼   cup all-purpose flour
6   egg whites
2   tablespoons vegetable oil

Topping:

½   cup fat-free yogurt
½   cup fat-free sour cream
1   teaspoon Japanese seasoned rice vinegar[*]

[*]Japanese seasoned rice vinegar can be found in the Asian food section of your supermarket.

Garnish:

¼ cup crumbled part-skim milk cheese
Fresh chopped Italian parsley
Red pomegranate seeds when available

1. To prepare fresh CHILES (page 148), soak *chiles* in 1 quart warm water with ½ teaspoon salt for 2 to 4 hours to make them less *picante*.

1. To prepare filling, coat a medium nonstick skillet with cooking spray (such as Pam); over medium heat, sauté onion and garlic until golden.
2. Add tomato sauce; lower heat and simmer until well blended and liquid is absorbed; stir occasionally.
3. Add beans and salt; continue to cook over low heat for 8 minutes; stir frequently.
4. Remove from heat; cool.
5. Stuff each *chile* with bean mixture.
6. Close with a toothpick.

1. To fry *chiles*, lightly dust each *chile* with flour.
2. In a large bowl, beat egg whites until they peak.
3. Cover each *chile* with beaten whites.
4. In a large nonstick skillet, heat 2 tablespoons of oil over medium heat; brown *chiles* on all sides.
5. Arrange *chiles* on a serving dish; cool.

1. To prepare sauce, in a small bowl blend yogurt, sour cream, and vinegar.
2. Spread sauce over *chiles*.
3. Sprinkle with crumbled cheese and parsley.
4. If pomegranates are in season, adorn with the red seeds for color.
5. If necessary, you may add a little half salt, half salt-substitute mixture from your shaker.

Serves 4.

Each Latina Lite serving contains: 305 calories
Total Fats: 10 gm
Saturated Fats: 2 gm   Protein: 19 gm
Unsaturated Fats: 8 gm   Sodium: 1226 mg
Carbohydrates: 37 gm

CHILES AND GARLIC WITH VEGETABLES—CHILES Y AJO CON VERDURAS

2   chiles guajillos *packaged dried, cored and seeded*
1   *cup warm water*
2   *teaspoons white vinegar*
½   *teaspoon half salt, half salt-substitute mixture*
1   *garlic head, peeled*
1   *tablespoon olive oil*
4   *tablespoons balsamic or cider vinegar*
1   *teaspoon fresh oregano or* ½ *teaspoon dried oregano*
1   *cup green beans, lightly steamed and cut into 1-inch*
         pieces
1   *cup carrots, lightly steamed and cut into 1-inch strips*
1   *cup cauliflower, lightly steamed and separated into*
         bite-size pieces
1   *cup yuca, steamed and cut into 1-inch pieces*
¼   *cup grated part-skim milk white cheese*
4   *raw onion rings*

1. Soak *chiles* in water with vinegar and salt for 1 hour; blot dry.
2. In a mortar, crush *chiles*, garlic, and oil to form a smooth paste; blend in vinegar and oregano.
3. Arrange vegetables on a serving platter; dribble sauce over them; sprinkle with cheese; adorn with onion rings.

Serves 4.

Each Latina Lite serving contains: 170 calories
Total Fats: 6 gm
Saturated Fats: 2 gm   Protein: 7 gm
Unsaturated Fats: 4 gm   Sodium: 400 mg
Carbohydrates: 23 gm

CHILE SAUCE FOR CHICKEN, LAMB, AND PORK—CHIRMOLE

3   chiles anchos, *packaged dried, cored and seeded*
3   chiles serranos, *canned, rinsed, dried, cored, and seeded*
2   *garlic cloves, halved*
1   *small onion, cut into chunks*
2   *cups tomato sauce*
2   *teaspoons vegetable oil*
¼   *teaspoon freshly ground black pepper*
1   *teaspoon ground annato (achiote) seeds*
½   *teaspoon ground cinnamon*
½   *teaspoon Tabasco sauce*
2   *teaspoons fresh oregano or 1 teaspoon dried oregano*
2   *tablespoons cornmeal*
¼   *cup fresh orange juice*
¼   *cup fresh lemon juice*
8   *almost ripe plums, diced*

1. Soak *chiles anchos* in warm water for 5 minutes.

2. Purée *chiles anchos* and *serranos*, garlic, onion, and tomato sauce in blender.

3. In a large nonstick pan, heat oil over low heat; add purée; simmer, covered, for 5 minutes.

4. Add pepper, annato, cinnamon, Tabasco, and oregano; simmer for 3 more minutes.

5. Dissolve cornmeal in orange juice until smooth; add to mixture, stir well; add lemon juice and plums; simmer for final 5 minutes.

Serves 8.

Each Latina Lite serving contains: 83 calories
Total Fats: 2 gm
Saturated Fats: 0 gm   Protein: 2 gm
Unsaturated Fats: 2 gm   Sodium: 158 mg
Carbohydrates: 17 gm

CHILE STRIPS AND ONION—
RAJAS DE CHILE CON CEBOLLA

4   *fresh* chiles **Californias** *(substitute any large green*
     fresh chile)
1   *teaspoon white vinegar*
1   *teaspoon half salt, half salt-substitute mixture*
1   *tablespoon vegetable oil*
1   *large white onion, thinly sliced*

1. To prepare *chiles*, roast *chiles* on all sides over stove burner until skin blackens and blisters.

2. Wrap in a damp cloth.

3. Peel, core, and seed; cut into 2-inch strips.

4. Soak *chile* strips in 1 cup water with vinegar and ½ teaspoon salt for 1 hour. Drain and dry *chiles*.

5. In a large nonstick skillet, heat oil over medium heat; sauté onion until translucent; add *chile*; lower heat; sauté for 5 minutes.

6. Add remaining ½ teaspoon salt just before serving.

Serves 4.

Each Latina Lite serving contains: 59 calories
Total Fats: 3 gm
Saturated Fats: 0 gm   Protein: 1 gm
Unsaturated Fats: 3 gm   Sodium: 393 mg
Carbohydrates: 7 gm

*C*HILE STRIPS IN CREAM— *RAJAS EN CREMA*

4   *fresh* chiles Californias, pasillas, *or* poblanos, *or 8 canned whole green* chiles, *cored, seeded, cut into strips*
1   *tablespoon vegetable oil*
1   *cup thinly sliced onion*
1   *tablespoon cornstarch*
¼   *cup water*
½   *cup fat-free plain yogurt*
½   *cup fat-free sour cream*
¼   *teaspoon half salt, half salt-substitute mixture*
¼   *cup grated white cheese*

1. To prepare *chiles*, roast *chiles* on all sides over stove burner until skin blackens and blisters.

2. Wrap in a damp cloth.

3. Peel, core, and seed; cut into 2-inch strips; set aside.

4. In a large skillet, heat oil over medium heat; sauté onion until translucent; add *chile* strips; sauté for 3 minutes more.

5. In a small saucepan, dissolve cornstarch in ¼ cup water; stir over low heat until thick.

6. Add yogurt and sour cream; stir; blend in salt and cheese.

7. Pour yogurt sauce over *chile*-onion mixture.

Serves 4.

Each Latina Lite serving contains: 132 calories
Total Fats: 6 gm
Saturated Fats: 2 gm   Protein: 8 gm
Unsaturated Fats: 4 gm   Sodium: 217 mg
Carbohydrates: 13 gm

VEGETABLES— VERDURAS

PICKLED ONIONS—*CEBOLLAS CURTIDAS*

4   medium red onions, sliced thinly
4   garlic cloves, sliced
¼   cup fresh lemon juice
¼   cup cider vinegar
2   teaspoons fresh oregano or 1 teaspoon dried oregano
½   teaspoon half salt, half salt-substitute mixture
1⅓ cups boiling water

1. Put onion slices in a rectangular glass dish.

2. Add garlic, lemon juice, vinegar, oregano, and salt; pour boiling water over mixture; cool.

3. Transfer to a glass jar with a lid; refrigerate for at least 24 hours.

4. If you double or triple the recipe, keep refrigerated and the onions will last up to 2 weeks.

5. Serve with *COCHINITA PIBIL* (page 140), *ENCHILADAS* (page 27), or other Mexican dishes.

Serves 4.

Each Latina Lite serving contains: 33 calories
Total Fats: 0 gm
Saturated Fats: 0 gm   Protein: 1 gm
Unsaturated Fats: 0 gm   Sodium: 210 mg
Carbohydrates: 8 gm

*G*RILLED SCALLIONS—
CEBOLLITAS VERDES ASADAS

16 scallions, cleaned (do not remove green tops)
2   tablespoons olive oil
1   teaspoon half salt, half salt-substitute mixture
4   lemons, halved

1. Brush oil entirely over each scallion.
2. Grill over hot coals; turn frequently, until outside begins to blacken.
3. Sprinkle with salt; serve with lemon.

Serves 4.

Each Latina Lite serving contains: 110 calories
Total Fats: 7 gm
Saturated Fats: 1 gm   Protein: 2 gm
Unsaturated Fats: 6 gm   Sodium: 393 mg
Carbohydrates: 13 gm

*M*USHROOMS WITH TOMATO AND
GARLIC—*CHAMPINONES TAPATIOS*

2   large chiles Californias or poblanos, *fresh or canned,*
     cored and seeded
2   tablespoons olive oil
1   cup diced onion
4   cups fresh small mushrooms, rinsed and dried with
     stems trimmed
4   garlic cloves, halved
1   cup tomato sauce
½   teaspoon half salt, half salt-substitute mixture

1. Roast *chiles* on all sides over stove burner until skin blackens and blisters.

2. Wrap in a damp cloth.

3. Peel, core, and seed; cut into 2-inch strips; set aside.

4. In a large skillet, heat oil over medium heat; sauté onion until lightly browned; add mushrooms and garlic; sauté for 3 minutes more; stir frequently.

5. Add *chiles* to mushrooms; sauté for another 3 minutes.

6. Add tomato sauce and salt; lower heat and simmer for 5 more minutes.

Serves 4.

Each Latina Lite serving contains: 149 calories
Total Fats: 8 gm
Saturated Fats: 1 gm   Protein: 5 gm
Unsaturated Fats: 7 gm   Sodium: 584 mg
Carbohydrates: 19 gm

CREAMED *CHAYOTE* SQUASH— *CHAYOTES HUAUTLA*

2   large chayote *squash, steamed and sliced*
1   *cup fat-free plain yogurt*
3   *tablespoons all-purpose flour*
⅓   *cup lowfat evaporated milk*
¼   *cup fat-free sour cream*
½   *cup chopped fresh Italian parsley*
8   *scallions, rinsed, dried, and chopped*
½   *teaspoon half salt, half salt-substitute mixture*

1. Arrange warm *chayote* slices on a platter.

2. In a small bowl, stir ⅓ cup yogurt with flour until there are no lumps.

3. In a small saucepan, heat evaporated milk over medium heat—careful not to scald the milk.

4. Slowly stir in yogurt and flour paste; when mixture thickens add sour cream, parsley, scallions, and salt; stir until well mixed.

5. Pour over *chayote*.

Serves 4.

Each Latina Lite serving contains: 106 calories
Total Fats: 1 gm
Saturated Fats: 0 gm   Protein: 7 gm
Unsaturated Fats: 1 gm   Sodium: 288 mg
Carbohydrates: 19 gm

STUFFED *CHAYOTES*— *CHAYOTES RELLENOS*

4   chayotes, *steamed*
2   *slices bread*
½   *cup milk*
1   *egg yolk*
½   *teaspoon half salt, half salt-substitute mixture*
4   *egg whites*
2   *tablespoons bread crumbs*
1   *tablespoon margarine*

1. Preheat the oven to 350°F.

2. Cut cooked *chayotes* in half; remove pulp; be careful not to break skins.

3. Place empty skins in a baking pan.

4. In a large bowl, soak bread in milk.

5. Mash *chayote* pulp with bread, egg yolk, and salt; mix well.

6. Meanwhile, in a large bowl, beat egg whites until stiff; gently fold into mashed *chayotes*.

7. Fill each half *chayote* with mixture; top with bread crumbs and dot with margarine.

8. Bake for 10 minutes until tops are golden brown.

Serves 4.

Each Latina Lite serving contains: 135 calories
Total Fats: 5 gm
Saturated Fats: 1 gm   Protein: 7 gm
Unsaturated Fats: 4 gm   Sodium: 391 mg
Carbohydrates: 15 gm

CAULIFLOWER WITH AVOCADO SAUCE— COLIFLOR CON AGUACATE

1   *medium head cauliflower, rinsed thoroughly and*
        broken into bite-size pieces
1   *medium avocado, ripe*
Juice of ½ lemon
½   cup fat-free sour cream
¼   cup fat-free milk
½   cup crumbled part-skim milk cheese
Freshly ground black pepper to taste

1. Steam cauliflower for 5 minutes. DO NOT OVERCOOK; cauliflower should not be wilted or mushy; cool.

2. Cut avocado in half; remove skin; sprinkle with lemon juice to avoid turning dark.

3. Mix avocado with sour cream, milk, cheese, and pepper.

4. Serve over cooled cauliflower.

Serves 4.

Each Latina Lite serving contains: 208 calories
Total Fats: 12 gm
Saturated Fats: 4 gm   Protein: 13 gm
Unsaturated Fats   8 gm   Sodium: 221 mg
Carbohydrates: 14 gm

CRILLED CORN—*ELOTE ASADO*

2   tablespoons margarine
4   fresh ears corn, husked
Aluminum foil
Ground red chile
1   teaspoon half salt, half salt-substitute mixture
4   lemons, halved

1. Spread 1 tablespoon margarine over corn; wrap in aluminum foil; grill over hot coals for 10 minutes, turning 3 times.
2. Open foil; spread remaining 1 tablespoon margarine on corn; sprinkle with *chile* and salt; drizzle with lemon.

Serves 4.

Each Latina Lite serving contains: 125 calories
Total Fats: 6 gm
Saturated Fats: 1 gm   Protein: 3 gm
Unsaturated Fats: 5 gm   Sodium: 456 mg
Carbohydrates: 18 gm

SPINACH WITH EGGS—*ESPINACAS CON HUEVOS REALES*

2   bunches fresh spinach, cleaned, or 1 pound frozen
      spinach
1   tablespoon margarine
1   cup fat-free milk
2   egg yolks
3   egg whites
½   teaspoon ground nutmeg
½   teaspoon half salt, half salt-substitute mixture
¼   teaspoon freshly ground black pepper

1. Heat oven to 350°F.

2. Steam spinach until wilted; or place in microwave on Medium for 4 to 5 minutes, turning 4 times; DO NOT OVER-COOK.

3. Drain and arrange in a glass baking dish.

4. Sprinkle small pieces of margarine over the spinach.

5. In a small saucepan, heat milk to boiling; cool to room temperature.

6. In a small bowl, beat egg yolks and whites together; add cooled milk to eggs gradually; stir constantly; add nutmeg, salt, and pepper; pour over spinach.

7. Cover baking dish with lid or aluminum foil; set in a larger pan half filled with water.

8. Bake for 45 minutes.

Serves 4.

Each Latina Lite serving contains: 140 calories

Total Fats:	7 gm	
Saturated Fats:	2 gm	Protein: 13 gm
Unsaturated Fats:	5 gm	Sodium: 450 mg
Carbohydrates:	8 gm	

CACTUS LEAVES—NOPALES

One of the most versatile vegetables is rarely consumed in Anglo homes—the *nopal* or cactus leaf. *Nopales* are consumed raw or cooked in soups, salads, *licuados*, and in *platos fuertes*—main dishes. The best *nopales* are the tender, freshly cut, purplish variety gathered and cleaned by Indian women in the northern states of Mexico during the spring and early summer. But succulent, tasty, despined cactus leaves can be found throughout the year in most Latin markets. They are also available canned.

Preparing *Nopales:*

8   small nopales *(thorns removed), cleaned*
3   *scallions*
1   *tablespoon white vinegar*
2   *copper pennies*

1. In a medium saucepan, bring 1½ quarts of water to a boil.

2. Add *nopales*, scallions, and vinegar.

3. When *nopales* begin to foam, heat the pennies in a small, dry skillet until they're red-hot; carefully drop the pennies into boiling water to cut excessive foaming.

4. Lower heat to medium and continue cooking for 20 minutes until *nopales* are tender.

5. Remove the pennies; rinse *nopales* with cold running water, drain; discard scallions.

*C*ACTUS LEAVES WITH *CHIPOTLE— NOPALITOS CON CHIPOTLE*

4   *cups* nopales, *cleaned*
2–4 chiles chipotles, *canned, rinsed, dried, cored, and seeded*
1   *cup tomato sauce*
½   *teaspoon half salt, half salt-substitute mixture*
1   *tablespoon cornstarch*
2   *tablespoons water*
½   *cup fat-free plain yogurt*
½   *cup fat-free sour cream*
¼   *cup grated white cheese*
4   *corn* tortillas *or* arepas

1. Preheat the oven to 400°F.

2. Prepare *Nopales* (above) cut into small squares; set aside.

3. Purée *chiles*, tomato sauce, and salt in blender; set aside.

4. In a small saucepan over low heat, dissolve cornstarch in 2 tablespoons water; stir constantly.

5. Stir in yogurt; then sour cream; remove from heat; set aside.

6. Arrange a layer of *nopales* in a rectangular glass baking dish; cover with a layer of tomato sauce, then yogurt.

7. Add a second layer: *nopales*, tomato sauce, and yogurt; end with a final layer of tomato sauce; sprinkle cheese on top.

8. Bake for 15 minutes.

9. Serve with hot corn *tortillas* or *arepas*.

Serves 6.

Each Latina Lite serving contains: 157 calories
Total Fats: 3 gm
Saturated Fats: 1 gm   Protein: 7 gm
Unsaturated Fats: 2 gm   Sodium: 632 mg
Carbohydrates: 27 gm

$\mathscr{C}$ACTUS LEAVES IN TOMATO SAUCE— *NOPALITOS NAVIGANTES*

4   *cups* nopales, *cleaned*
1   *cup tomato sauce*
½   *cup onion, cut into chunks*
2   *garlic cloves, halved*
1   *cup chicken broth or 1 bouillon cube or 1 teaspoon consommé granules with 1 cup water*
2   *fresh* chiles poblanos *or* Californias, *seeded and cored, cut into strips (you may substitute any available fresh large long green* chiles*)*
½   *teaspoon fresh chopped oregano*
½   *teaspoon half salt, half salt-substitute mixture*
1   *egg*

1. Prepare *Nopales* (page 164); cut into small squares; set aside.

2. Purée tomato sauce, onion, and garlic in blender.

3. Transfer to a large saucepan and simmer for 5 minutes; add remaining ingredients except egg.

4. Continue to simmer just below boiling point for 15 minutes.

5. Just before serving, beat egg and dribble into sauce.

Serves 6.

Each Latina Lite serving contains: 79 calories
Total Fats:　　　　 1 gm
Saturated Fats:　　 0 gm　　　 Protein:　　 3 gm
Unsaturated Fats:　 1 gm　　　 Sodium: 706 mg
Carbohydrates:　　 15 gm

POTATOES IN MILK— *PAPAS CON LECHE*

4　 medium potatoes, thinly sliced
1½ cups fat-free milk
1　 leek, rinsed thoroughly and chopped
2　 teaspoons margarine
1　 teaspoon half salt, half salt-substitute mixture
1　 cup chopped fresh cilantro
¼　 cup grated white cheese

1. Place potatoes, milk, leek, margarine, and salt in a large skillet; simmer, uncovered, for 25 minutes until potatoes are cooked and milk thickens.

2. While hot, sprinkle with cilantro and cheese.

Serves 4.

Each Latina Lite serving contains: 131 calories
Total Fats: 5 gm
Saturated Fats: 2 gm   Protein: 8 gm
Unsaturated Fats: 3 gm   Sodium: 571 mg
Carbohydrates: 15 gm

BAKED PLANTAINS— PLATANOS ASADOS

4   plantains, very ripe (completely black-brown skin)
4   teaspoons margarine

1. Preheat the oven to 350°F.
2. Slit skin of plantain lengthwise; place on cookie sheet.
3. Bake for 20 minutes; turn plantains; bake for another 20 minutes.
4. Melt margarine.
5. Serve in peel drizzled with margarine.

Serves 4.

Each Latina Lite serving contains: 192 calories
Total Fats: 4 gm
Saturated Fats: 1 gm   Protein: 1 gm
Unsaturated Fats: 3 gm   Sodium: 49 mg
Carbohydrates: 36 gm

Squash Dumplings— TORTITAS DE CALABAZA

8   medium Italian zucchini
1   cup grated part-skim milk cheese
2   tablespoons all-purpose flour
3   egg whites
½   teaspoon half salt, half salt-substitute mixture
2   tablespoons vegetable oil

1. Rinse and dry squash; trim both ends; steam for 2 minutes.
2. Quarter each squash lengthwise; gently cut a 1½-inch slit and insert cheese into each quarter; lightly dust with flour.
3. In a medium bowl, beat egg whites until they peak.
4. Coat each zucchini quarter with beaten egg white.
5. Heat oil until very hot in a large nonstick skillet; fry *tortitas* until golden brown on all sides; reserve oil.
6. Blot excess fat on paper towels.
7. Set aside.

Sauce:
½   cup thinly sliced onion
2   cups tomato sauce
½   teaspoon half salt, half salt-substitute to taste
Tabasco sauce to taste

Garnish:

½   cup thinly sliced red onion

1. In a large skillet, sauté onions over low heat in reserved oil used to fry *tortitas*; add tomato sauce, salt, and Tabasco; simmer for 5 minutes.

2. Add *tortitas*; heat, covered, for 5 minutes more.
3. Garnish with red onion rings.

Serves 8.

Each Latina Lite serving contains: 159 calories
Total Fats: 8 gm
Saturated Fats: 3 gm   Protein: 11 gm
Unsaturated Fats: 5 gm   Sodium: 400 mg
Carbohydrates: 11 gm

SPINACH DUMPLINGS— *TORTITAS DE ESPINACA*

2   bunches spinach
2   medium potatoes, boiled and mashed
1   tablespoon cider vinegar
½   cup grated part-skim milk cheese
1   egg
1   egg white
3   tablespoons vegetable oil

1. Clean spinach; discard stems; put each bunch in a large bowl; microwave on High for 4 minutes rotating bowl 4 times.
2. In a large bowl, combine spinach and mashed potatoes; add vinegar and cheese.
3. In small bowl, beat the egg with egg white; add beaten egg to spinach-potato mixture.
4. When everything is thoroughly mixed, form dumplings into 2-inch-diameter rounds.
5. In a large skillet, heat 2 tablespoons oil over medium heat; brown *tortitas* on both sides until golden brown; blot excess oil on paper towels.
6. Set aside.

Sauce:

½ cup thinly sliced onion
2   cups tomato sauce
½   teaspoon half salt, half salt-substitute mixture
Tabasco sauce to taste

GARNISH:

½ cup thinly sliced red onion

1. In a large skillet, heat remaining 1 tablespoon oil over low heat; sauté onions; add tomato sauce, salt, and Tabasco; simmer for 5 minutes.
2. Add *tortitas*; heat, covered, for 5 minutes more.
3. Garnish with red onion rings.

Serves 8.

Each Latina Lite serving contains: 318 calories
Total Fats: 8 gm
Saturated Fats: 2 gm   Protein: 8 gm
Unsaturated Fats: 6 gm   Sodium: 349 mg
Carbohydrates: 15 gm

PLANTAIN FRITTERS—*TOSTONES*

Plantains are used extensively in Cuban cuisine. *Tostones* are twice-fried plantain slices.

3   tablespoons vegetable oil
2   medium green plantains, peeled and cut into 1-inch-
        diagonal slices
½   teaspoon half salt, half salt-substitute mixture

1. In a large nonstick frying pan, warm oil over medium heat; sauté plantain slices until golden brown on both sides; reserve oil.

2. Remove slices with slotted spoon; press plantain slices between 2 pieces of paper towel until about ½ their original thickness.

3. Soak *tostones* for 5 minutes in a bowl of warm water with ½ teaspoon dissolved salt; dry between paper towels.

4. Reheat reserved oil in skillet; fry *tostones* on both sides again.

5. Blot between paper towels again to remove excess oil.

6. Serve immediately.

Serves 4.

Each Latina Lite serving contains: 157 calories
Total Fats: 10 gm
Saturated Fats: 1 gm   Protein: 0 gm
Unsaturated Fats: 9 gm   Sodium: 210 mg
Carbohydrates: 18 gm

 ## STUFFED CARROTS— *ZANAHORIAS RELLENAS*

3   chiles mulatos, *packaged dried* (chiles guajillos *or* pasillas *may be substituted)*
1   tablespoon red wine vinegar
1   teaspoon half salt, half salt-substitute mixture
2   teaspoons vegetable oil
½   cup diced onion
1   cup chicken broth or 1 bouillon cube or 1 teaspoon consommé granules dissolved in 1 cup water
½   cup tomato sauce
½   cup fat-free cottage cheese
1   egg
2   tablespoons all-purpose flour
12   large carrots, peeled and cooked whole

1. Soak *chiles* in 1 cup water with vinegar and ½ teaspoon salt for 2 hours.

2. Rinse, drain, seed, and core.

3. Purée *chiles* in blender.

4. In a large skillet, heat oil over low heat; sauté onion until translucent; add *chiles*, broth, and tomato sauce; simmer for 5 minutes.

5. Meanwhile, combine cottage cheese, egg, flour, and remaining ½ teaspoon salt.

6. With a sharp knife, cut a V-shaped wedge lengthwise in each carrot; reserve wedges.

7. Hollow out inside of carrot; stuff with cottage cheese mixture; top with V-shaped carrot wedge.

8. Use toothpicks to keep wedges in place.

9. Place carrots in sauce; simmer for 5 minutes more. Serve hot.

Serves 6.

Each Latina Lite serving contains: 113 calories
Total Fats: 3 gm
Saturated Fats: 1 gm   Protein: 7 gm
Unsaturated Fats: 2 gm   Sodium: 590 mg
Carbohydrates: 16 gm

Salads—Ensaladas

Although fresh vegetables are abundant, salads are not as popular in Latin America as in the United States. Cooked salads are more common than fresh, leafy green salads. Yet, one of the most popular lettuce salads—Caesar Salad—has its origin in Mexican cuisine. César Cardini created this salad about fifty years ago, while he was employed as a waiter at *Aguas Calientes*, the racetrack in Tijuana. He returned to Mexico City and opened Cardini's Restaurant, which was recognized worldwide as the home of the original Caesar Salad. In the midsixties, my family enjoyed Caesar Salad prepared by the *maestro*. César used a whole raw egg in his original salad; this recipe calls for fresh and healthy egg whites.

Caesar Salad—Ensalada Cesar

2　large garlic cloves
4　anchovies
4　tablespoons olive oil
2　tablespoons Worcestershire sauce
4　tablespoons fresh lemon juice
1　teaspoon prepared mustard
2　egg whites (be sure to use fresh cold-storage eggs)
16　romaine lettuce leaves
Freshly ground black pepper to taste
4　tablespoons grated Parmesan cheese

1. Rub garlic on a large wooden salad bowl.

2. After the *ensaladera* is covered with the scent of fresh garlic, use a garlic press to crush garlic into the salad bowl; add anchovies and olive oil; mash anchovies; combine them with garlic and oil until a smooth paste is formed.

3. Add Worcestershire, lemon juice, mustard, and egg whites; beat with a fork until everything is well blended.

4. Add lettuce leaves (César Cardini served 3 to 5 whole large leaves per person, but you may wish to cut them in bite-size pieces); carefully toss lettuce with dressing.

5. Sprinkle pepper and cheese over salad.

Serves 4.

Each Latina Lite serving contains: 211 calories
Total Fats: 17 gm
Saturated Fats: 4 gm   Protein: 9 gm
Unsaturated Fats: 13 gm   Sodium: 499 mg
Carbohydrates: 5 gm

ZUCCHINI AND TOMATO SALAD— ENSALADA DE CALABACITA Y JITOMATE

1   cup peeled and chopped Italian zucchini
1   medium green bell pepper, cored, seeded,
        and chopped
2   medium tomatoes, chopped
½   cup diced celery
5   scallions, chopped
4   large lettuce leaves
1   6-ounce jar red pimientos, drained
        and diced

Dressing:

3   tablespoons olive oil
1   tablespoon balsamic vinegar
1   garlic clove, minced
1   tablespoon freshly chopped Italian parsley
½   teaspoon half salt, half salt-substitute mixture
¼   teaspoon freshly ground black pepper

1. Combine zucchini, bell pepper, tomatoes, celery, and scallions in a large bowl.
2. Place olive oil, vinegar, garlic, parsley, salt, and pepper in a jar; tighten lid; shake well.
3. Pour dressing over vegetables; mix well.
4. Chill for 3 hours.
5. Arrange on lettuce leaves; garnish with red pimiento.

Serves 4.

Each Latina Lite serving contains: 140 calories
Total Fats: 10 gm
Saturated Fats: 1 gm   Protein: 2 gm
Unsaturated Fats: 9 gm   Sodium: 234 mg
Carbohydrates: 12 gm

COLD CHAYOTE SQUASH SALAD— ENSALADA DE CHAYOTE

2   large chayotes
1   large avocado, ripe
1   large orange

1. Quarter and steam *chayotes* for about 5 minutes until tender but firm; cool and peel; thinly slice each quarter.

2. Peel, quarter, and slice avocado.

3. Rinse and dry orange; do not peel; cut in half rounds.

4. Alternate *chayote*, avocado, and orange slices on a platter.

5. Chill.

Dressing:

2   *tablespoons olive oil*
¼   *cup fresh orange juice*
1   *teaspoon fresh lemon juice*
1   *tablespoon Japanese seasoned rice vinegar**
1   *tablespoon grated orange peel*
¼   *teaspoon ground cayenne pepper*
¼   *teaspoon half salt, half salt-substitute mixture*

1. Briskly blend all ingredients with a wire whisk.

2. Serve chilled over salad.

Serves 4.

Each Latina Lite serving contains: 176 calories
Total Fats: 15 gm
Saturated Fats: 2 gm   Protein: 2 gm
Unsaturated Fats: 13 gm   Sodium: 110 mg
Carbohydrates: 13 gm

*Japanese seasoned rice vinegar can be found in the Asian food section of your supermarket.

BLACK BEAN AND MANGO SALAD— ENSALADA DE FRIJOL NEGRO CON MANGO

2   cups black beans, cooked or canned, rinsed and
       drained
¼   red onion, minced
2   medium ripe mangos, peeled and chopped
1   cup chopped fresh cilantro
½   cup grapefruit juice
1   tablespoon fresh lemon juice
1   teaspoon ground cumin
1   fresh chile jalapeño, cored, seeded, and minced
2   tablespoons chopped fresh Italian parsley
½   teaspoon half salt, half salt-substitute mixture
4   large lettuce leaves

1. Combine all ingredients except lettuce in a large *ensaladera*—salad bowl; chill for at least 2 hours.
2. Arrange on lettuce leaves.

Serves 4.

Each Latina Lite serving contains: 209 calories
Total Fats: 1 gm
Saturated Fats: 0 gm   Protein: 9 gm
Unsaturated Fats: 1 gm   Sodium: 221 mg
Carbohydrates: 44 gm

CHICKPEA AND RED PEPPER SALAD—
ENSALADA DE GARBANZO Y PIMIENTO MORRON

1   red bell pepper, cored, seeded, and finely chopped
1   cup chickpeas (garbanzos), cooked or canned,
       drained
1½ cups finely chopped celery
½   cup finely chopped red onion
½   cucumber, peeled and finely chopped
4   large lettuce leaves

Dressing:

2   tablespoons olive oil
1   tablespoon fresh lemon juice
1   tablespoon Japanese seasoned rice vinegar[*]
1   teaspoon consommé granules
1   teaspoon mustard
Freshly ground black pepper to taste

1. Combine all vegetables except lettuce in a large salad bowl.

2. In a small bowl, briskly whisk dressing ingredients; pour dressing over vegetables; toss lightly.

3. Refrigerate for at least 1 to 2 hours before serving.

4. Arrange on lettuce leaves.

Serves 4.

Each Latina Lite serving contains: 157 calories
Total Fats: 8 gm
Saturated Fats: 1 gm   Protein: 5 gm
Unsaturated Fats: 7 gm   Sodium: 314 mg
Carbohydrates: 18 gm

[*]Japanese seasoned rice vinegar can be found in the Asian food section of your supermarket.

$\mathcal{S}$ALAD FOR CHRISTMAS EVE—
ENSALADA DE NOCHE BUENA

2 cups sliced beets, freshly steamed or canned
1 cup beet juice from cooked or canned beets,
    or water
3 oranges, peeled and cut into bite-size pieces
2 ripe bananas, peeled and cut into bite-size
    pieces
2 apples, peeled and chopped
1 medium jícama, peeled and chopped
½ head iceberg lettuce, grated
6 packets sugar substitute
2 tablespoons Japanese seasoned rice vinegar*

1. Combine everything except lettuce, sugar substitute, and vinegar in a large *ensaladera*—salad bowl; chill.

2. Just before serving, mix in lettuce, sugar substitute, and vinegar.

Serves 6.

Each Latina Lite serving contains: 147 calories
Total Fats: 1 gm
Saturated Fats: 0 gm   Protein: 3 gm
Unsaturated Fats: 1 gm   Sodium: 46 mg
Carbohydrates: 36 gm

*Japanese seasoned rice vinegar can be found in the Asian food section of your supermarket.

ARIZONA CHICKEN SALAD—
ENSALADA DE POLLO ESTILO ARIZONA

1   tablespoon vegetable oil
2   cups skinless chicken breast, cut into chunks
2   cups red kidney beans, cooked or canned, drained
¼   cup finely diced onion
2   tomatoes, chopped
1   teaspoon red chile powder

Dressing:

½   teaspoon Tabasco sauce
½   cup fat-free sour cream
2   tablespoons fat-free plain yogurt
2   tablespoons Japanese seasoned rice vinegar*
2   tablespoons mayonnaise

2   cups grated lettuce
½   avocado, sliced
4   TORTILLAS TOSTADAS (page 203), in strips

1. In a large skillet, heat oil over medium heat; brown chicken; add beans, onion, tomato, and *chile* powder; reduce heat; sauté for 8 minutes; cool; set aside.
2. Whisk Tabasco, sour cream, yogurt, vinegar, and mayonnaise together.
3. Place chicken and beans into a large *ensaladera*—salad bowl; add lettuce; mix with dressing.
4. Top with avocado slices and *tortilla* strips.
5. MEXICAN RED SAUCE (page 64), GREEN SAUCE (page 65), or *PICO DE GALLO* (page 61) goes well with this salad.

Serves 4.

*Japanese seasoned rice vinegar can be found in the Asian food section of your supermarket.

Each Latina Lite serving contains: 395 calories
Total Fats: 15 gm
Saturated Fats: 2 gm   Protein: 25 gm
Unsaturated Fats: 13 gm   Sodium: 585 mg
Carbohydrates: 4 gm

CACTUS LEAF SALAD— ENSALADA DE NOPALES

8   small nopales *leaves, cleaned and despined*
12 *small red radishes, diced*
2   *tomatoes, chopped*
3   *sprigs fresh cilantro, chopped*
1   *medium white onion, diced*
1   *fresh* chile serrano, *cored, seeded, and minced*
4   *tablespoons crumbled part-skim milk cheese*
1   *teaspoon chopped fresh oregano*

1. To prepare *NOPALES* (page 164), cut into small squares.
2. Combine cooked *nopales* with all ingredients in a large *ensaladera*—salad bowl.
3. Refrigerate.
4. Serve cold with a *SALSA ROJA MEXICANA* (page 64).
5. If necessary, season with half salt, half salt-substitute mixture from your shaker at table.

Serves 4.

Each Latina Lite serving contains: 131 calories
Total Fats: 4 gm
Saturated Fats: 2 gm   Protein: 6 gm
Unsaturated Fats: 2 gm   Sodium: 441 mg
Carbohydrates: 22 gm

UACAMOLE

My grandmother served avocado in its shell instead of butter with almost every meal. Lots of times, avocado was prepared as *guacamole*, which spreads easily on almost everything. Delicious on chips, *tortillas*, in sandwiches, it also adds a magnificent flavor to chicken, meat, fish, rice, and beans. Unfortunately, avocados contain a lot of fat; one half of an avocado contains 15 grams of fat.

2   *ripe medium avocados, peeled and mashed with a*
       wooden spoon
1   *fresh* chile serrano, *seeded, cored, and finely minced*
3   *sprigs fresh cilantro, chopped*
¼   *cup finely diced onion*
1   *tomato, finely chopped*
1   *teaspoon fresh lemon juice*
½   *teaspoon half salt, half salt-substitute mixture*

1. Mix everything together on a serving dish.

2. When mixed, place 1 or more avocado pits in the *guacamole* to help retain the fresh green color.

3. Try putting some on your sandwich instead of mayonnaise.

Serves 4.

Each Latina Lite serving contains: 166 calories
Total Fats: 15 gm
Saturated Fats: 2 gm   Protein: 2 gm
Unsaturated Fats: 13 gm   Sodium: 471 mg
Carbohydrates: 9 gm

Asparagus Spread—
GUACAMOLE DE ESPARRAGOS

4   cups asparagus, cooked or canned, drained
½   medium onion, cut into chunks
2   teaspoons fresh lemon juice
2   tomatoes, chopped
½   cup chopped fresh cilantro
1   fresh chile serrano, cored, seeded, and minced
4   teaspoons olive oil
1   teaspoon half salt, half salt-substitute mixture

   1. Purée asparagus and onion in blender; stir in lemon juice, tomato, cilantro, *chile*, olive oil, and salt.
   2. Use as spread.

Serves 4.

Each Latina Lite serving contains: 103 calories
Total Fats: 5 gm
Saturated Fats: 1 gm   Protein: 6 gm
Unsaturated Fats: 4 gm   Sodium: 418 mg
Carbohydrates: 12 gm

Jicama, Orange, and Pineapple
SALAD—JICAMA, NARANJA Y PINA

1   jícama, peeled and cut into 2-inch strips
3   oranges, peeled and cut into slices
2   1½-inch slices pineapple, cored and cut into
        2-inch strips
2   tablespoons fresh lemon juice
½   tablespoon ground red chile
1   teaspoon half salt, half salt-substitute mixture

1. Arrange all fresh fruit on a large platter.
2. Sprinkle with lemon juice, *chile*, and salt.

Serves 6.

Each Latina Lite serving contains: 83 calories
Total Fats: 0 gm
Saturated Fats: 0 gm   Protein: 1 gm
Unsaturated Fats: 0 gm   Sodium: 262 mg
Carbohydrates: 16 gm

SHREDDED CHICKEN OR SEAFOOD SALAD—*SALPICON*

Salpicón salad has always been a favorite *plato fuerte*. Mexican salads do not look or taste like Anglo salads. The chicken or meat is shredded and combined with lettuce or cabbage, grated immediately before serving. In the coastal states, *Salpicón* is often prepared with cooked shellfish chunks (unshredded). It may also be prepared with canned, rinsed, drained, and crumbled tuna fish. A great, quick, easy meal for family or guests served year-round.

1   *10-ounce package frozen green peas*
3   *medium chicken breasts, cooked and shredded**
1   *large onion, thinly sliced*
2   *tomatoes, cut into 8 sections each*
6   *cups grated lettuce*

---

*To shred chicken or meat, cook until tender and cool. Then separate the strands like threads one by one.

Dressing:

3   tablespoons vinegar from canned chiles
2   tablespoons olive oil

GARNISH:

10 chile jalapeño *strips, canned (reserve liquid)*
½   cup red pimiento, canned and drained, cut into strips
1   avocado, peeled and sliced
4   tablespoons grated part-skim milk cheese

1. Steam green peas for 3 minutes; cool.

2. Combine chicken, onion, tomatoes, peas, and lettuce in a large *ensaladera*—salad bowl.

3. Whisk vinegar from canned *chiles* and oil together; pour over salad; lightly toss.

4. Garnish with *chile jalapeño* strips, red pimiento, and avocado slices; sprinkle cheese on top. If necessary, season with half salt and half salt-substitute mixture from your salt shaker at table.

Serves 6.

Each Latina Lite serving contains: 257 calories
Total Fats: 13 gm
Saturated Fats: 3 gm   Protein: 21 gm
Unsaturated Fats: 10 gm   Sodium: 136 mg
Carbohydrates: 16 gm

SHREDDED CHICKEN SALAD IN LIME DRESSING—*SALPICON YUCATECO*

Geographically, Yucatán is closer to Cuba and Florida than to Mexico City. *Yucatecan* food employs Mexican, Caribbean, and European seasonings. This version of S*alpicón* is less spicy than that of the central plateau. Try it. If you cannot live without *picante*, serve with a side of *PICO DE GALLO* (page 61).

4   *medium chicken breasts, cooked and shredded**
1   *bunch red radishes, diced*
½   *cup chopped fresh cilantro*
½   *head lettuce, grated*

Dressing:

¼   *cup fresh lime or lemon juice*
4   *tablespoons olive oil*
2   *garlic cloves, minced*
½   *teaspoon half salt, half salt-substitute mixture*
Freshly ground black pepper to taste

1. Whisk lime or lemon juice, oil, garlic, salt, and pepper until well mixed and frothy.
2. Refrigerate for 30 minutes.
3. Just before serving, place salad ingredients in a large *ensaladera*—salad bowl.
4. Pour dressing over salad; toss.

Serves 4.

---

*To shred chicken or meat, cook until tender and cool. Then separate the strands like threads one by one.

Each Latina Lite serving contains: 289 calories
Total Fats: 17 gm
Saturated Fats: 3 gm   Protein: 28 gm
Unsaturated Fats: 14 gm   Sodium: 296 mg
Carbohydrates: 6 gm

TOMATOES STUFFED WITH CHEESE— TOMATES RELLENOS A LA VERACRUZ

6   large ripe tomatoes, peeled*
½   cup fat-free cottage cheese
3   tablespoons mayonnaise
3   tablespoons fat-free yogurt
1   cup chopped celery
1   cup fresh pineapple, diced (discard core)
1   teaspoon half salt, half salt-substitute mixture
4   mint leaves

1. Cut one thin slice across core of tomato; remove core; reserve slice.

2. With a curved sharp spoon or knife, like a serrated grapefruit spoon or knife, remove pulp and seeds; place each hollow tomato upside down on a paper towel to drip dry.

3. In a medium bowl, combine cottage cheese, mayonnaise, and yogurt; stir in celery and pineapple.

4. Lightly salt inside of each tomato and stuff.

5. Top each tomato with reserved tomato slice.

*To peel tomatoes, gently scorch tomato skin over stove burner until it blisters; wrap tomatoes in a cool damp cloth for a few minutes. The peel will separate easily.

6. Decorate hole left by removed core with a mint leaf.
7. Refrigerate.

Serves 6.

Each Latina Lite serving contains: 121 calories
Total Fats: 6 gm
Saturated Fats: 1 gm   Protein: 6 gm
Unsaturated Fats: 5 gm   Sodium: 608 mg
Carbohydrates: 12 gm

Beans, Rice, and Breads—*Frijoles, Arroz y Panes*

Whether they are called *alubias, fréjoles, frijoles, habichuelas, granos, habas, judías,* or *porotos en vaina,* beans are popular in all Latin countries. Nutritious, economical beans are consumed worldwide. In Boston, baked beans are eaten; in the Middle East, *hummus*; in Asia, soybeans. Jewish people prepare barley-lima soup; the Greeks, white beans; the French serve their *casseroles cassoulets*; in India, kidney beans are eaten with pepper and lemon; and Palestinians and Spanish favor *fava* beans. Most Latin menus include beans as a side or main dish daily.

Although the current vogue is to preboil beans for ten minutes and then soak for only an hour before cooking, I like the flavor after they have been immersed in cool water overnight without salt. Most beans are sold dried and packaged. Some beans may be old and tough, twelve or even eighteen months old. The more water absorbed, the less digestive gas will be produced. Water should be changed at least once during the soaking period. During hot weather, refrigerate soaking beans to prevent fermentation. After soaking, drain off water, and cover with fresh water. For one to two cups of dry beans, add half an onion cut into chunks, two bay leaves, and one teaspoon salt while cooking. Boil beans in a large covered pot from one to five hours, depending on the bean, until tender.

BEANS, COLOMBIAN-STYLE—
FRIJOLES COLOMBIANOS

½   pound red kidney beans
1   tablespoon vegetable oil
1   medium onion, chopped
2   garlic cloves, minced
4   slices smoked lean turkey ham, chopped
3   cups diced green plantain
1   cup tomato sauce
1   teaspoon half salt, half salt-substitute mixture

1. The night before you plan to cook beans, rinse and drain; in a large bowl, cover with water; soak overnight.

2. The following day, drain beans; set aside.

3. In a large saucepan, heat oil over low heat; sauté onion and garlic until onion becomes translucent; add turkey ham, beans, and 5 cups of water.

4. Cover and simmer for 2 hours until beans are cooked.

5. Add plantain, tomato sauce, and salt; cook another 30 minutes.

6. Remove from stove; cool.

7. Refrigerate; allow flavors to absorb at least 4 to 5 hours before serving.

Serves 6.

Each Latina Lite serving contains: 187 calories
Total Fats: 4 gm
Saturated Fats: 1 gm   Protein: 7 gm
Unsaturated Fats: 3 gm   Sodium: 691 mg
Carbohydrates: 35 gm

ƁEANS, COUNTRY-STYLE—
FRIJOLES CRIOLLOS

2   teaspoons vegetable oil
½   onion, cut into chunks
1   green bell pepper, cored, seeded, and cut into chunks
2   garlic cloves, minced
1   cup tomato sauce
¼   cup water
½   teaspoon chicken consommé granules
2   cups beans, cooked or canned, drained

1. In a medium saucepan, heat oil over low heat; sauté onion until translucent; add bell pepper; sauté for 3 minutes.

2. Add garlic, tomato sauce, water, and consommé; simmer for 5 minutes more.

3. Add beans; cover and simmer for another 15 minutes.

Serves 4.

Each Latina Lite serving contains: 168 calories
Total Fats: 3 gm
Saturated Fats: 0 gm   Protein: 8 gm
Unsaturated Fats: 3 gm   Sodium: 230 mg
Carbohydrates: 29 gm

BEANS IN A POT—
FRIJOLES DE OLLA

½ pound beans (black, pintos, navy, etc.)
5 cups water
1 medium onion, sliced
1 tablespoon vegetable oil
1 tablespoon dried oregano
1 bay leaf
1 teaspoon half salt, half salt-substitute mixture

1. The night before you plan to cook the beans, rinse and drain; in a large bowl, cover with water; refrigerate.

2. The following day, drain beans and rinse.

3. In a large saucepan, add all ingredients.

4. Cover and simmer for 2 to 4 hours until beans are tender. (Cooking time varies with different beans.)

5. Discard bay leaf.

Serves 8.

Each Latina Lite serving contains: 59 calories
Total Fats: 2 gm
Saturated Fats: 0 gm   Protein: 3 gm
Unsaturated Fats: 2 gm   Sodium: 196 mg
Carbohydrates: 8 gm

฿EANS, BLACK VENEZUELAN-STYLE— *FRIJOLES NEGROS ESTILO VENEZOLANO*

½   cup diced onion
1   tablespoon **ACHIOTE CUBANO** *(page 50)*
½   cup diced celery
½   cup diced red bell pepper
½   cup long-grain white rice, rinsed and drained
2   cups water
1   chicken bouillon cube or 1 teaspoon consommé
       granules
½   teaspoon ground turmeric
½   teaspoon dried oregano
2   cups black beans, cooked or canned, drained
1   teaspoon red cayenne pepper
Lemon wedges

1. In a large saucepan, heat *Achiote* oil over medium heat; sauté onion until translucent; add celery, red bell pepper, and rice; stir constantly for 2 to 3 minutes.

2. Lower heat; add water, bouillon, turmeric, and oregano.

3. Cover and cook for 20 minutes until rice is soft; fluff with a fork; add beans.

4. Sprinkle with red pepper; serve with lemon wedges.

Serves 4.

Each Latina Lite serving contains: 202 calories
Total Fats: 4 gm
Saturated Fats: 1 gm   Protein: 9 gm
Unsaturated Fats: 3 gm   Sodium: 270 mg
Carbohydrates: 34 gm

ℬEANS, REFRIED CUBAN STYLE— *FRIJOLES REFRITOS CUBANOS*

"Refried beans" is really a misnomer. The beans are not fried twice as their name implies. Actually, "*re-fritos*" is a shortened version of "*retebién frijoles fritos*" which means better than best fried beans.

1   *tablespoon vegetable oil*
3   *tablespoons finely minced onion*
2   *small garlic cloves, minced*
2   *cups cooked beans*
1   *cup bean broth (liquid from cooked beans)*
2   *tablespoons* **SOFRITO** *(page 66)*
1   *beef bouillon cube*
½   *teaspoon dried oregano*
¼   *cup tomato sauce*
1   *tablespoon dry red wine (optional)*

1. In a large nonstick skillet, heat oil over medium heat; sauté onion and garlic until lightly browned.

2. Mash 1 cup beans; add to onion and garlic; stir in bean broth gradually; allow mixture to boil until bean paste thickens and liquid is absorbed.

3. Add *Sofrito*, bouillon, oregano, tomato sauce, wine, and the remaining 1 cup beans; continue cooking for 10 minutes.

Serves 4.

Each Latina Lite serving contains: 180 calories
Total Fats: 5 gm
Saturated Fats: 1 gm   Protein: 9 gm
Unsaturated Fats: 4 gm   Sodium: 480 mg
Carbohydrates: 27 gm

REFRIED BEANS, LATINA LITE—
FRIJOLES REFRITOS LATINA LITE

1   tablespoon vegetable oil
3   tablespoons finely minced onion
2   small garlic cloves, minced
2   cups cooked beans
2   cups bean broth (liquid from cooked beans)
1   teaspoon half salt, half salt-substitute mixture

1. In a large nonstick skillet, heat oil over medium heat; lightly brown onion and garlic.
2. Mash 1 cup beans; add to onion and garlic; sauté; stir frequently.
3. Add bean broth gradually; stir until thoroughly mixed.
4. After all liquid is added, allow mixture to boil until bean paste thickens and excess liquid is absorbed.
5. Add the remaining 1 cup beans and salt; continue cooking for 5 minutes.

Serves 4.

Each Latina Lite serving contains: 152 calories
Total Fats: 4 gm
Saturated Fats: 1 gm   Protein: 7 gm
Unsaturated Fats: 3 gm   Sodium: 145 mg
Carbohydrates: 23 gm

BEANS AND RICE, NICARAGUAN-STYLE—*GALLO PINTO NICARAGUENSE*

2   tablespoons vegetable oil
3   tablespoons diced onion
1   garlic clove, minced
2   cups cooked pinto beans
1   cup cooked long-grain white rice
½   teaspoon half salt, half salt-substitute mixture
¼   teaspoon ground cumin
1   bay leaf
Freshly ground black pepper to taste

1. In a large skillet, heat oil over medium heat; sauté onion and garlic until onion is translucent; add beans, rice, salt, cumin, bay leaf, and pepper.
2. Fry rice-bean mixture, scraping off the crust that sticks to the bottom of pan with a spatula.
3. Mixture is ready to serve when sufficiently crusty.
4. Discard bay leaf.

Serves 4.

Each Latina Lite serving contains: 215 calories
Total Fats: 7 gm
Saturated Fats: 1 gm   Protein: 8 gm
Unsaturated Fats: 6 gm   Sodium: 185 mg
Carbohydrates: 30 gm

CHICKPEAS IN ADOBO— GARBANZOS ADOBADOS

2 chiles anchos *(packaged and dried)*
2 cups chickpeas (garbanzos), cooked or canned, drained
1 cup bean broth from cooked or canned beans
2 garlic cloves, halved
1 tablespoon cider vinegar
1 tablespoon Japanese seasoned rice vinegar*
1 teaspoon dried oregano
½ teaspoon ground cumin
4 slices smoked lowfat turkey ham, cut into bite-size pieces
2 teaspoons olive oil

1. Soak dried *chiles* in warm water until pliable; remove core and seeds.

2. Purée *chiles*, beans, bean broth, garlic, vinegars, oregano, and cumin in blender.

3. Transfer purée to a large saucepan; add turkey ham; stir in oil; simmer for 15 to 20 minutes.

Serves 4.

Each Latina Lite serving contains: 199 calories
Total Fats: 6 gm
Saturated Fats: 1 gm   Protein: 13 gm
Unsaturated Fats: 5 gm   Sodium: 290 mg
Carbohydrates: 25 gm

*Japanese seasoned rice vinegar can be found in the Asian food section of your supermarket.

BEANS, KIDNEY SOUTH AMERICAN-STYLE—*HABICHUELAS ROJAS SUDAMERICANOS*

2   cups red kidney beans, cooked or canned
1   cup bean broth from cooked or canned beans
½   beef bouillon cube or ½ teaspoon consommé granules
1   tablespoon vegetable oil
1   cup diced white onion
4   garlic cloves, minced
1   pound ground turkey breast
2   cups canned and peeled tomatoes
2   bay leaves
1   teaspoon ground cumin
½   teaspoon red cayenne pepper
¼   cup chopped fresh Italian parsley
Salt and freshly ground black pepper to taste

1. Heat beans and broth in a casserole; stir in bouillon.
2. In a large skillet, heat oil over medium heat; sauté onion until translucent.
3. Add garlic and ground turkey; brown; add tomatoes, bay leaves, cumin, and cayenne pepper.
4. Lower heat and simmer for 5 minutes; transfer meat mixture to beans in casserole.
5. Simmer and stir for 6 to 8 minutes.
6. Discard bay leaves. Serve hot garnished with parsley.
7. Add pepper and half salt, half salt-substitute mixture from your shaker at table.

Serves 6.

Each Latina Lite serving contains: 309 calories
Total Fats: 13 gm
Saturated Fats: 4 gm   Protein: 27 gm
Unsaturated Fats: 9 gm   Sodium: 677 mg
Carbohydrates: 22 gm

BEANS, CUBAN BLACK AND RICE (MOORS AND CHRISTIANS)—*MOROS Y CRISTIANOS*

1	tablespoon olive oil
½	cup diced onion
2	garlic cloves, minced
1	medium green bell pepper, cored, seeded, and diced
2	cups cooked black beans
¾	cup long-grain white rice, washed and drained
2	cups water
1	beef bouillon cube or 1 teaspoon consommé granules
1	bay leaf
¼	teaspoon ground cumin

Freshly ground black pepper to taste

1. In a large skillet, heat oil over medium heat; sauté onion until translucent.
2. Add garlic and green bell pepper; sauté for 5 minutes.
3. Add remaining ingredients except pepper.
4. Cover; cook over low heat for 20 minutes until rice is soft.
5. Add pepper; serve hot.

Serves 6.

Each Latina Lite serving contains: 196 calories
Total Fats: 3 gm
Saturated Fats: 1 gm   Protein: 7 gm
Unsaturated Fats: 2 gm   Sodium: 171 mg
Carbohydrates: 35 gm

BREAD SUBSTITUTES— SUSTITUTOS DE PAN

Bread, the "staff of life," shares top billing with beans as a standard food. Flat breads, leavened breads, filled breads, braided breads, white breads, black breads, wheat breads, rye breads, corn breads, potato breads, cheese breads, and barley breads can all be found in some area of the world. In the Middle East, pita bread is prevalent, in Mexico, *tortillas*, in France, *baguettes*, in Chile, Venezuela, and Puerto Rico, *arepas*, and in New York, pizza and bagels.

CORNMEAL PATTIES—AREPAS

Fried cornmeal cheese patties are popular throughout South America. A great accompaniment to any meal instead of *tortillas* or bread.

½   cup yellow cornmeal
1½ cups water
½   teaspoon sugar
½   cup grated white cheese
2   tablespoons vegetable oil

1. In a small saucepan, combine cornmeal, water, and sugar.

2. Cook over low heat; stir constantly until mixture thickens; cool.

3. Add cheese; mix thoroughly.

4. In a large nonstick frying pan, heat oil over medium heat; form dough into small balls 1 tablespoon at a time; flatten with spatula and fry until golden brown on both sides.

Makes 8 arepas. Serves 4.

Each Latina Lite serving contains: 204 calories
Total Fats: 12 gm
Saturated Fats: 4 gm   Protein: 9 gm
Unsaturated Fats: 8 gm   Sodium: 125 mg
Carbohydrates: 15 gm

PUERTO RICAN "*TAMALES*"—*GUANIMES*

Typical Puerto Rican food, similar to Mexican *tamales* or Chilean *arepas*. *Guanimes* taste best wrapped in a plantain leaf or corn husk—tied at both ends—and steamed. Both types of wrappers are available in Latino food markets and in many supermarkets. Even if you have never eaten them before, I am sure they will be pleasing to your palate.

8   *corn husks or plantain leaves*
1   *cup milk*
1   *teaspoon coconut extract*
2   *cups cornmeal*
2   *tablespoons margarine*
½   *teaspoon half salt, half salt-substitute mixture*
2   *teaspoons sugar*
1   *tablespoon* ACHIOTE CUBANO *(page 50)*

1. Before using, soak corn husks in tepid water until pliable.

2. In a small bowl, mix milk with coconut extract; set aside.

3. In a medium bowl, combine cornmeal, margarine, salt, and sugar; mix well.

4. Add milk; stir mixture until a soft dough forms; divide into 8 pieces.

5. Rub each plantain leaf or corn husk with a little *Achiote* oil; place dough in middle of leaf or husk; flatten each piece; fold husk or leaf around dough; tie with kitchen string at both ends.

6. Steam for 35 minutes.

Makes 8 *guánimes*. Serves 4.

Each Latina Lite serving contains: 362 calories
Total Fats: 10 gm
Saturated Fats: 2 gm   Protein: 8 gm
Unsaturated Fats: 8 gm   Sodium: 307 mg
Carbohydrates: 59 gm

QUESADILLA EXPRESS

I grew up eating *quesadillas*, the Mexican competition to pizza. These popular anytime snacks are prepared the "fast-food way" by putting cheese inside a folded *tortilla* and grilling on both sides. They may also be made from *masa-tortilla* dough; recipes for *quesadillas* prepared from scratch are included in the chapter for *ANTOJITOS* (page 16). For a variety of quick *quesadillas*, insert a slice of lean turkey ham or mushrooms or squash or refried beans and a strip of *chile* with the melted cheese.

1   *ounce part-skim milk cheese*
1   *corn* tortilla

  1. Add cheese on the *tortilla*; fold.
  2. Grill on both sides on a nonstick griddle.

Makes 1 *quesadilla.*

Each Latina Lite serving contains: 146 calories
Total Fats: 5 gm
Saturated Fats: 3 gm   Protein: 10 gm
Unsaturated Fats: 2 gm   Sodium: 198 mg
Carbohydrates: 15 gm

TORTILLA, TOASTED—*TOSTADA*

According to the old form, *tostadas* were fried *tortillas* that oozed oil, but now you can prepare them without fat. Toast a *tortilla* in the toaster-oven, on the griddle, or in the oven. A fresh corn *tortilla* tastes better than an old one. Eat *tostadas* with *ceviche*, refried beans, *nopales* salad, *salsas*, and dips, among countless other dishes.

TAMALES

Each night at sunset in Mexico City the melodious whistle of the *tamale* vendor stimulated my appetite. "Red *Tamales, Chile Tamales, Mole Tamales, Tamales de Piña Y Fresa*, and glorious *Tamales Especiales de Pollo*," he crooned. Unfortunately, I had to control myself—his *tamales* were chock-full of tasty but unhealthy *manteca*—lard. Latina Lite chicken, pineapple, and fresh ground corn *tamales* are packed with flavor instead of fat.

CHICKEN TAMALES— TAMALES DE POLLO

4   tablespoons margarine
1   cup yellow cornmeal (Maseca)
⅔   cup powdered fat-free milk dissolved in ¾ cup water
2   tablespoons finely minced onion
½   teaspoon half salt, half salt-substitute mixture
Freshly ground black pepper to taste
2   eggs
2   egg whites
1½ cups cooked and shredded chicken breast
2   cups cooked and diced chayotes
4   tablespoons finely minced carrots

½   teaspoon baking powder
Corn husks for wrapping, immersed in warm water until
      pliable
Strips of chile jalapeño (optional)

1. In a large saucepan, melt margarine over low heat.

2. Add cornmeal; stir until smooth paste is formed; add milk, onion, salt, and pepper; stir until smooth; remove from heat.

3. Add eggs and egg whites whisked together, chicken, chayote, and carrots; mix well; add baking powder.

4. Divide mixture into 8 parts; put each part into a corn husk wrapper; if desired, add a chile strip to each tamal; tie at both ends.

5. Place tamales on a steamer rack in a large casserole.

6. Steam for 1 hour, until tamal separates from corn husk.

7. Delicious alone or with SALSA ROJA or VERDE (pages 64 and 65).

Serves 4.

Each Latina Lite serving contains: 401 calories
Total Fats: 16 gm
Saturated Fats: 3 gm   Protein: 23 gm
Unsaturated Fats: 13 gm   Sodium: 534 mg
Carbohydrates: 41 gm

PINEAPPLE *TAMALES— TAMALES DE PINA*

4   tablespoons margarine
1   cup yellow cornmeal (Maseca)
⅔   cup powdered fat-free milk dissolved in ¾ cup water
½   cup sugar
4   packets sugar substitute
2   cups canned unsweetened pineapple, drained and cut
        into small cubes
½   teaspoon half salt, half salt-substitute mixture
½   teaspoon baking powder
8   corn husk wrappers, soaked in water until pliable

1. In a large saucepan, melt margarine over low heat.
2. Add cornmeal; stir constantly until smooth paste is formed.
3. Add milk, sugar, sugar substitute, pineapple, and salt; mix well; add baking powder.
4. Divide dough into 8 parts; put each part into a corn husk wrapper; tie at both ends.
5. Place *tamales* on a steamer rack in a large casserole.
6. Steam for 1 hour, until *tamal* separates from corn husk.
7. Serve for lunch or light evening meal.

Serves 4.

Each Latina Lite serving contains: 413 calories
Total Fats: 12 gm
Saturated Fats: 2 gm   Protein: 5 gm
Unsaturated Fats: 10 gm   Sodium: 403 mg
Carbohydrates: 74 gm

TAMALES, SWEET SAN LUIS POTOSI-STYLE—*TAMALES HUICHEPOS*

4   *ears corn with their husks*
2   *tablespoons margarine*
¼ *cup sugar*
4   *packets sugar substitute*
1   *teaspoon vanilla extract*
½ *teaspoon baking powder*

1. Clean corn husks and set aside.

2. Remove corn kernels from cobs; grind kernels in blender or processor.

3. In a medium bowl, whisk margarine until light and fluffy; add ground corn kernels, sugar, sugar substitute, and vanilla.

4. Stir until well mixed; carefully add baking powder.

5. Divide dough into 4 parts; put each part into a husk; fold husk; tie with kitchen string at both ends.

6. Steam for 1 hour until dough gently pulls away from husk.

Serves 4.

Each Latina Lite serving contains: 170 calories
Total Fats: 6 gm
Saturated Fats: 1 gm   Protein: 2 gm
Unsaturated Fats: 5 gm   Sodium: 110 mg
Carbohydrates: 30 gm

Desserts—Postres

Latinos love sweets. We grow up sucking the sweet juice from *la caña*, sugarcane; eating sticky-sweet coconut-sugar confections; and surrounded by candies and *pan dulce* wherever we turn. You can continue to humor your sweet tooth, stay slim, and enjoy candies, pies, and desserts prepared with our healthier, less-fattening recipes.

Rice Pudding, Puerto Rican-Style—Arroz con Dulce

Rice pudding is scrumptious. Chill it; add a little fat-free milk to dilute the consistency, and dress it up with diced papaya, pineapple, mango, strawberries, or guava.

2   cups water
¼   teaspoon half salt, half salt-substitute mixture
2   cinnamon sticks
¼   teaspoon ground cloves
1   1-inch-square piece fresh ginger, peeled and thinly sliced
1   cup water
1   cup short-grain white rice, rinsed and drained

¾ *cup raisins*
1 *teaspoon coconut extract*
⅓ *cup sugar*
1 *12-ounce can lowfat evaporated milk*
10 *packets sugar substitute*
Ground cinnamon to taste

1. In a large saucepan, combine water, salt, cinnamon sticks, cloves, and ginger.
2. Bring to a boil; reduce heat; simmer for 3 minutes; strain and discard spices, except for a few pieces of ginger and cinnamon bark.
3. Return mixture to the saucepan; bring to a boil; add 1 cup water, rice, raisins, coconut extract, and sugar.
4. Cover; simmer over lowest heat for 20 minutes. (Note: Use a large saucepan to avoid liquid bubbling over the top.)
5. Remove cover; cook over lowest heat for 10 minutes more until all liquid is absorbed; stir in milk with a wooden spoon.
6. Cool; stir in sugar substitute.
7. Place in a serving dish and sprinkle with cinnamon.
8. Refrigerate.

Serves 6.

Each Latina Lite serving contains: 191 calories
Total Fats: 1 gm
Saturated Fats: 1 gm   Protein: 6 gm
Unsaturated Fats: 0 gm   Sodium: 145 mg
Carbohydrates: 42 gm

CORN PUDDING—*BUDIN DE ELOTE*

1   cup fresh corn kernels or canned and drained kernels
1   tablespoon cornstarch
¼   cup water
1   cup evaporated lowfat milk
1   cup evaporated fat-free milk
¼   cup sugar
1   teaspoon ground vanilla bean
4   tablespoons raisins
4–6 packets sugar substitute

1. Purée corn in blender; set aside.
2. In a large saucepan, dissolve cornstarch in ¼ cup water over low heat; stir constantly until cornstarch becomes translucent.
3. Slowly add the lowfat evaporated milk; then the fat-free evaporated milk, sugar, vanilla, and raisins.
4. Stir until mixture begins to thicken; add ground corn; stir until mixture assumes pudding consistency.
5. Remove from heat; stir in sugar substitute.
6. Pour into a serving bowl.
7. Refrigerate.

Serves 4.

Each Latina Lite serving contains: 223 calories
Total Fats: 2 gm
Saturated Fats: 1 gm   Protein: 11 gm
Unsaturated Fats: 1 gm   Sodium: 290 mg
Carbohydrates: 46 gm

*T*ORTILLA-BREAD PUDDING— *CAPIROTADA*

Traditional Mexican dessert for *cuaresma*—Lent. Although the recipe is designed for 4, you may want to double or triple the quantities to have enough for other family members and guests.

Syrup:

3   *cups water*
½   *cup sugar*
1   *tablespoon ground cinnamon*
2   *cinnamon sticks*
12 *whole cloves*

5   *teaspoons margarine (divided)*
4   *corn tortillas, cut into bite-size squares*
4   *apples, cored, peeled, and cubed*
4   *tablespoons raisins*
15 *packets sugar substitute*
4   *bolillos (Mexican French-style rolls), toasted and cubed*
8   *ounces grated white cheese*

1. Preheat the oven to 400°F.
2. To prepare syrup, boil water; add sugar, cinnamon, cinnamon sticks, and cloves; simmer for 5 minutes; remove cloves and cinnamon sticks and cool; set aside.
3. Grease bottom of a glass baking pan with 1 teaspoon margarine.
4. Arrange *tortillas* cut into squares on bottom of pan; place ¾ of apple cubes on top; sprinkle with 2 tablespoons raisins, and only 10 packets sugar substitute; dot with 2 teaspoons margarine; cover with ½ cup syrup.

5. Add half of toasted bread cubes, remaining ¼ apple cubes, 4 ounces cheese, the remaining 2 tablespoons raisins, and more syrup; dot with remaining 2 teaspoons margarine.

6. Repeat procedure with other half of bread and remaining 4 ounces cheese; cover with remaining syrup.

7. Bake for 25 to 30 minutes; remove from oven; sprinkle with remaining 5 packets of sugar substitute.

8. Serve hot or cold.

Serves 6.

Each Latina Lite serving contains: 411 calories
Total Fats: 11 gm
Saturated Fats: 5 gm   Protein: 14 gm
Unsaturated Fats: 6 gm   Sodium: 411 mg
Carbohydrates: 67 gm

Fruit compote in cream— COMPOTA DE FRUTAS

1   cup papaya or mango, peeled, seeded, and cubed
½   cup fat-free yogurt
4   tablespoons fruit liqueur (any flavor)
4   packets sugar substitute
1   cup cantaloupe melon, peeled, seeded, and cubed
1   cup grapes
½   banana, sliced

1. Purée papaya or mango, yogurt, and fruit liqueur in blender; pour into a serving bowl.

2. Add sugar substitute and fresh fruit. Substitute any seasonal fruit for others.

3. An easy, quick healthy dessert!

Serves 4.

Each Latina Lite serving contains: 177 calories
Total Fats: 1 gm
Saturated Fats: 0 gm   Protein: 3 gm
Unsaturated Fats: 1 gm   Sodium: 30 mg
Carbohydrates: 34 gm

WHIPPED CREAM—
CREMA CHANTILLY

Can you have whipped cream and still lose weight? Yes, if you follow my instructions. My *Crema Chantilly* has little fat, yet satisfies the craving for something sweet and creamy.

1   *12-ounce can lowfat evaporated milk*
½   *teaspoon vanilla extract*
4–6 *packets sugar substitute*

1. Chill unopened can of evaporated milk together with a mixing bowl and whipping blades in the freezer for 20 minutes.
2. When well chilled but not frozen, pour milk into cold bowl; add vanilla and sugar substitute; whip until peaks are formed.
3. Use immediately!

Serves 4.

Each Latina Lite serving contains: 75 calories
Total Fats: 2 gm
Saturated Fats: 1 gm   Protein: 7 gm
Unsaturated Fats: 1 gm   Sodium: 110 mg
Carbohydrates: 11 gm

$\mathcal{C}$USTARD—*FLAN*

This Spanish national dessert was inherited by all Latin people. After serving this recipe a few times, try creating variations by stirring 1 cup of sliced strawberries or canned crushed drained pineapple into the custard before pouring it into the *flaneras*. Rum, coconut, or almond *flan* can be created by substituting ¾ teaspoon of one of these flavors with ¼ teaspoon vanilla extract. Blend ½ cup cottage cheese into the custard for a cheese *flan*. Apart from different flavors, experiment with forms; make a circular *flan*, a square one, or a standard small custard-cup *flan*.

2   *whole eggs*
4   *egg whites*
¼   *cup sugar*
4   *packets sugar substitute*
1   *teaspoon vanilla or coconut extract*
1   *12-ounce can lowfat evaporated milk*

1. Preheat the oven to 350°F.
2. In a large bowl, beat eggs, egg whites, sugar, sugar substitute, and vanilla together; set aside.
3. In a small saucepan, heat milk over low heat; stir constantly; slowly add egg mixture; continue to stir.
4. When mixture begins to thicken, remove from heat; separate into 6 *flaneras*—Pyrex custard cups.
5. Set the *flaneras* in a flat pan filled with 1½ inches of water; bake for 45 minutes until a knife or toothpick comes out clean when inserted into custard.

Serves 6.

Each Latina Lite serving contains: 129 calories
Total Fats: 2 gm
Saturated Fats: 1 gm   Protein: 9 gm
Unsaturated Fats: 1 gm   Sodium: 146 mg
Carbohydrates: 16 gm

Mango Gelatin—
GELATINA DE MANGO

2   mangos, peeled and diced
1   0.3-ounce (small) package sugar-free lime gelatin
1   cup lowfat evaporated milk, well chilled
¼   cup sugar
¼   teaspoon mint extract
A few drops green food coloring
4   mint leaves

1. Reserve ¼ of diced mango.
2. Dissolve ½ package of gelatin in ¼ cup boiling water; purée gelatin and ¾ of the mango in blender.
3. In a medium bowl, beat milk, sugar, mint extract, and food coloring until peaks are formed; gently fold into gelatin with reserved ¼ of diced mango.
4. Divide into 4 dessert cups; chill.
5. Decorate each with a mint leaf.

Serves 4.

Each Latina Lite serving contains: 172 calories
Total Fats: 1 gm
Saturated Fats: 0 gm   Protein: 7 gm
Unsaturated Fats: 1 gm   Sodium: 79 mg
Carbohydrates: 37 gm

RUM AND ALMOND CREAM GELATIN— GELATINA DE ROMPOPE

1   cup lowfat evaporated milk
¼   cup sugar
1   teaspoon almond extract
1   teaspoon rum extract
1   egg yolk
1   0.6-ounce (large) package sugar-free strawberry
        gelatin
2   cups fresh strawberries, cleaned and halved
4   packets sugar substitute
2   tablespoons rum (optional)

1. In a small saucepan, simmer milk and sugar; stir constantly with a wooden spoon; when mixture begins to thicken add almond and rum extracts; stir until thoroughly mixed; remove from heat; cool.

2. In a small bowl, beat egg yolk; add to cooled milk.

3. In a small bowl, dissolve gelatin in 1 cup boiling water; add cooled milk mixture in place of additional cold water.

4. Pour into ring mold; refrigerate.

5. Fifteen minutes before serving, remove from ring mold; place strawberries in center of the gelatin.

6. Sprinkle strawberries with sugar substitute and if you like, 2 tablespoons of rum.

Serves 4.

Each Latina Lite serving contains: 165 calories
Total Fats: 2 gm
Saturated Fats: 1 gm   Protein: 10 gm
Unsaturated Fats: 1 gm   Sodium: 84 mg
Carbohydrates: 25 gm

NOTE: Pineapple gelatin may be used in place of strawberry with fresh pineapple in center; or lemon gelatin with mango in center.

Prickly Pear Gelatin— Gelatina de Tuna

6 prickly pears
1 0.6-ounce (large) package sugar-free lemon gelatin
Juice of 1 lemon

1. Peel cactus fruits; force fruit through a strainer to catch seeds; discard seeds.
2. Dissolve gelatin in 1 cup boiling water; add strained fruit in place of additional cold water.
3. Add lemon juice.
4. Refrigerate in a mold.

Serves 4.

Each Latina Lite serving contains: 41 calories
Total Fats: 0 gm
Saturated Fats: 0 gm   Protein: 4 gm
Unsaturated Fats: 0 gm   Sodium: 10 mg
Carbohydrates: 6 gm

Coconut Fudge—Jamoncillo de Coco

If you love sweets and prefer to eat your milk instead of drinking it, try preparing this quick, easy candy. It resembles the fudge sold in stores specializing in old-fashioned candies.

⅓ cup powdered fat-free milk
3 tablespoons water
½ teaspoon coconut extract
3–4 packets sugar substitute

1. Mix powdered milk with water to form a thick paste; add coconut extract and sugar substitute; if necessary add a little water.

2. Use your fingertips to press fudge into the bottom of a 4-inch-diameter bowl; refrigerate for ½ hour; cut into small pieces.

3. For variety, substitute vanilla, almond, maple, or rum extract.

4. For chocolate flavor, add 1 tablespoon unsweetened cocoa, ½ teaspoon liquid chocolate flavor, 1 to 2 additional packets sugar substitute, and ½ tablespoon water.

Serves 1.

Each Latina Lite serving contains: 80 calories
Total Fats: 0 gm
Saturated Fats: 0 gm   Protein: 8 gm
Unsaturated Fats: 0 gm   Sodium: 123 mg
Carbohydrates: 12 gm

RANGE MOUSSE—
MOUSSE DE NARANJA

1   *cup lowfat evaporated milk*
1   *cup fat-free milk*
1   *egg*
½   *cup strained fresh orange juice*
1   *0.6-ounce (large) package sugar-free orange gelatin*
½   *teaspoon vanilla extract*
4   *packets sugar substitute*

1. Place evaporated milk in freezer for 20 minutes; do not freeze.

2. In a small saucepan, heat fat-free milk over medium heat; avoid boiling; lower heat; beat the egg; slowly add

beaten egg; stir constantly until milk begins to thicken; remove from heat and cool.

3. In a small saucepan, heat orange juice almost to boiling; dissolve gelatin in juice; cool; add vanilla.

4. Carefully blend fat-free milk and egg mixture into gelatin dissolved in orange juice.

5. Place a small bowl on a bed of ice; remove evaporated milk from freezer; pour into bowl with sugar substitute; whip and fold into gelatin.

6. Divide into 4 tall dessert glasses.

7. Refrigerate until set.

Serves 4.

Each Latina Lite serving contains: 117 calories
Total Fats: 2 gm
Saturated Fats: 1 gm   Protein: 12 gm
Unsaturated Fats: 1 gm   Sodium: 129 mg
Carbohydrates: 14 gm

ᗷAKED ORANGES— NARANJAS HORNEADAS

1   cup water
2   teaspoons fresh lemon juice
2   cinnamon sticks
4   oranges, washed thoroughly
4   tablespoons sugar
4   teaspoons margarine
1   teaspoon ground cinnamon

1. Preheat the oven to 350°F.

2. Put water, lemon juice, and cinnamon sticks in bottom of covered casserole.

3. Place oranges in casserole; cover; bake for 1½ hours; discard liquid on bottom of pan.

4. Remove 1 slice from top of each orange; add sugar, margarine, and cinnamon.

5. Replace slice.

6. Serve hot.

Serves 4.

Each Latina Lite serving contains: 145 calories
Total Fats: 4 gm
Saturated Fats: 1 gm   Protein: 1 gm
Unsaturated Fats: 3 gm   Sodium: 44 mg
Carbohydrates: 29 gm

VANILLA-ALMOND CREAM CUSTARD PUDDING—*NATILLA*

2   tablespoons cornstarch
3   cups lowfat milk
¼   cup sugar
2   pieces lemon peel
3   egg yolks
4   egg whites
½   teaspoon almond extract
1   teaspoon vanilla extract
4   packets sugar substitute

1. In a large saucepan, dissolve cornstarch in ¼ cup water; over medium heat, stir until smooth; add milk, sugar, and lemon peel; stir constantly with a wooden spoon.

2. In a small bowl, beat egg yolks and whites with almond extract; add egg mixture to milk; stir constantly.

3. When mixture begins to thicken, remove from heat; add vanilla and sugar substitute.

4. Discard lemon peel.
5. Empty into a serving bowl.
6. Cool to room temperature.
7. Refrigerate.

Serves 6.

Each Latina Lite serving contains: 143 calories
Total Fats: 5 gm
Saturated Fats: 2 gm   Protein: 8 gm
Unsaturated Fats: 3 gm   Sodium: 101 mg
Carbohydrates: 17 gm

CORN CAKE—*PASTEL DE ELOTE*

2   cups fresh tender corn kernels, ground and then
        measured
2   egg yolks
¼   teaspoon half salt, half salt-substitute mixture
¼   cup sugar
5   packets sugar substitute
2   tablespoons margarine, melted
½   cup all-purpose flour
3   teaspoons baking powder
6   egg whites
1   teaspoon margarine

1. Preheat oven to 300°F.
2. Put corn into a large bowl with the 2 yolks; whisk briskly until mixed; add salt, sugar, and sugar substitute; mix well.
3. Add melted margarine; continue mixing.
4. Combine flour and baking powder; gently add to dough.
5. Meanwhile, in a large bowl, beat egg whites until they peak; carefully fold into dough.

6. Grease a nonstick loaf pan with 1 teaspoon margarine; empty dough into pan; bake for 25 minutes until an inserted knife or toothpick comes out clean.

Serves 4.

Each Latina Lite serving contains: 300 calories
Total Fats: 10 gm
Saturated Fats: 2 gm   Protein: 11 gm
Unsaturated Fats: 8 gm   Sodium: 798 mg
Carbohydrates: 45 gm

WEET POTATO-PUMPKIN PIE— PAY DE BONIATO Y CALABAZA

Boniatos are Cuban staples fit for a gourmet. They make a luscious pie combined with pumpkin, *estilo New Yorkino*.

Pie Crust:

¾   *cup corn flakes*
6   *packets sugar substitute*
2   *tablespoons margarine*

1. Make coarse crumbs by crushing corn flakes in a plastic bag with a rolling pin; add sugar substitute; with a fork, press margarine into corn flake crumbs.
2. When margarine is totally combined with crumbs, use your hands to mold crust into an 8-inch pie pan.

Filling:

1   cup boniato, *unpeeled, cut into chunks*
¾   *cup canned or cooked pumpkin*
2   *eggs*
3   *egg whites*
¾   *cup sugar*
½   *teaspoon half salt, half salt-substitute mixture*
½   *teaspoon ground cinnamon*
¼   *teaspoon ground nutmeg*
¼   *teaspoon ground ginger*
⅛   *teaspoon ground cloves*
⅔   *cup fat-free evaporated milk*
10   *packets sugar substitute*

1. Preheat oven to 425°F.

2. Cover *boniato* with water in a saucepan; bring to a boil; cover; lower heat; simmer for 30 minutes until tender; drain *boniato*; cool; mash.

3. Combine *boniato* with pumpkin.

4. In a small bowl, beat eggs and egg whites together; add to *boniato* and pumpkin; add remaining ingredients; mix thoroughly.

5. Pour mixture into crust; bake for 15 minutes at 425°F; lower heat to 350°F; bake for 45 minutes until toothpick comes out clean when inserted into center.

Serves 6.

Each Latina Lite serving contains: 247 calories
Total Fats: 6 gm
Saturated Fats: 2 gm   Protein: 7 gm
Unsaturated Fats: 4 gm   Sodium: 249 mg
Carbohydrates: 43 gm

NOTE: If *boniato* is unavailable, substitute additional pumpkin or yams.

PINEAPPLE, COUNTRY-STYLE—
PINA CAMPESINA

1   *cup fresh orange juice*
½   *teaspoon ground cinnamon*
¼   *cup sugar*
2   *cups canned, unsweetened pineapple chunks*
½   *cup grated white cheese*
4   *packets sugar substitute*

1. In a medium saucepan, heat orange juice with cinnamon and sugar to boiling; lower heat; cover; simmer for 5 minutes.

2. Add pineapple; simmer, covered, for 5 minutes more.

3. Remove from heat; sprinkle cheese and sugar substitute on top.

Serves 4.

Each Latina Lite serving contains: 231 calories
Total Fats: 5 gm
Saturated Fats: 3 gm   Protein: 9 gm
Unsaturated Fats: 2 gm   Sodium: 151 mg
Carbohydrates: 40 gm

SWEET FRIED PLANTAINS— PLATANOS DULCES

An extraordinary dessert whose delightful sweet taste depends on the ripeness of the plantains. Generally, plantains are purchased when still green and are considered ripe and ready to use when they appear to be rotten: soft and black-brown all over.

4   teaspoons margarine
½   cup fresh orange juice
Juice of 1 lemon
2   tablespoons dark-brown sugar
1   large ripe plantain, peeled and sliced diagonally
2   tablespoons sugar
1   ounce cognac or rum
CREMA CHANTILLY—WHIPPED CREAM (page 213)

1. In a medium skillet, melt margarine over medium heat; be careful not to burn margarine.
2. Add orange and lemon juices, and sugar; stir constantly.
3. Add plantain slices; move them around pan; bathe in margarine-juice mixture until tender.
4. Remove from heat.
5. Arrange plantain slices on a platter; just before serving, sprinkle with sugar and cognac or rum.
6. At the very moment of serving, light platter with a match.
7. Top with Latina Lite Crema Chantilly.

Serves 4.

Each Latina Lite serving contains: 257 calories
Total Fats: 4 gm
Saturated Fats: 1 gm   Protein: 8 gm
Unsaturated Fats: 3 gm   Sodium: 160 mg
Carbohydrates: 45 gm

RICE CAKE WITH FRUIT— *TESORO DULCE*

2   cups cooked short-grain white rice
2   cups fresh orange juice
2   bananas, ripe
1   tablespoon fresh lemon juice
1   egg yolk
3   egg whites
1⅓ cups fat-free powdered milk
⅓   cup sugar

1. Preheat the oven to 350°F.
2. Purée all ingredients in blender; transfer to a glass baking dish.
3. Set baking dish in a larger pan filled with 2 to 3 inches of water.
4. Bake for 30 minutes.

Serves 6.

Each Latina Lite serving contains: 276 calories
Total Fats: 2 gm
Saturated Fats: 1 gm   Protein: 10 gm
Unsaturated Fats: 1 gm   Sodium: 113 mg
Carbohydrates: 56 gm

BREAD CUBES, SWEET AND TOASTED WITH SYRUP—*TORREJAS*

½   cup fat-free milk
½   cup sweet red wine
4   slices French bread, toasted and cubed

1 egg
2 egg whites
1 teaspoon ground cinnamon
1 tablespoon vegetable oil

1. In a medium bowl, mix milk and wine together; carefully soak each bread cube in mixture; remove with slotted spoon and place cubes on piece of aluminum foil.

2. In a small bowl, beat egg and egg whites together; sprinkle bread cubes with cinnamon; coat each with egg mixture.

3. In a large nonstick skillet, heat oil over medium heat; brown each *torreja* on all sides.

4. Carefully remove cubes with a slotted spoon; blot excess oil on paper towels.

Syrup:

⅓ cup sugar
½ cup water
1 stick cinnamon
Pinch of half salt, half salt-substitute mixture
4 packets of sugar substitute

1. In a small saucepan, dissolve sugar in water; heat until boiling; stir constantly.

2. Lower heat; add cinnamon and salt; continue stirring.

3. When syrup begins to thicken, remove from heat; cool; add sugar substitute.

4. Pour over *torrejas* just before serving.

Serves 4.

Each Latina Lite serving contains: 250 calories
Total Fats: 6 gm
Saturated Fats: 1 gm   Protein: 8 gm
Unsaturated Fats: 5 gm   Sodium: 340 mg
Carbohydrates: 37 gm

Drinks—Bebidas

⿻ED HIBISCUS TEA—*AGUA DE JAMAICA*

Dried *Jamaica*, red hibiscus flowers, may be purchased in bulk in most Latin markets. If you cannot find them, various brands of Red Zinger Tea (red hibiscus tea) are available.

3   cups water
½   pound dried **Jamaica** *blossoms*
Sugar substitute to taste

    1. Heat water in a medium saucepan until water reaches boiling point; add blossoms; cover; simmer flowers for 20 minutes at boiling point to extract maximum flavor and ensure sterilization.
    2. Cool concentrated mixture; refrigerate in glass container.
    3. One-quarter to one-third cup of concentrate makes an 8-ounce glass of *Jamaica* Water.
    4. Sweeten with sugar substitute to taste.
    5. Drink as much as you want hot or cold.

Serves 11.

Each Latina Lite serving contains: 1 calorie

Total Fats:	0 gm		
Saturated Fats:	0 gm	Protein:	0 gm
Unsaturated Fats:	0 gm	Sodium:	1 mg
Carbohydrates:	0 gm		

ẞOURSOP OR *GUANABANA* WITH MILK— *CHAMPOLA DE GUANABANA*

A refreshing tropical drink popular in Cuba, Puerto Rico, and Mexico. At first, you may not like the exotic taste, but the haunting, sweet-sour flavor remains on your palate, compelling you to try it again.

1   *fresh soursop or* guanábana *(about 1 pound)*
½   *cup sugar*
10–15 packets sugar substitute
1   *quart fat-free milk*
Cracked ice
Sugar substitute to taste

1. Peel *guanábana.*
2. Cut it in half; discard seeds.
3. Place pulp in a large bowl; sprinkle sugar on pulp.
4. Allow sugar to penetrate at least 1 hour.
5. Purée mixture in blender with 1 cup milk.
6. Mix thoroughly with remaining milk; pour into pitcher.
7. Serve over cracked ice, adding sugar substitute to taste.

Serves 8.

Each Latina Lite serving contains: 113 calories
Total Fats: 0 gm
Saturated Fats: 0 gm   Protein: 5 gm
Unsaturated Fats: 0 gm   Sodium: 71 mg
Carbohydrates: 24 gm

RICE WATER—
HORCHATA DE ARROZ

½   cup uncooked short-grain white rice
2½ cups water
2   cups fat-free evaporated milk
1   tablespoon vanilla extract
2   teaspoons almond extract
2   teaspoons coconut extract
1   tablespoon ground cinnamon
½   cup sugar
12 packets sugar substitute
Cracked ice

1. Soak rice in water for at least 2 hours.
2. Purée swollen rice grains with remaining ingredients in blender; chill.
3. Serve over cracked ice.

Makes 8 8-ounce glasses.

Each Latina Lite serving contains: 152 calories
Total Fats: 0 gm
Saturated Fats: 0 gm   Protein: 6 gm
Unsaturated Fats: 0 gm   Sodium: 74 mg
Carbohydrates: 32 gm

FRUIT SMOOTHIES—
LICUADOS OR BATIDOS

Formerly, forcing fruit pulp through a sieve was a tedious chore, but now you can purée wonderful fruit *licuados* or *batidos* instantly in the blender. *Batidos* or *licuados* are made from papaya, strawberries, bananas, peaches, berries, cantaloupe, tropical fruits, and even lettuce, watercress, *nopales*, alfalfa, and other vegetables. An easy satisfying drink that helps adults and kids to drink their milk. Water may be substituted for milk in a *licuado* or *batido*.

1   **cup fat-free milk**
½   **teaspoon vanilla, almond, or coconut extract**
3–6 packets sugar substitute
4–6 ice cubes
½   **banana, or**
1   **cup strawberries, or**
¾   **cup papaya, or other fruit**

1. Place all ingredients in blender, except ice and fruit.
2. Blend at high speed, add ice cubes one by one until blended.
3. Add fruit and blend for only 3 to 4 seconds to avoid bruising.
4. Results: A thick, delicious fruit milk shake.

Serves 2.

Each Latina Lite serving contains: 60 calories
Total Fats: 0 gm
Saturated Fats: 0 gm   Protein: 5 gm
Unsaturated Fats: 0 gm   Sodium: 63 mg
Carbohydrates: 10 gm

NOTE: Another method is to freeze 1 cup of fat-free milk in ½-cup containers. Instead of 4 to 6 ice cubes, use only 2 to 3.

HOT COFFEE SHAKE—
LICUADO DE CAFE CALIENTE

1   *cup strong hot coffee*
¼   *cup powdered fat-free milk*
½   *teaspoon vanilla extract (or other flavor)*
2   *packets sugar substitute*
2   *scoops frozen fat-free, sugar-free vanilla yogurt*

1. In the blender, process coffee, milk, vanilla, and sugar substitute.
2. Pour into a glass.
3. Top with yogurt.

Serves 2.

Each Latina Lite serving contains: 111 calories
Total Fats: 0 gm
Saturated Fats: 0 gm   Protein: 7 gm
Unsaturated Fats: 0 gm   Sodium: 103 mg
Carbohydrates: 20 gm

TRADITIONAL HOT PUNCH—
PONCHE TRADICIONAL

8   *guayabas (guavas), cut in half*
16 *small plums or prunes*
8   *cups water*
2   *lemons, cut into wedges*
½   *cup sugar*
20 *cinnamon sticks*
4   *cups fresh orange juice*
16 *ounces rum*

1. In a medium saucepan, boil *guayabas* and plums in 2 cups water until fruit is very soft; add more water if necessary.

2. Remove from heat; purée in blender; strain liquid; discard seeds.

3. Return liquid to saucepan, add lemon, remaining 6 cups water, sugar, 4 sticks cinnamon, and orange juice.

4. Bring to boiling point; lower heat; simmer for 3 minutes.

5. Serve hot; put 1 stick of cinnamon and 1 ounce of rum in each glass.

Makes 16 glasses.

Each Latina Lite serving contains: 114 calories

Total Fats:	1 gm		
Saturated Fats:	0 gm	Protein:	1 gm
Unsaturated Fats:	1 gm	Sodium:	3 mg
Carbohydrates:	28 gm		

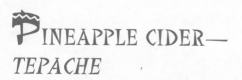

PINEAPPLE CIDER—
TEPACHE

1   large ripe pineapple (about 3 pounds)
2   quarts water
1   cup light-brown sugar
4   whole cloves
2   cinnamon sticks (about 4 inches each)
1   cup light beer
12   packets sugar substitute

1. Do not peel pineapple; wash thoroughly; core; cut the flesh and skin into chunks.

2. Place into a large covered jar (like a pickle jar); add water, sugar, cloves, and cinnamon.

3. Cap jar; store in warm place for 48 hours; uncap; stir.

4. Add beer; allow *tepache* to continue to ferment for 24 hours more.

5. Strain liquid; discard fruit; add sugar substitute.
6. Chill.
7. Serve cold over cracked ice.

Makes 10 glasses.

Each Latina Lite serving contains: 100 calories
Total Fats: 0 gm
Saturated Fats: 0 gm   Protein: 0 gm
Unsaturated Fats: 0 gm   Sodium: 10 mg
Carbohydrates: 24 gm

Part
TWO

· ·

DIET AND NUTRITION

The Light Goes On— Se Prende la Luz

Recognizing What Makes Us Fat

Siempre Te Contestaré, Mi Amor, Cuando Me Llamas—Call and I Will Always Answer, My Love

Rosita was so proud. She had been chosen as the godmother of her favorite niece's first child. She was looking forward to the baptism, to seeing her whole family at the *misa* in church. Secretly, Rosita was also anticipating the sumptuous meal that would follow. In preparation, she had not eaten since noon of the previous day, contemplating the delicious food.

Rosita was not disappointed. After the beautiful ceremony, she rushed down to the fiesta and eagerly approached the table overflowing with *sopas, flautas, carne asada, frijoles refritos, cochinita pibil, tamales, enchiladas,* and countless other tempting dishes. Rosita piled her plate high and went over to a table where several of her cousins were already enjoying the wonderful banquet.

Rosita exchanged a few appreciative comments about the ceremony and the fiesta with her cousins and was about to take her first bite of a *tamal* when she heard what she thought was her husband's voice affectionately call, "*Gorda!*" She turned to wave only to see six or seven other women also responding to the salutation.

It was not Rosita's husband who was looking for his "Fatty."

Rosita felt embarrassed and self-conscious. She tried to laugh the incident off, but it had upset her intensely. All her life she had been called *Gorda*. The label was so deeply ingrained in her own self-image, she did not even think about it. Rosita had always been heavy and had never made an effort to lose weight. She identified herself as a fat person and lived accordingly.

Suddenly, Rosita felt trapped by her lifelong label. She wanted to leave the "ranks of the *gordas*."

Sadly, thousands and thousands of women are overweight because they identify themselves as fat. If you think of yourself as fat, you will be. It is a trap that is set for many of us in childhood. An adorably chubby toddler coos happily when her mother hugs and kisses her, saying "*Gordita*." But with every hug and kiss, the child is learning to think of herself as fat and of being fat as something that brings love. Those are the first seeds of a *mente gorda*—a way of thinking that encourages a fat body.

The first step in losing weight is changing your mind-set. Find in your heart the picture of how you would like to be— the trimmer, younger-looking, sexier you. Get to know that person. That is your *mente delgada*—thin mind—and she will help you overcome the obstacles you may encounter and achieve your weight-loss goal.

WHAT FEEDS OUR *MENTES GORDAS*

There are very few people who can honestly say, "I like being fat and want to stay that way." Most of us are miserable being overweight and know deep inside that it destroys our self-esteem, our health, and our social and family lives. Yet, many Latinas have an emotional dependence on fattening food as a result of being raised with the traditions of our cultures that equate food with health and love.

They Loved Me So Much,
I Was the Fattest Kid in Town

Olivia was brought up in Las Vegas. Her mom worked to support the family, and her *abuelita* took care of her while her mother was at the office. All day long, her grandmother filled Olivia with delicious snacks and rich Puerto Rican foods to fatten her up and keep her *nieta* "chubby and healthy." Almost every day when she came home from work, Olivia's mother brought her sweets.

Both her mother and grandmother assured Olivia of their love by constantly feeding her. "I guess I was the most loved, since I was the fattest kid in my class," Olivia says. "I know their intentions were to make me happy, but the fact was that I was really unhappy. My classmates ridiculed me; I particularly remember one mean skinny little boy who regularly hid behind the mailbox on the way home from school. He would jump out taunting, 'Fatso! *Gorda!*' Delighted, he teased me unmercifully until the tears streamed down my face. Terribly upset, I would waddle home and quietly slip in, to avoid my mother and grandmother. I always headed directly to the *cocina*—kitchen—to soothe my hurt with conveniently available *frituras de yautía, tostones, guanimes o mofongo balls.*"

Being overweight made Olivia terribly unhappy. But she could not give up the delicacies she associated with her mother and grandmother's love. Her *mente gorda* told her that she could find comfort in food and that only a miracle could make her thin. It did not take a miracle for Olivia to lose weight; with the help of the Latina Lite system, she took control of her *mente gorda* and changed her eating habits.

Most people, like Olivia, eat with their minds, not their mouths. Unfortunately, the unsightly, unhealthy fat that accumulates in their bodies is not imaginary. And it takes a lot of hard work and dedication to get rid of it.

Understanding and controlling your *mente gorda* is essential to losing weight and remaining trim. So begin by listening to that part of your mind that entices you to overindulge. What is it asking for? What does it promise you?

For many of us, our relationship with food can be difficult and confusing. Let's face it, warm, savory, rich dinners and delectable, sweet desserts can take our minds off our anxieties, troubles, and insecurities. But only while they last. After they are gone, what we are left with are the same anxieties, troubles, and insecurities, plus the embarrassment of being out of control and the shame of being overweight. That is when our *mentes gordas* spring the trap. "*Come!* Food will make you feel better," the fat mind-set whispers. And so we eat to forget the sadness and loneliness of being *gordas*.

Equal Opportunity: He Goes Out Dancing. She Stays Home and Eats.

Edelmira was desperate. She found herself spending too many sad lonely nights, waiting for her husband, Ramón, to come home. More often than not he would arrive in the wee hours of the morning offering no explanation. Every night, Edelmira watched television alone imagining to herself, "Ramón is at a nightclub, having a wonderful time dancing with a slim, attractive woman."

After fifteen years of marriage and four children, Edelmira admitted to herself that she was obese and that her obesity had made her unattractive. She was distressed by her appearance and recognized that Ramón—who was still a slim, attractive man—also felt humiliated by her condition. But she felt powerless to do anything about her weight.

The more Edelmira fantasized about Ramón's exciting nights out, the worse she felt. She became more tense, feeling trapped, lonely, and abandoned. She seldom slept well, because her mind raced incessantly. Every night, when Edelmira reached the darkest moment of her lonely depression, the little friend inside her head began to advise: "Drink some beer to help you sleep and eat some chips with dip. That will calm you. Ramón is out somewhere having a won-

derful time, you are entitled to a drink to cheer yourself up!"
Edelmira trusted her *mente gorda* and, feeling justified, began
to drink and eat in order to sleep. She gained ten to fifteen
pounds each and every year, until she tipped the scales at
more than three hundred pounds.

Edelmira spent fifteen solitary years before she acknowl-
edged the destructive nature of her *mente gorda*. With the
help of the Latina Lite system, she began to defy her fat mind-
set. Edelmira took control over her *amiga traidora*—trai-
torous friend—who beguiled her into isolating herself within
thick layers of unattractive fat. She learned to resist her per-
sistent *mente gorda* by distracting herself whenever it admon-
ished, "You'll never be thin. Why try?" When her destructive
inner voice was most vocal, Edelmira called friends, or her
supportive brother and sister-in-law.

After Edelmira lost sixty-five pounds in the first year, some
members of her family began to implore her to stop *adel-
gazando*, "You are getting too thin, you don't look good." She
agreed to take a six-month vacation from reducing.
Fortunately, she had already learned to ignore her *mente
gorda*'s advice and did not gain any weight during her hiatus.
She resumed her weight-loss plan and within eighteen
months lost another hundred pounds, slimming down from a
size *XXXXL* to a size 8.

Edelmira and Ramón just celebrated their twentieth wedding anniversary. They declare that the last five years have
been the happiest of their marriage.

Your *mente gorda*, like Edelmira's, might tell you that trying
to change your life for the better—to confront your problems,
take control, lose weight—is useless. It may encourage you to
forget yourself with another heaping helping of french fries or
a big piece of cake. Do not listen to it. You know that in the
long run the food will do nothing to change your life except
make you heavier.

I'll Do Anything to Keep You Safe

Lucero had had weight problems as a teenager, but had kept her eating under control and reached her thirty-eighth birthday in good shape. Then something happened. In the space of six months, Lucero gained fourteen pounds. She became alarmed but could find no explanation for the sudden weight gain.

So what had happened in those six months? As it turned out, it was during that time that Lucero's seventeen-year-old son, Alfonso, started driving a car. Lucero was terribly worried about her *niño*, especially when he went out at night. "What time are you coming home?" she would interrogate Alfonso as he got ready to leave. Often, he was late, leaving a nervous Lucero to pace the floor with images of car wrecks and gang members swirling in her head. "Is he okay? Has he had an accident? Maybe he has been attacked."

The more worried she became, the louder a long-dormant inner voice wheedled: "Eat something to calm yourself." Before long, she would find herself obeying, invading the refrigerator to find something, anything, to allay her fears. Naturally her weight went up.

Lucero was able to stop and ask herself, "Does my eating make Alfonso come home sooner? Does my gaining weight protect him from harm?" Of course, the logical answers were "no." Surprised that her long-silent *mente gorda* had suddenly exerted its control over her again, Lucero made a concerted effort to think before she ate. Thoughtful awareness allowed her to stop overeating and send her *mente gorda* packing.

Awareness is crucial in the battle with your *mente gorda*. You must eat to nourish your body, but be careful not to use food to satisfy other needs. Your *mente gorda* will try to trick you into eating for hundreds of different reasons: because you are anxious, or happy, or tired; because you should not waste food; because you must not appear impolite when your friend worked hard to prepare a special dessert just for you; because you can lose weight anytime you want.

Remember, the only time to eat is when you are hungry, and then you should eat responsibly and only enough to satisfy that hunger.

Marriage Demands Sacrifice, But Not My Body

Ricardo left his wife, Clara, and their baby daughter in Nicaragua to come to Arizona to build a new life for the family. Industrious and energetic, Ricardo quickly landed a good job and called for his wife to join him. For eighteen-year-old Clara, the trip was a dream come true. It was the first time she had traveled away from the small town where she was born, and she could not wait to see all the wonders of the United States and to be with her husband again.

As she stepped off the plane, Clara could not even imagine what her new life would be like. The first surprise came right at the airport; Ricardo came to meet her and the baby in their very own new car.

Ricardo continued to be extraordinarily successful in his job. The family prospered and put down roots in their new home. During the next three years, Clara and Ricardo were blessed with two more children. Life could not be sweeter.

But with every promotion he got, Ricardo had less and less time to spend at home. Left alone to care for three young children, Clara keenly felt the absence of family support. Her heart yearned for her mother, sisters, cousins, and aunts far away in Nicaragua. To chase away the loneliness, Clara began looking for ways to make her life happier. She discovered that other *señoras* separated from their families gathered most afternoons at the local fast-food restaurant with their kids. The children played while their *mamas* passed the time chatting and munching on their burgers and fries.

Clara quickly got into the habit of spending two to three hours daily with her new *amigas*. She drank sweet cola and ate french fries, plus she finished what her children left over. Clara knew that she was gaining weight because of the change in the way she ate, but her *mente gorda* kept encouraging her. "*Cuesta mucho comer, come todo!*" It instructed her to down leftovers because to waste food would be a sin. It persuaded her that she was a married woman with children and expected to be fat. Obligingly, Clara ate and ate.

Finally, after Clara had gained four sizes, Ricardo called her attention to her body. "You look old and unattractive with the extra weight," he told her. "I work with women much older than you who are also mothers of three and four children. They are slim and look young. You are no longer the same Clara that I married!" Ricardo's stark words shocked Clara into realizing that if she continued to follow her *mente gorda*'s advice, she risked losing her husband and her happiness.

It was the stress of change that let loose Clara's insatiable *mente gorda*, but it was her change to a *mente delgada* that helped her regain control, eat in moderation, and accept the glorious rewards of being slim.

Mentes gordas come in all shapes and sizes—except small. The key for you is to identify your own. Learn its tricks. When does it demand to be fed? What kinds of food does it want? What does it promise in return?

Remember, the first step in becoming thin is learning what makes us fat.

¿Quién Manda?—Who Is in control?

Most of us have lived with our *mentes gordas* since childhood. They are second nature to us. We have learned to accommodate them—to build our lives around them. You may not even notice how your *mente gorda* controls you.

I Brought Back Ten Pounds of Chicago Fat

Perla was ecstatic. She had dropped a whole dress size in just four weeks. She could not wait to show off her new figure on her upcoming Christmas visit to her family in Chicago. But as the time for the trip neared, Perla became concerned. "What can I do? They are arranging so many parties," she fretted. "And my mother prepares wonderful homemade *tamales*. I know I am not going to be able to resist. I'll probably regain ten pounds during my two-week visit."

Sure enough, after two weeks in Chicago, Perla came back ten pounds heavier. Discouraged, she abandoned her weight-loss plan and resigned herself to being overweight. Her *mente gorda* had succeeded in undermining Perla's commitment to slimming down. Even before she went to Chicago, Perla had (1) accepted the inevitability of gaining weight; (2) declared complete loss of control over her eating in the face of familial pressure; (3) prepared herself to overindulge; and (4) rehearsed the excuse for her overeating, "*No es mi culpa.* I am not to blame."

Fortunately, Perla had tasted the pride and self-esteem that comes with losing weight. She quickly realized that the decision to abandon herself to fat was a last-ditch effort by her *mente gorda* to remain in control. Perla fought back by resuming her weight-loss plan. She listed every obstacle she was likely to encounter on her way to permanent slimness. Determined to lose every ounce of excess fat, Perla ate wiser and exercised. With every food encounter, good eating decisions became easier. She has lost thirty pounds of body fat, looks more beautiful, and feels terrific about herself.

Perla is returning to Chicago in a few weeks for her cousin's wedding. This time she is ready to withstand any food temptations.

"Making a verbal commitment was easy," Perla explains. "The hard part was actually taking the first step: admitting that I was fat and that my nonrational side controlled me. For some reason, I always told myself that I could lose weight whenever I wanted to. And I did, for a short time. But I could never keep it off. Every time I regained a little weight, I would just quit. I know now that a few blunders on the road to permanent weight loss are to be expected. They do not mean, 'Give up, there is no hope.' Now I know I'm stronger. When I'm tempted to pig out, I just think of the compliments I get on my figure. This time I'm going to return from Chicago just as thin as I am now!"

To lose weight, you will have to control your food rather than allow your *mente gorda* to dictate what and how much to eat. Do not underestimate how difficult this is going to be. But do not give in to the temptation to give up—or even give an inch. With the help of the Latina Lite system you can uproot your fat mind-set and achieve permanent weight loss.

Fat, Family, and Friends

As you begin to *adelgazar*—lose weight—not everyone may share your joy and enthusiasm. You may encounter resistance from family and friends. "You must not change the way you were taught to eat," these "well-wishers" may try to convince you. "Stop losing weight and return to the way you were."

There Ought to Be a Law Against Thin Women

During the time I was casting off unwanted pounds, a puzzling thing happened. Some of my heavier women friends openly discouraged my efforts. "Lolita, you are wasting your time," they said, "and you're setting yourself up for heartbreak and disappointment."

They truly did not want me to succeed. It was shameful, they said, for me to take only a nibble or actually refuse the marvelous delicacies they served. "*No seas sangrona*—you mustn't be rude. I made *flan de coco* especially because I know how much you love it."

"You're almost thirty with two children," my friends would say. "You can't expect to look like a *quinceañera*—fifteen-year-old." I politely listened to their comments and suggestions but lovingly declined their offerings.

You have to be prepared for this kind of peer pressure from friends, family, and coworkers. The best way to handle it is to find people who will support you in your efforts to lose weight. And always remember that only *you* have the right to decide how *you* will eat and look.

Birds of a Feather Eat Together

Herminia worked the nightshift in a factory. The work was hard, with two twenty-minute breaks and an hour for lunch. Many Latinas worked on the same shift, and every night during the breaks and lunch, Herminia and her group took comfort in home-cooked food. Everybody took turns bringing something—*dulces, tostones, pastelitos, flan, tamales, arroz, pupusas*—to enjoy together.

Herminia always ate with her coworkers. "The other *muchachas* will spurn you if you refuse their goodies," her *mente gorda* said to her. When it was her turn, she felt obligated to compete with the others by preparing even richer dishes.

Almost all of the *señoritas* were overweight. They lamented their bulging figures, yet encouraged one another to perpetuate their bad eating habits. When any one of the group made an effort to resist the daily "pig-out" sessions, the others pressured her. "We work so hard, *el gusto más grande*, the greatest pleasure for us is eating. If we do not treat ourselves well, who will?"

Herminia really wanted to become thin. She made several attempts to resist the pressure of the group, but each time her mind ordered her, "*Ceda*, give in, avoid the risk of breaking with the group." Herminia started to resent her "fat mind" and her friends. She felt conflicted and trapped.

Herminia began to change only after she had banded with two other young women in the group who also felt communal eating was not in their best interest. Through mutual support, they made a conscious effort to resist consuming too many snacks at work. The three were able to oppose their *mentes gordas*, and regain their teenage figures.

Formando una Mente Delgada— Shaping a Mente Delgada

"*Come poco, amigo Sancho, y cena menos, que el estómago es la oficina donde se fragua la salud y vida,*" Don Quixote counseled Sancho Panza. "Dine scantily, friend Sancho, and sup even less. The stomach is the office in which health and life are forged." For those of us whose eating habits were controlled for a long time by our *mentes gordas*, this is hard advice to swallow. It is, however, a perfect expression of a *mente delgada*—the foundation of permanent weight loss.

Make a List

Start shaping your *mente delgada* by listing the disadvantages of excess weight on a 3 by 5 card similar to the reminder card at the end of this chapter. List the ways in which being overweight negatively affects your life. Some examples may be: I can't buy clothes that I like; I've got a double chin; My tummy is too big; Climbing stairs makes me gasp for air; I suffer from indigestion; The zippers in my pants and skirts keep breaking. Make copies of your personal card to carry with you. Every time your *mente gorda* tempts you to eat something succulent and fattening, or seduces you to go back for seconds, or tells you to choose the biggest piece, take out your card and review it. Then decide whether eating that second helping is worth the unhappiness that excess weight brings.

Lo Que Veo, Lo Como—I Eat It Because It's There

About a year ago, Amelia, a woman who had lost four sizes with my program, invited me to join her for lunch at a popular local restaurant, an "all-you-can-eat" buffet serving Latin food. There were counters of fried food, meats, turkey, pastas, salads, vegetables. A "fix-your-own-taco" stand. A whole section was devoted to freshly baked breads. And, of course, a dessert island, overflowing with *arroz con leche, natilla, pastelitos,* and three self-serve frozen yogurt machines.

Discreetly, we spied the most overweight people precariously balancing plates piled high. We eavesdropped on an overfed gentleman ardently examining his companion's food. "What are you eating? That looks so good. Your selections are always better than mine. I didn't get any of that!" The woman with him, accustomed to his "yours-is-*más sabroso*" attitude, answered: "Jorge, that's the *tortas de calabaza*. They were on your plate under the fried chicken and the *Moros y Cristianos*. You couldn't taste yours because you combined it with the *boliche asado*."

All around us, we noticed many *gordas y gordos*, looking tired from so much eating, forging ahead with the breads and desserts. "I marvel at how dedicated fat people are to their eating," Amelia commented. "When I was heavy, I was afraid that I would miss something that I had already paid for, so I ate two and three of everything. My *gordita* advised, 'Get your money's worth. Stuff in as much as you can!' I'm so grateful I'm not that way anymore."

Our *mentes gordas* encourage us to eat beyond reasonable capacity. You know ahead of time that you are going to feel uncomfortable afterward, but most of the time you feel powerless to stop. To avoid overeating, set a specific limit on how much you are going to eat and stick to it. Let your *mente delgada* determine the amount of nourishment your body needs.

Out of Sight But on My Mind

Rebecca had a weakness that dominated her life, the rich and creamy *quesos sabrosos* available in Little Havana. Every time Rebecca went to the market, the cheeses seemed to beckon: "Don't you understand? I was created for you. Buy me! Buy me now!" How could she remain strong? So many cheeses, so many voices.

There was always at least one *trozo*—chunk of cheese—in Rebecca's refrigerator. Often, she would be in bed reading, watching television, or attempting to sleep, when she heard the cheese call out in a sweet, enticing voice: "*Visítame!* You don't have to eat me, just check me out and see how good I look! Make sure no one has made off with me!" She tried very hard to summon up the strength to refuse, but all too often she succumbed and devoured *el trozo completo*—the whole thing.

Rebecca started to regain control over her desires only after she admitted that she had given in to her *mente gorda*. She realized that she could not coexist with fatty temptations. Rebecca lost all of her unwanted weight and has kept it off by refusing to buy any more cheese or other high-fat foods.

Our *mentes gordas* never forget. Even now, after thirty years of self-control, I have to keep a vigilant eye on my *gordita*. Just recently, I was waiting in line at the *cajera* to check out my groceries, when my inner voice began cajoling, "*Compra una bolsita de pulpa de tamarindo.* Buy it. You haven't had spicy sweet gooey tamarind in so long. No one will know." I turned up the music on my Walkman and drowned out the nagging voice.

Count on your *mente delgada* to help you maintain healthy eating habits. Whether you refrain from buying fattening foods you cannot resist or learn to overcome temptation, eating sensibly and nutritionally is the key to permanent weight loss. And always remember that you are in control.

LET'S SUMMARIZE

Hay Esperanza Para Ti—Yes, There Is a New Horizon

To lose weight and keep it off, you must recognize and **CONTROL** your *mente gorda*, the part of your mind that drives you to eat without reason or restraint. Defy it, whether you feel frustrated, angry, unhappy, depressed, bored, or contented.

Use the list below to make a reminder card to help control your *mente gorda*. Copy those highlighted words that apply specifically to you onto an index card. Carry the card with you and read it when you feel tempted to eat too much, eat unhealthy food, or when you hear your *mente gorda* beckoning, "Oh, come on, just this once. It's time to party! You deserve it!"

REMINDER CARD—
Temptation

Think of yourself: **I'm a lean person.**

List **obstacles** that prevent weight loss.

Disregard unconfirmed dietary information.

Avoid pills and **quick weight loss schemes**.

Network with a friend for verbal support.

Disregard negative, unhelpful comments.

Contact family and loved ones for support.

Team-up *con delgados*—lean, active people.

Avoid people who routinely "*tragar*, pig out."

Walk away from fatty food temptation.

Be aware of irrational, **destructive urges.**

When tempted, **review** this list.

When tempted, get busy—**distract** yourself.

When tempted, **call** a friend.

When tempted, **change environments.**

There are *obstáculos*—**pitfalls**—during weight loss.

Temporary **setbacks** may occur. It's okay.

You can **succeed.** *Sí, se puede.*

EXCUSES THAT KEEP YOU FAT— *PRETEXTOS MARAVILLOSOS*

We saw in the preceding chapter how completely our *mentes gordas* control our lives when we are overweight. For most of us, this loss of control over our own lives feels terribly shameful. So to deal with the shame and the pain, we invent excuses—excuses that hide the truth and keep us fat. There are thousands of them. You have probably heard hundreds and used a few yourself. You might have blamed those around you or the customs of your culture: "I want to be slim, but my Latin family, my work, my *amor*, and my genes all stand in my way." You may have justified your excess pounds by saying: "If I lose weight, I am going to look older." Or, "I don't have big breasts or buns to begin with, and I am afraid that weight loss will make what I have disappear." You might have even tried to deny being overweight by hiding beneath billowing clothes.

But all our excuses are just that. A few examples will illustrate how we use excuses to avoid slimming down. In working toward permanent weight loss, it is very important to examine the excuses you have relied on in the past, to understand them, and to move beyond them.

"FAT IS MY DESTINY—
MI DESTINO ES LA GORDURA"

I often hear people say, "I want to be thin, but my body has a mind of its own. I just can't slim down." There are many variations on this theme, but the basic excuse is the same: "I am not in control of my body." These excuses, designed to absolve you of responsibility for your weight and your eating habits, are in reality fat traps. In pinning the blame for your extra pounds on something outside of your control, you give up the possibility of taking charge and losing weight.

Remember, the key to permanent weight reduction is acknowledging that you make choices about what you eat, when you eat, how much you eat, and ultimately how much you weigh.

THE MOTHER OF ALL EXCUSES

Not long ago I came across an article about Latina "genetics." I was flabbergasted to read that Latina women cannot expect to be slim because our bodies are designed to carry more weight than those of Anglo women. *Qué pretexto increíble!* The Latinas I know come in all shapes and sizes: Some are tall and willowy; others are petite, with delicately formed figures; and still others spend their lives looking for "scientific" explanations to justify the extra pounds they carry.

Genetics do play a role in determining your body type but not your weight. We can all be slim. We just have to stop hiding behind excuses and exercise our willpower.

WHY BLAME YOUR BODY?

Before she even stepped on the scale for her weekly weigh-in, Amparo declared, "I just got my period, and I always swell up." Sure enough, she had gained three pounds. Amparo had tried to lose weight several times before but always ended giving up in frustration.

Amparo was further convinced her excess weight was caused by contraceptive pills. "Everybody gets fat on the pill. So why try to reduce?" she argued. She had armed herself with an ironclad, no-fault excuse for failure based on incorrect information. Women on birth control pills do retain extra body water, but the pills do not cause an increase in body fat.

Amparo finally put aside her excuses, began to eat sensibly, added more water to her diet, cut down on salt, started walking four or five times a week, lost weight, and continued her monthly menstruation.

BLAME IT ON MY GLANDS!

Few women actually have thyroid disease. Carrying extra pounds, however, burdens every system and organ in your body, and therefore many overweight people do suffer from a malfunctioning thyroid. In most cases, though, symptoms disappear and normal functioning resumes with weight loss.

LOVE AND POUNDS—*PESO Y AMOR*

In talking about *mentes gordas*, we touched on the intimate connection that often exists between our relationship to food and our need for love. The excuses we use for remaining overweight also frequently involve our romantic interests, our sexuality, or our reproductive lives.

PAPER FACES ON PARADE

Hortensia, at nineteen, had been overweight all of her life. Obesity had made her unattractive, and men did not pay her much attention. She had never had a boyfriend and fantasized about having an *amor*. This motivated Hortensia to lose thirty-seven pounds in seven months.

As the layers of fat melted away, Hortensia's natural beauty emerged. She looked sensational. Tall, willowy, with long blond hair and light eyes, she could have been a model. No wonder that now men showered her with attention wherever she went.

Most women would be delighted to be so admired. For Hortensia, though, unaccustomed as she was to being noticed, every compliment or appreciative look was a source of discomfort. She cringed inside each time an unknown admirer flattered her with *piropos*—flowery compliments. The more attention she got, the more dismayed she became.

Hortensia's sense of being constantly harassed because of her looks finally reached an unbearable point. She had gone to apply for employment at a local firm. The young man who was interviewing her paid more attention to her lovely face and figure than to her qualifications for the job. He expressed his admiration and invited Hortensia for lunch. Frustrated and alarmed, she gathered up her belongings and marched out of the office.

After that, Hortensia decided that she could not tolerate being attractive. She chose to cover herself up again with a protective layer of fat, regaining all of the weight she had lost and then some.

Sex is powerful. Hortensia wanted to be attractive to men, but she did not know how to handle the attention. She felt objectified, ashamed, and out of control. And she returned to the "comfort" of her obesity. Unfortunately, she will probably remain there until she realizes that she is as much in control of her sexuality as she is in control of her weight.

THE SUPREME TEST—*LA ÚLTIMA PRUEBA*

Pola and Frank had had a loving, committed relationship for several years before deciding to move in together. With the stress of the move and the new domestic arrangements, Pola put on a few pounds. Frank, for his part, did not hesitate to tell her that he preferred her thinner. He encouraged her to slim down and commented on her eating habits. Pola was annoyed by his relentless nagging and suspicious of his motives. "If he really loved me," she concluded, "he wouldn't care whether I am a little overweight. I am going to have to test him."

And test him she did, until she was a size fourteen. Deep down, Pola wanted to lose weight to please Frank. She loved him and feared losing him. Yet, her insecurity invigorated her *mente gorda*, who told her, "Keep testing." Not surprisingly, the only thing Pola accomplished was to make Frank feel as if she did not care enough about him. Frank finally left for a trial separation. While he and Pola were apart, he fell in love with a slim, shapely woman. He is now married and living in another state, while Pola is alone. She is convinced that Frank never loved her and blames him for her being fat.

Pola, like so many women, was not confident enough to believe that her man truly loved her. She wanted proof that he would be committed to her through thick and thin—or in this case, thick and fat. She sacrificed her body and her relationship to her insecurities and continues to use the disappointment as an excuse for staying overweight.

OVERWEIGHT HERITAGE

Our families are a source of strength, the root of identity, a connection to our heritage. Our families are also critical in shaping our images of our bodies, our attitudes toward food, and our eating and exercise habits. It is no surprise, therefore, that families and family beliefs are often the excuses we use for being overweight.

I NEVER LIE! (WELL, MAYBE, OCCASIONALLY)

Berta, a striking thirty-seven-year-old brunette, was constantly vacillating between wanting to be trim like the models in popular magazines and "remaining sensually sumptuous."

Actually, she bordered on obesity and periodically waged war against her excess weight, turning to the usual weight-loss pills, preparations, and crash diets with no lasting success. "All my life I have been assured that *niños gorditos y mujeres llenitas*—chubby children and fleshy women—are lovable and desirable," Berta complained. "I cannot slim down, and my family and Latin heritage are at fault." To relieve the stress of her conflict, Berta consulted endlessly with trusted family members about her body. "What do you think? Do I need to lose weight? Or, *estoy bien*, am I all right the way I am?" Predictably, everyone gave her the answer they thought she wanted to hear.

Berta only succeeded when she became convinced that she needed to rely on her own judgment to lose weight. She began without uttering a word to anyone. She made weight loss a priority, choosing her food carefully and following a strict exercise regimen. She pasted pictures of her face onto cutouts from magazines—pictures of models in slinky dresses, bathing suits, and lingerie—to help her visualize how she wanted to look. And above all, Berta kept her own counsel about the way her body looked.

Berta's family saw that she was serious. Seeing her slim down, they rejoiced and became her proud allies. In fact, Berta's husband has been so inspired by her example, he has vowed to stay slim and young-looking with her.

Too Much Family

Berta's thirty-four-year-old cousin, Carolina, also used her family as an excuse for extra pounds. Always struggling to trim down, she defends her rolls of body fat by saying "What can I do? How can I lose weight with so many *reuniones*? My social calendar overflows."

Carolina lives in Houston, Texas, surrounded by parents, grandparents, her six brothers and sisters, and her husband's four siblings—all married with children—her in-laws, her and her husband's uncles and aunts, nieces and nephews, and all of the *primos*—cousins. This family is so abundant, she can count on at least one or two *eventos* every week of the year.

One Saturday morning, Carolina woke up eagerly anticipating the day's eating itinerary. "Three fiestas," she counted. "Breakfast at the *iglesia*—church—a shower in the afternoon, and a *quinceañera* at night. *Qué maravillosa es mi vida!* Life is wonderful." Carolina's *mente delgada*, alarmed by her fatty fantasies, protested: "You are still full from last night's dinner in honor of your father's *Día del Santo*. Try to eat a little less today." In response, her alert *mente gorda* promptly reminded her that she wanted to have a good time, and once again, Carolina postponed the decision to eat sensibly.

Carolina's *pretexto*—excuse—was never-ending. She could always depend on an upcoming party as a reason to delay taking off the excess weight.

"Why do you go to parties?" I asked Carolina. "Just to eat?" She shot back defensively, "No." As we continued talking, though, it became clear that Carolina did not really enjoy any aspect of the parties except eating. Embarrassed by her body, she did not dance, did not mingle, did not talk to the other guests. She always joined the group of fat women huddled next to the food, feasting for the duration of the fiesta.

Finally fed up enough with her appearance to stand up to her *mente gorda*, Carolina worked hard to change her behavior. She stopped fasting so as to have extra room for the *guisados sabrosos*—delicious dishes at the *reunión*. In fact, she started eating a small, low-calorie, high-fiber meal about thirty minutes before going to parties. Feeling full, she was less tempted and stopped constantly maneuvering herself over to the food.

"I know what fun is now that I stopped making excuses," Carolina says. "Instead of eating my way through every party, I move around and make a point to chat with everyone. I don't miss a dance. And I have more friends than ever." Best of all, Carolina is four sizes smaller.

THE WAY TO A MAN'S HEART IS
THROUGH MY STOMACH

Belén was puzzled. In just three years of marriage she had become seriously overweight, even though she was convinced that she ate sparingly. "I eat like a little bird. I can't understand why I gain weight. Just a small breakfast and nothing all day until my husband comes home. I make a grand dinner for him, but I really don't eat much."

Belén had been raised to believe that as a traditional homemaker, she was expected to prepare sumptuous meals for her husband every day. Since the first day of marriage, she had spent hours cooking *pastelitos, arepas de maíz,* and other *frituras,* continuously proving that her husband had found an extraordinary wife.

Belén is a culinary artist. She has strict standards, and every special creation is taste-tested numerous times to ensure that the seasoning, consistency, and aroma are just right. For sampling she uses a ladle with a half-cup capacity, which she fills for each test, analytically slurping the contents. *Cada pastelito y fritura* was subjected to similar thorough sampling. Guaranteeing the excellency of her *comida* "forces" Belén to consume the equivalent of an extra meal each and every day. No wonder she keeps putting on pound after pound.

Unfortunately, Belén has not been able to recognize that it is her *mente gorda* that is driving her behavior. "I must keep my husband well fed and happy," she insists and continues to sacrifice her well-being and self-esteem.

THE ANTHROPOMORPHIC TRASH CAN

Lupita's parents left their beloved Puerto Rico for the continent to seek a better life. Both worked hard to offer their children all the advantages possible. Lupita became a registered nurse and has a very good job in a research laboratory. But having grown up in a family that "knew the true value of work," she still regards food as something precious, a blessing that is not to be wasted.

"I prepare nutritious food for my family," Lupita complains. "But my children don't appreciate it. They leave half their portions on their plates. *La comida sobrante me da lástima.* It hurts me to throw away leftover food."

To relieve her anxiety about wasting food, Lupita has worked out a system for dealing with leftovers. After dinner, she gathers her children's plates and places them on the counter next to the kitchen sink. She stands so that no one can see her working, turns on the garbage disposal, and cleans each plate by quickly and efficiently shoveling the leftovers into her mouth. No wonder Lupita is extremely heavy. And she will remain so until she rejects the excuse that only *she* can protect the world from "leftover abuse."

If you worry about wasting food, here are a few tips: Buy only what you need. Select more lowfat items. Use smaller plates. Do not take seconds. Save others' leftovers for a future meal.

... *Más Pretextos*—
... and Yet More Excuses

Soy Una Víctima de "Mañanitis"—
I Am Absolutely Going to Possibly Start
Losing Weight Tomorrow, Maybe

Some of us still live with the *"mañanitis"* syndrome: "I'll do it *mañana!*" Socorro, for example, was so astonished by her friend's success at slimming down with my program, she decided to give it a try. "I'll start my diet after the first of the year," she said, "because I know I am going to eat during Christmas." In January, she said, "I think I'll wait until after Valentine's Day, because *mi novio* always gives me chocolates." And so it went. The right time never came.

That's a Great Excuse. May I Borrow It?

One woman's excuse is often another woman's remedy. Teresa blames the fact that she is a housewife for her excess weight. "I can't get thin because I stay home all day surrounded by readily available food," she complains. "It's less difficult to lose weight when you work outside the home." Carmen, on the other hand, claims that she is overweight because she is forced to grab fast food for lunch while at the office. She thinks being at home would make weight loss easier.

As you can see, many of us subconsciously create alibis that keep us powerless victims of out-of-control poundage.

Elevators Also Have Their Ups and Downs

There are those who assert that they are in complete control of their weight. Irene proudly claimed, "I can lose weight whenever I want. I don't have to follow any program." Every time she decided to go on a diet, she did—usually a strict crash diet. After two weeks of near starvation, she would lose eight to fifteen pounds. Then, she would gain it all back in the next two weeks. On average, Irene lost thirty-five pounds a year and regained thirty-eight.

In over thirty years of counseling more than 100,000 clients, I have never seen anyone use a starvation diet to achieve long-term weight loss. At one time or another, you may have starved yourself to slim down quickly for a special occasion. You had set your goal to be thin only for the event, and the moment it was over you reverted to your old familiar eating habits. The lost pounds were recovered in half the time it took to lose them. Actually, you did reach your objective, which was to lose the extra pounds for that specific occasion. It was accomplished in a way that set you up for failure. Anybody can endure self-imposed torture for short periods. But to stay thin for a lifetime, you have to set this lifelong objective: "I never want to be fat again." Staying slim demands altering the way you think about yourself, relinquishing all excuses, modifying your eating habits, and making exercise a regular part of your life.

As children learning to walk, we would fall but would immediately get up and go at it again. Our desire to explore the world and reassuring, supportive parents helped us to keep trying. To succeed at losing weight, we also need resolve and encouragement. You must realize that you create excuses to avoid committing to weight loss; you must recognize when you are inventing an excuse; stop before you start believing your own alibi; save time and energy by not defending excuses; and find the specific catalyst—"hot button"—that will help keep you motivated. In the next chapter we will push several hot buttons in hopes of finding the one that launches you into a lifestyle that assures permanent weight loss.

Make your Reminder Card using only the words that apply to you.

REMINDER CARD—
Stop Making Excuses

I can't help it.

At home, I'm surrounded by food.

At the office, I eat out all the time.

I can lose anytime I want.

I have no time to exercise.

I don't have the time to lose weight now.

I am going to start tomorrow, really.

My menstrual cycle keeps me fat.

Birth control pills make me gain extra pounds.

My prescription medicine makes me fat.

If I continue having babies, I can't be thin.

It's my glands, really.

If I look too good, men will stare at me.

Men will want to do something to me.

He should love me even if I am fat.

I'll slim down to earn a present.

My breasts or buns will shrink.

My face will develop wrinkles.

I will lose my chubby friends.

It's not healthy to be thin.

It's my **destiny** to be tubby.

It's my **culture, heritage, genes, luck**.

I am just **pleasingly plump**, really.

I can't be **rude** and refuse a second helping.

I have absolutely **no control** over my weight.

I paid good money for it, I am **eating it all**.

I can't bear seeing food **wasted**.

Being on a diet is too **expensive**.

Tienes Razon— You Cannot Lose Weight Without the Right Reason

To paraphrase a well-known joke, going on a diet is easy— we have all done it lots of times. Losing weight and keeping it off is an entirely different matter. We overeaters are like drug addicts in that we have to "hit bottom" in order to begin to change. Our *mentes gordas* are so firmly in control of our lives, it usually takes a shock to get us to think about what being overweight is doing to us. Panic over the possibility of losing our *amores*, fear about our health, or shame about the way we look, and so on, are the hot buttons that jolt most people into taking action to finally get serious about losing weight.

Since you are reading this book, you have probably already had the unpleasant experience of having one of your hot buttons pushed. Remember, you are on your way to permanent weight loss, when the need to stay slim is stronger than your *mente gorda*.

THE LOVE BUTTON—*EL BOTON DEL CARINO*

There is probably nothing that will get you to trim down faster than the realization that fat is getting in the way of you and your *amado*. In most cases, our need for love is more powerful than our *mentes gordas*, and we gladly give up our overeating ways to be with the one we love.

I'll Never Leave Your Side

At forty-two, Xochi had been happily married for twenty years and had four children. She was robust and careless about her appearance, dutifully obeying her *mente gorda*. She claimed that she had no reason to slim down, since her husband, "loved her just the way she was." And besides, she felt that at her age she could not really change.

But neither Xochi's marriage nor her mind were as tranquil as she professed. In a moment of doubt, she admitted to a trusted friend that she had become uneasy lately because her slim, attractive husband was spending more and more time away from home. Xochi also confessed that she felt terribly unattractive.

"But I know he still adores me," Xochi added quickly, pushing away the uncomfortable thoughts. "From our wedding night until this day, he has always slept cuddled up against me."

The next day, while making the bed, Xochi noticed that the mattress slanted down to a deep depression on her side. Suddenly she realized that her *viejo* did not have a choice but to sleep next to her: Gravity pulled him down the incline, and he ended up wedged against her voluminous body.

After this dose of reality, Xochi examined herself in a full-length mirror. "I'm huge!" she admitted to herself. "This is not the same woman my husband fell in love with."

The following weekend, the family went to the beach. Xochi, too self-conscious to wear a bathing suit, covered herself from head to toe in a loose robe. She spent the whole day huddled under her umbrella, discreetly observing as every slim *guapa* who walked by turned her husband's head.

The very next day, Xochi took a vow to lose weight. She faithfully adhered to a diet for the next year, exercised, toned her body, lost all the weight she wanted to lose, bought a new bathing suit—and a new mattress. Xochi happily reports her husband is sleeping closer to her than ever.

Xochi had thought about losing weight many times in the past. She even went so far as to promise, "I am starting my diet *mañana!*" But she was never really motivated until she realized that her excess fat could cause her to lose her man.

Many of us are just like Xochi. We do not face our fat facts. Instead of facing the truth, we avoid looking at ourselves in photographs and full-length mirrors. We deny any connection between our fat and our emotional pain or physical discomfort. But when a "hot" button is pushed, we are compelled to give up our old familiar habits. You do not forget how it feels when you finally let yourself see what your body really looks like. There is no choice but to stick to your vow to trim down.

I Nominate Slimness; I Second the Motion— *Nombro Delgadez*

For Alicia, the moment of truth came at a fund-raising dinner held by the Northern New Jersey Cuban Community that had backed her husband's successful campaign for congressman. A well-groomed, charismatic champion of Latino causes, Alicia's husband is a social and political leader who lives in the public eye. Alicia—an unwieldy size sixteen—had always felt awkward, insecure, and self-conscious at the many events to which she had to accompany her husband. She knew she looked matronly no matter what she wore or how much makeup she had on, but did not make an effort to overcome her *mente gorda*.

On this particular occasion, though, Alicia realized that she was not the only one who disapproved of her appearance. As she and her husband walked arm in arm through the ballroom, greeting the many prominent people from his district who had gathered that night, Alicia heard a group of women whispering: "Look at the *señor*, such a distinguished, good-looking gentleman. He could have his choice of women. Isn't it surprising that he chose that *vieja*—old wife."

Alicia was mortified. The conflict she found herself in was

so intense it almost brought her to a nervous breakdown. She knew her presence at events was imperative to her husband's career, yet she could not face appearing in public.

Fortunately, Alicia bounced back quickly and went to work on her body. With intense dedication, she pared down thirty-nine pounds and four sizes in seven months. Now, she eagerly accompanies the congressman everywhere and smiles graciously as the ladies whisper about her. What she hears most often these days, though, is, "*¿Quién es la jovencita guapa, su querida?* Who is that good-looking young woman, his girlfriend?"

Of Course You're Right, But . . .

As is the case with any major life change, the motivation to lose weight must come from inside. It is unlikely that you will succeed because your mother or the man in your life insists that you slim down.

Rosa de Lima, a third-year medical student, was literally compelled to try to lose weight by her *novio*—fiancé. She felt resentful and rebellious. "I'll show him," was her attitude. "He can't tell me what to do." The rebellion was successful; Rosa de Lima was not. She lost a few pounds at the beginning but gleefully regained them, plus a pound for good measure. The engagement was called off.

We all want to be loved just the way we are. Just like Rosa de Lima, in the face of pressure from others to slim down, many of us rebel and purposely gain weight to exert control and assert our independence.

THE HEALTH BUTTON—*EL BOTON SALUDABLE*

Ah, Sweet Misery of Life

For some of us, even the life-threatening consequences of obesity are not sufficient to break the hold of the *mente gorda.* Carmelita gained forty-two extra pounds over ten years. The excess weight strains her petite frame and compromises all of her organs. She can no longer climb even a few stairs without becoming breathless. Her legs swell after a short outing. She had developed diabetes, cardiac problems, and hypertension. Although she has been repeatedly hospitalized for one or another of her many ailments, Carmelita refuses to give up her terrible eating habits, which she has generously passed on to her children.

During one of Carmelita's many hospital stays, her oldest daughter came to visit, absentmindedly snacking on freshly baked *churros.* Carmelita was immobilized in bed, with oxygen tubes in her mouth and nose, her breathing impaired by excessive body fat. But even though she was hardly able to breathe, her *mente gorda* was hard at work. *"No seas malita, ponga una en la esquina de mi boca,"* she gasped. "Don't be mean to your mother. Slip one into the corner of my mouth."

Life Is Too Short to Be Miserable— *Vida Solo Hay Una*

Fortunately, most of us value life more than eating. Griselda was double Carmelita's size. She experienced the same shortness of breath, swelling in her joints, and exhaustion. She could not walk without a cane. In addition, her sleep was disturbed nightly by cramps and indigestion. She woke up five times a night or more, urgently gulping antacid preparations and indigestion pills. Her life had been reduced to agonizing, lifeless days followed by sleepless nights. At forty-eight, Griselda looked and felt ancient.

Finally, Griselda had had enough. After one particularly uncomfortable night, she told her husband that she wanted to do something about her weight and enlisted his help. Together, they followed my diet and eating plan. They walked the recommended one hour each day at a brisk pace. In just one year and five months, Griselda lost 134 pounds. She now shares her youngest daughter's wardrobe and dances with her spouse at every family outing.

What About the Children?
¿Qué Pasa Con Los Niños?

Tita loved her eleven-year-old son, Carlitos. She did everything to assure his future success. But neglectful of her own body, Tita helped Carlitos develop terrible eating habits. Together, mother and son indulged their *mentes gordas* on secret "eating excursions," consuming fat-filled pizzas, hamburgers, *frituras*, and rich ice creams and desserts. They concealed their excessive eating from *el jefe*—Dad—who disapproved of his wife and son's obesity.

Carlitos wanted to lose weight. He felt disliked by his classmates, and their constant taunts depressed him. He seldom participated in extracurricular activities, usually spending his after-school hours at his mother's side. Tita chose to interpret Carlitos's dependence on her as a sign of love and ignored the omens of his distress.

Approaching his thirteenth birthday, Carlitos began to drag his left leg ever so slightly. It was almost imperceptible. His parents did nothing, ascribing the condition to "growing pains." During the following six months, Carlitos began to drag his leg more and more. An orthopedist discovered that fat deposits had obstructed the arteries supplying blood to his right leg, and the leg had stopped growing. His limp was caused by his diet and lack of physical activity. The doctor advised that the boy lose weight *pronto*. Tita, frightened and guilty, talked about wanting to change her son's eating habits but had no idea how to prepare the needed diet.

About one month later, Carlitos collapsed in his bathroom, his right leg having gone numb. He fractured his hip and was rushed to the hospital for the first of nine reconstructive surgeries to repair the joint. The major part of his fourteenth year was spent in recuperating and physical therapy. Although immobilized in the hospital, Carlitos did not gain weight. In fact, restricted to a lowfat, high-fiber diet combined with custom-designed vigorous exercise, he reduced. After returning home, he has continued his healthy regimen.

Happily, Carlitos now has a girlfriend and is trim and well-adjusted. He still faces more surgeries, but the reduction in body fat and improved muscle strength greatly improve his prognosis for full recovery.

THE SHAME BUTTON— EL BOTON DE LA VERGUENZA

One of the most common hot buttons that push people to break with their *mentes gordas* is the feeling of shame caused by the embarrassing, painful situations that excess weight often creates. Whether it is not being able to fit behind the wheel of a car or seeing the fear in the eyes of the other passengers on an airplane as they pray that you do not sit next to them, once you have experienced the humiliation of being too fat to do the everyday things others do, chances are you will let your *mente delgada* help you change your life.

I Don't Want to Be Buried with My Fat

Older women of substantial size often feel their bodies are beyond hope. Indoctrinated to believe that it is harder to lose weight after forty, they resign themselves to a "fat future." The fact is, once the right hot button is pressed, you can lose weight and keep it off no matter what your age.

Lupe was sixty-four years old and sixty-four pounds overweight. She had been heavy for the past thirty years, yet had always defended her *panza*—stomach. "My stomach is *mi curva de felicidad*—my happiness curve," she asserted. "It shows how well I treat myself. I feed it whatever it wants."

The death of her sister, however, inadvertently became the catalyst for Lupe's wanting to trim her stomach. When her sister died, Lupe took an emergency leave from her job in a day-care center and rushed back to Puerto Rico for the *velorio*—night vigil. It was also up to her to help make arrangements for the burial.

The first pressing problem for the family was to find a

caja—coffin—that would accommodate the deceased, who had always been obese and had done nothing about it. All of the ready-made caskets were too small, and there was no other choice but to order a very expensive custom-made one. The problems did not stop there: Instead of the customary four pall bearers, it took six men to handle the weight of the coffin.

Lupe felt mortified for her sister and vowed to herself that she would not humiliate her family in the same way after her demise. During the three years after her sister's death, Lupe lost weight in order to prepare for her own death. After trimming sixty-seven pounds from her body, however, she was rejuvenated. She has no intentions of expiring, has retired from the day-care center, travels a lot, and is enjoying life to the fullest.

Lady, Take a Taxi

Once a hot button has been pressed, most of us make an unshakable commitment to slimming down. Take the example of Candelaria, for whom a painfully shaming experience served as the reason to break with her *mente gorda*.

Candelaria was born and brought up in an inaccessible pueblo, in the high sierra of the *Tierra Caliente*, in the state of Guerrero, Mexico. She had left her pueblo and moved to Acapulco, where she fell in love with and married a man from Houston, Texas. After ten years, three children, and fifty extra pounds, she yearned to return to visit her parents.

Candelaria was jubilant as she boarded the plane to Mexico City. Once back in Mexico, she journeyed seven hours by bus to Iguala, where she tried to hire a mule for the arduous trip deep into the high sierra. The mule's owner took one look at the overfed would-be rider and refused to rent his animal to the *gorda*, even for double the usual price. Depressed, Candelaria had no choice but to turn around and go home.

The intense heartache of this disappointing journey left such a deep impression, Candelaria was obliged to embrace the voice of sensible restraint—her *mente delgada*. She was ready to stop eating in her usual unhealthy way, recognizing that the extra pounds kept her from enjoying her most treasured activities. She vowed to take off the weight and lost fifty pounds. One year later, Candelaria mounted a grateful mule, endured the fifteen-hour trek to her pueblo, and happily embraced her parents.

THE SELF-ESTEEM BUTTON—
EL BOTON DE LA AUTO-ESTIMA

Finally, what helps many of us to make the decision to lose weight is the reality that being overweight is depressing and emotionally draining. Whether you cannot get the job you really want or buy a sexy dress because of your extra pounds, what ultimately suffers is the way you see yourself in relation to the world—your self-esteem. That alone can be enough to get you to embrace your *mente delgada*.

Your Honor, I Rest My Case

Diana is a brilliant young attorney. She graduated number one in her class and passed the New York Bar Exam on the first try. Ambitious and eager to prove herself, she wanted a position on Wall Street. She diligently reviewed the want ads in the *New York Times* and *Wall Street Journal* every week and mailed out her résumé. Her credentials were sensational, so almost every company where she applied was anxious to interview her. A year and a half later, however, a discouraged Diana still did not have a job.

It was always the same story. Every personnel manager who contacted her seemed eager to employ her before the personal interview. After the interview, though, she heard nothing or a canned excuse: "You are overqualified"; or "We'll let you know"; or "I am so sorry, we hired a previous candidate." Yet, the same ads reappeared in the paper.

Diana—a size twenty-two—realized that her appearance

was her downfall. She had to trim down in order to be hired. She took an interim at-home job translating legal documents and started on my weight-reduction program. She changed bad eating habits, substituted water for soft drinks and coffee, and began walking instead of taking taxis and buses. She now wears a size ten, lives in Manhattan, and is researching corporate law for a major investment firm.

A Dress by Any Other Size

Many overweight women think that their extra pounds are their "little secret." They think that no one will notice, because they so cleverly hide the fat under loose, dark clothing specifically designed to camouflage a shapeless body. Do not fool yourself into thinking clothes will make fat disappear. Large clothes only disguise the location of the fat; they do not make you look thinner.

Clothing for a robust shape can be a problem. How many times has this happened to you? You go into a store hoping to buy the cute little dress in the window. You ask for a size fourteen, let's say, and are delighted when the saleswoman informs you that she has that size. Then when she brings it out, it looks totally different—large and distorted, not at all adorable.

How often have you gone into a boutique to purchase an outfit for a special event only to have the salesclerk say, "Sorry, I don't think we have anything here to fit you." Many of us have permanently changed our lives after experiences such as this.

The Hips That Broke the Camel's Back

A delighted Susana wrote to me: "I have always felt that the only person who can decide that she or he will (or must) lose excess weight is that person her(him)self. I made that decision after the costly purchase of a size eighteen formal that had to have the hip seams let out, so I could wear it with comfort to a ball. Although I looked 'nice,' that was not the comment I wanted from my friends. A few days after the ball I saw the photos. Inside my gown, I looked like two people with one head. That was it! The next day I adopted the Latina Lite way . . . I can't explain the thrill when the scale moved below the 150 mark . . . it was like a personal pat on the back . . . I am now at the weight that my doctor says is right for me . . . keeping a close check on what I eat will be a way of life for me from now on."

All of us can successfully lose weight, but it may take a jolt of truth to move us to action. Is your body adversely affecting your life? Are there things that you would like to do, but cannot because you are heavy? Can you squeeze into the clothes you would like to wear? Does your child invite you to school functions? Do you complain that your husband never invites you out? Inside, we know the reason for so much rejection. We suffer from hurt feelings too much of the time. If your weight is affecting your life, it is time to change.

The World Is a Stage—
El Teatro de la Vida

It is not necessary to wait for disaster to strike. Why go through the pain of having your hot buttons pushed by events outside your control? You can take charge and inspire yourself to face the truth. Here is how: Cut two eyeholes in an ordinary brown paper bag. Undress with your back to a full-length mirror. Place the bag over your head. Then turn around and pose.

It's show time! Try not to laugh! If you are relatively pleased with what you see, you need not slim down. But if you are not satisfied, you will be happy to know you have just pressed one of your hot buttons, alerting yourself to the fact that the time has come to trim down.

REMINDER CARD

··

GRASA NO MAS—
READ MY LIPS, NO MORE FAT!
I'm not going to be fat because I don't want:
to **lose my spouse**
my lover **looking** at leaner prospects
to **miss out** on any physical activities
to **die sooner** than I have to
to **give up** wearing my fabulous wardrobe
to be disadvantaged when I apply for a **job**
to **look old**
to be **ashamed** of how I look
to look in a **mirror** and see a fat person
to have to wear "fat folks" **clothing**
to look unattractive or **lose my sex appeal**
to always be trying to **conceal** my body fat
to **look** like a **bulging** sack of potatoes
to **hide my body** under billowing, bulky clothes
to wear a baggy T-shirt at the **beach**
to feel **ridiculed** by my "friends"
to **disappoint** myself and fail at my goal
to feel like a **failure**

to feel **self-conscious, awkward, unacceptable**

to be **rejected** when I want to have a date

to be **discriminated against** in job promotions

to have to listen to "fat person" **jokes** about me

to have the **discomfort** of carrying extra pounds

to have to constantly **think** about my fat problem

to constantly be **worried** about my health

to have to **avoid** weight **scales** or **mirrors**

to worry about having a **heart attack**

my **sibling** to be **thinner** than I am

Unrealistic
Expectations—
Esperanzas
Inalcansables

MIRACLES AND DISAPPOINTMENTS

Once our hot buttons are pushed and we finally decide to lose weight, we want immediate results with little effort. You want to be thin *de la noche a la mañana*, overnight, and the last thing in the world you want to hear is that slimming down is a gradual process that involves total commitment, a change of eating habits, and a dedication to an active, healthy lifestyle.

In the search for a quick way to shed their extra pounds, many people spend enormous amounts of energy and money on "*milagros*—miracle cures." These range from extreme starvation diets to thinning creams and reducing pills to acupuncture and magic potions. I have even heard of a woman so desperate to find an instant weight-loss miracle she allowed a "doctor" to inject her with goat urine.

Needless to say, these schemes only help you lose hope and money. Reducing plans and products that promise fast, painless, effortless weight-loss almost never produce lasting results and can often cause damaging side effects.

Patience—*Paciencia*

Maria de Alba was desperate. She rushed into my office almost in tears. "I was just diagnosed with atherosclerosis. My doctor told me that I am in great danger of having a heart attack because of my weight and must begin to reduce immediately." *La doctora* had pushed Maria's hot button—the button for survival. The doctor's warning finally instilled in her an understanding of the consequences of continuing to indulge her *mente gorda* and remaining overweight.

At age forty-seven, Maria was desperate to trim down fast. Fear for her health motivated her, she wanted to go on a near-starvation diet in order to drop pounds quickly and solve her medical problems. She begged for Fen-Phen. The kind of diet she had in mind, however, would have had the exactly opposite effect, endangering her health. Extreme, low-calorie diets never work, and in cases such as Maria's are outright dangerous. Starvation diets produce weight loss that is mostly body water and muscle protein—with part of the protein loss being vital heart tissue. Along with the water, essential minerals—potassium, chloride, and sodium—are lost, depriving the body of necessary electrolytes that protect the heart from "shorting out" with irregular and possibly fatal heartbeats.

In consultation with her doctor, I helped Maria develop a diet and exercise program designed to enable her to lose no more than one pound a week over the span of a year. She was on her way to shedding fifty-two pounds, more than enough to dispel her doctor's concern.

Fat Memory—*Gordos Recuerdos*

Anyone who has ever tried to slim down knows the hardest part is not dropping the weight but keeping it off. Imelda, a thirty-seven-year-old Ecuadoran, is a perfect example. She had repeatedly lost weight only to gain it all back. "I feel *hechizada*—jinxed," Imelda complained. "I try so hard, but I just cannot stay slim."

Imelda's pattern had been the same for many years: She would go on a starvation diet, lose two sizes quickly, feel satisfied, and then return to her regular eating habits. She could not maintain her reduced weight because she did not "reeducate" her fat cells.

Our bodies are composed of about sixty trillion cells. In a woman of average size, thirty to thirty-five billion of these are fat cells. Each cell has a "memory" of its own. Over the years, Imelda's fat cells had become accustomed to being filled to near capacity. When she went on a crash diet, her fat cells reduced in size and immediately began sending signals to the brain that something was wrong. At this point, Imelda began to experience intense, urgent hunger. Predictably within two weeks, she would be so miserable, she would abandon her punishing diet and go on an eating binge to satisfy her "starved" fat cells.

Imelda would have been much more successful had she tried to lose weight gradually. If she had lost only one pound a week until she reached her desired weight and then held steady for two months, her fat cells would have had time to adjust to their new size. That way, Imelda would not have experienced the endless, gnawing hunger that drove her back to her old eating habits and would have been able to maintain her new weight.

There Must Be a Pill for Me

As you can see, many people are willing to spend extravagantly and act recklessly to lose weight. They are constantly on the lookout for new *trampas*—schemes—that promise easy success. Cecilia, for example, spent $125 for a small jar of a reducing cream she saw advertised on her local Chicago television station. As directed, she applied it to her thighs, buttocks, and stomach every night. After only twenty-five days she needed more cream. And then more. Five hundred dollars later, she still had the rolls of fat she wanted to get rid of, but her bank account had gotten substantially slimmer.

Fat blockers are regularly released by drug companies with a flurry of publicity. "THIS IS THE MIRACLE YOU HAVE ALL BEEN WAITING FOR! Buy our new formula and melt the fat from your body." So far, these drugs have been little better than snake oil, producing few lasting positive results and numerous long-term adverse side effects.

The newest arrivals in the diet pill market are appetite suppressants—fenfluramine/phentermine and dexfenfluramine. These drugs are designed to help you lose weight by tricking your body into feeling full by stimulating the production of serotonin. Additional serotonin calms your brain's satiety center and elevates your mood. Sounds great: Take a pill and feel happily satiated.

There is a caveat, though. Most pharmaceutical firms manufacturing and marketing these drugs have ethically admitted that no information is available about the safety and effectiveness of their product beyond one year's use. Long-term exposure to the drugs has produced brain damage in some laboratory animals, and withdrawal has been shown to cause drastically lowered levels of serotonin and depression in some human subjects. In addition, the use of anorexigens—antiappetite drugs—is associated with a serious, potentially life-threatening cardiovascular condition affecting the lungs. A rash of recent deaths has caused speculation that fenfluramine/phentermine (fen-phen) and dexfenfluramine (Redux) may produce deadly heart and lung deterioration.

When fen-phen first appeared on the market Dr. Brian A. Joseph, Chairman of the Ethics Committee of the American Association of Bariatric (Obesity) Physicians, was quoted in *Time* Magazine as saying: "These are legitimate medications when used in a responsible manner as an adjunct to a weight loss program." The scientists who developed these new miracle drugs believe their products work but advise using them judiciously. They further advise that to sustain permanent weight loss the user must adhere to a plan of balanced nutrition and exercise. Physicians and scientists agree that pills alone will not ensure permanent effortless slimness.

Several other wonder drugs are currently being tested—e.g., a hormone pill, a fat gene mutation pill, a stimulant/caffeine pill, and a neurotransmitter pill. But those who choose to wait for one of these "miracle cures" will have to remain *gorda* for the next five to seven years, the time it takes to gain FDA approval.

It is much quicker and safer to exercise regularly and follow the four-week nutrition plan on page 344. It does take more work and more self-discipline, but instead of adverse **side** effects, you will get thinner **sides**.

LET'S TALK ABOUT REALITY—
HABLEMOS DE LA REALIDAD

Clearly, realistic expectations of what it takes to achieve permanent weight loss are essential if you are to be successful. It is equally important, though, to have realistic expectations of how much weight you are going to lose, how long it will take to achieve your goal, how your body will change as you reduce, and the effect weight loss may have on your life.

Selecting Your Goal Weight

There is no such thing as your "correct" weight. We all have three distinct body weights: 1. Our actual weight, as registered on the scale—the one we tend to understate; 2. Our optimal or goal weight—the weight at which our bodies function best; and 3. Our "set" weight—the weight to which our bodies have become accustomed over time. After you lose or gain weight, your body tries to drift back to the set weight. The secret to permanent weight loss is to select a reasonable goal weight, gradually achieve it, and then allow your body to adjust, holding steady for two to three months, while a new set weight is established.

It is very important that you be the one to decide how

much weight you want to lose. It is your choice to work toward a slimmer body—and to succeed you must remember that you have the power and the control throughout the process. You are unique, and your objective should be personal and suitable for you. Most important is that your goal be reasonable and attainable.

How do you pick a goal weight? I will illustrate using an example and then explain how you can do it yourself. Carmen, who measures 5' 4", will be our model. Look at Table I. In the height column, find 5' 4", then match the height with the corresponding weight range. You will see "117 to 139." Carmen's target will be between 117 and 139 pounds. With a range of twenty-two pounds, what weight would be **optimal**? To start, it is best to choose a moderate objective, near the upper end of the range. For Carmen, an initial goal of 137 pounds seems reasonable. Her current weight is 152 pounds and to get down to 137 she needs to lose 15 pounds—and that should take between 8 to 15 weeks. If, after losing 15 pounds, she is satisfied with the way she looks she can stop losing and maintain that weight. But if she wants to be slimmer, she can set a new goal. Perhaps, 130 pounds or less. The key is to set a comfortable goal—one that does not set you up for failure by being too ambitious.

Now, let's determine your goal weight. Find your height in Table 1. Match it to the corresponding weight range. Decide on a goal weight somewhere within that range. Try to choose a number near the upper end of the range, as we did for Carmen. Once you achieve this target, you can maintain it for a while, then reassess and choose a new target weight in the middle or the lower end of the range.

Table I
DETERMINING WEIGHT

HEIGHT	OPTIMAL WEIGHT RANGE
4' 4"	52 to 68
4' 5"	58 to 75
4' 6"	63 to 79
4' 7"	69 to 86
4' 8"	74 to 92
4' 9"	79 to 97
4' 10"	85 to 103
4' 11"	90 to 110
5' 0"	94 to 117
5' 1"	99 to 122
5' 2"	107 to 128
5' 3"	112 to 135
5' 4"	117 to 139
5' 5"	121 to 145
5' 6"	128 to 149
5' 7"	132 to 155
5' 8"	137 to 159
5' 9"	142 to 166
5' 10"	148 to 169
5' 11"	154 to 176
6' 0"	149 to 182
6' 1"	153 to 187
6' 2"	158 to 193
6' 3"	164 to 196
6' 5"	173 to 200

Record your present weight here: _____ pounds

Record your initial goal weight here: _____ pounds

Subtract and record the weight to be lost: _____ pounds[*]

[*]Optimal weight loss is about one pound per week.

Age Is Not a Factor—
Para El Peso No Hay Edades

Notice that Table I does not allow for any differentiation based on age. That is because how old you are has nothing to do with your optimal weight. You may be thinking, "I am not a teenager, I am expected to be a bit more filled out." Actually, you do not have that luxury. Burdening an older body with excess weight can produce serious consequences. Organs and bones are more susceptible to malfunction as they age. And, in fact, they become smaller and weigh a little less. So your goal weight should be well within the optimal range.

Furthermore, it is a myth that it is harder for older women to lose weight and remain slim. Rosalia is a perfect example. At fifty, she was convinced that she was too old to rehabilitate her *cuerpo amplio*—generous figure. Rather than participate herself, Rosalia encouraged her overweight married daughter to try my reducing program. She continued to prepare meals for the whole family but was now using my lowfat recipes. Rosalia lost sixty-two pounds without even trying. Now, Rosalia is approaching age fifty-five with the figure of a twenty-five-year-old, while her daughter, who did not adhere to the plan, has the body of a fifty-year-old.

Aiming Too High

Setting your expectations too high can be a real obstacle to losing weight. Clara wanted very much to reach her optimal weight of 126 pounds. But the thought of having to lose thirty-five pounds terrified her. So instead of having an attitude of "Yes, I can do it," all Clara could say was, "I could never weigh that little again. I'd better settle for 146 pounds." Not surprisingly, she had trouble reaching her goal weight.

At my suggestion, Clara tried to set her target differently. She resolved to lose one dress size. She achieved this objective easily, shedding eight pounds. After maintaining her new weight for two months, Clara felt more confident and reassessed her goal. She decided to lose another twenty-seven pounds to reach her optimal weight.

Two years later, Clara is still a slim 126 and is amazed at how easy it is to maintain this weight. "I don't know what I was worried about," she says happily.

Enough Is Enough

San Francisco de Sales, the bishop of Geneva in the seventeenth century, once observed: "If the body is very fat, we cannot endure it, and if it is very skinny, it cannot endure us." Elena is dissatisfied with the goal weight she has reached. At 5' 7" and 127 pounds, she is five pounds below the lower limit of her optimal weight range. However, she wants to achieve the waiflike look of fashion-magazine models and is starving herself in order to lose another seven pounds. Her body, for its part, is instinctively trying to safeguard its well-being. Elena suffers from endless hunger, headaches, and mental discomfort. She is vulnerable to illnesses and does not look well, the victim of an unrealistic goal.

A Watched Scale Never Moves

Our bodies are efficient machines that run on the food we eat. Some of us make the mistaken assumption that our bodies can be efficient and machinelike in shedding accumulated extra weight. Evita, for instance, calculated that it would take her eight weeks to lose thirty-five unwanted pounds. She expected to drop four and a half pounds a week, and not an ounce less.

Evita was delighted after the first week of her reducing program: She had lost five pounds. She was disappointed after the second week, having trimmed off only two and a half pounds. After the third week, during which she lost only three quarters of a pound, Evita began to get frantic. And after losing only one more pound during the fourth week, she was ready to quit.

Meaningful weight loss is always gradual but never consistent. There is usually a dramatic change in the first week of a reducing program—as was the case with Evita—that is primarily due to the loss of body fluid. In the second week, more fat is eliminated. After about the third week, your body begins to fear famine, tries to economize energy, and enters into a period of slower weight loss. In this phase, your weight will appear to remain the same, even though your fat cells are actually shrinking in size. By week five, your body will make the necessary adjustment, and the scale indicator will begin to move down again. The only realistic way to judge progress is to calculate the average pounds lost over a period of six to eight weeks.

Luckily Evita did not give in to her fears and *huirse*—quit. In eight weeks, she had reduced almost two sizes, having lost an average of one and a half pounds a week.

Inches and Pounds—*Medidas y Peso*

Lorena also expected consistent progress and was dismayed when her weight seemed to plateau above her target. She dropped twenty-nine pounds and then appeared to stop. "It doesn't work for me anymore," she worried.

In reality, Lorena's body was adapting to its new weight and allowing its tissues and skin to contract before resuming weight loss. As we lose our unwanted fat, the indicator on the scale moves down for several months and then comes to a "plateau" for anywhere from two to five weeks. Reducing programs cannot be measured solely by the scale. Usually, it is exactly during plateau times that inches disappear.

Generally, our bodies are able to eliminate up to one pound of pure body fat a week by eating sensibly and exercising. A weight loss of four pounds or more in the first week of a program or by following a "crash" diet always consists of 75 percent water and muscle loss. Anything over a pound weekly is easily regained. Eight pounds represent one dress size for a woman of average build—seven pounds for smaller women, and up to eleven pounds for larger women. In a year, you can easily lose from twenty-five to fifty pounds—that is three to six sizes.

To help measure progress, do not just weigh yourself. Instead, use the "tight-pant-test." Find a tight skirt or pair of pants and try them on every two weeks. They are sure to feel looser and looser, even if the indicator on the scale is not moving down as fast as you think it should.

Which Came First, the Thigh or the Breast?— ¿Qué Fue Primero, el Muslo o el Seno?

Aurora, seated, looked so slim that I could not understand why she wanted to lose weight. She had a thin, pretty face and a petite, trim torso to the waist. Her problem became painfully clear when she stood up, though. Aurora wore a size seven top and a size thirty-eight bottom. Understandably, she wanted to even out her proportions.

I explained to Aurora that spot reducing is physiologically impossible but in her case, a lot of leg exercise and upper body weight training will increase the size of her muscles and help match her top to her bottom. Bulges occur in specific areas because those locations contain a greater concentration of fat cells. Short of liposuction, there is no way to remove fat from one region exclusively. When you reduce calorie intake or burn off calories, all the fat cells in your body begin to shrink evenly. Sensible eating and exercise will gradually reduce bulges, then tone and shape all the parts of the body making them strong and attractive.

Motherhood Should Not Weigh You Down

There are times in a woman's life when even the most diligent dieter cannot lose weight, no matter how hard she tries. Before the arrival of her child, Linda, a 5' 7" fashion model, weighed 128 pounds. Four months after her daughter was born, Linda was still 139 pounds and out of work.

Linda was distraught and confused. Throughout the pregnancy, her program of sensible eating and moderate exercise had kept her weight exactly at the level recommended by her doctor. But now it was not working. She simply could not lose the stubborn eleven pounds and was losing hope instead.

Linda felt reassured after I explained the double-nine rule—nine months of gestation and nine months of reduction after terminating lactation. During pregnancy, fat accumulates at a steady pace. During the time you are breastfeeding, your body becomes more efficient at retaining fat in order to ensure a rich milk supply for the baby. It is nearly impossible to lose those last ten to fifteen pounds while nursing. But do not allow breastfeeding to stop you from starting to diet and exercise with doctor's approval. By faithfully maintaining a diet-exercise program you can expect to recoup your former figure—maybe even make it better—within nine months after the baby is weaned from the breast. Be patient.

"I Am Thinner, but . . ."

Some of us believe that if only we could lose weight, our lives would be magically transformed. In fact, they are: We look and feel younger and more attractive. Our self-esteem grows with the satisfaction of having achieved a difficult goal. Our health improves. But with all its wonderful benefits, weight loss is not the answer to all of life's problems. And like any major change, it can have some unexpected consequences.

You know how important it is to be completely committed to losing weight and keeping it off. Be careful not to set yourself up for failure by having unrealistic expectations of how your life will change once you are slim. Be especially watchful for your *mente gorda*'s attempts to seduce you into giving up when the weight loss may temporarily produce an unexpected result.

The Incredible Shrinking Woman

Flor had decided to lose weight and, after losing thirty-five pounds, was halfway to her goal. She was especially motivated by the prospect of losing the fat pads on the back of her upper arms that made her so self-conscious, dreaming of wearing sleeveless shirts and dresses. There was a problem, though. The overstuffed pads had been replaced by unattractive hanging folds of skin. Flor felt deceived and determined to stop reducing.

Unfortunately, Flor simply did not give herself enough time. With much of her excess weight having been deposited on the back of her upper arms, her skin had expanded over a long period of time to accommodate the accumulation of enlarged fat cells. Eventually it would shrink, but not overnight. Skin requires three to six months or more to adjust and shrink.

Be Careful What You Wish For— *Cuida Lo Que Quieres*

Norma, too, discovered that losing her excess weight was not a panacea. She had been *llenita*—plump—for as long as she could remember. Now, at twenty-two, her natural good looks were obscured by 123 extra pounds that made her look lumpy and square. Her face as well as her body was distorted by overstuffed fat cells.

Norma had grown up heavy in Las Vegas and had a large circle of friends. Her lifelong girlfriends invited her to every party, depended on her to supervise the food, often sending their boyfriends to pick her up and drive her to the *reuniones*. Norma was happy but wanted her own boyfriend. "Slimming down will enhance my social life even more," she daydreamed.

Norma worked really hard to achieve her goal, and in fact lost seven pounds more than the necessary 123. A striking beauty emerged. Now, with not even a trace of extra fat remaining, Norma was so stunning she was invited to compete for the title of *Señorita Latina* of Las Vegas.

Suddenly, Norma's party invitations ended. Her girlfriends, now concerned that their *novios* would find Norma irresistible, stopped including her in their events. Norma was unprepared for her friends' reaction and was almost ready to sacrifice her new sense of pride and satisfaction. "I was happier fat," she faltered. "I was popular, with lots of friends. Now, I am slim and lonely. What should I do?"

Of course, being slim and having friends are not mutually exclusive. With encouragement and support, Norma began to look for new companions. It was not long before the word got around the Latino network that a beautiful *señorita* was available. Her social life took off. She is now engaged to a young Latino television sports announcer, and together they attend nonstop social events. Norma's old friends call often, hoping to be invited to one of her glamorous parties.

Saying Good-bye to Your *Mente Gorda*— Un *"Adios"* a la Mente Gorda

Our *mente gorda* has been with us for many years. It is unrealistic to think that you can bid it good-bye without feeling an emptiness. Even after you remove her influence from your life, there will be times when that familiar friend, your inner *gordita*, will try to reenter your life.

She is like an old love that you never forget. Have you ever adored someone who hurt you? Most of us have. You recognize the harm and want to end the relationship, but the thought of separation is painful and frightening. After the relationship is severed, there will be times when you yearn for your *mente gorda*, just as you sometimes long for a poorly chosen former sweetheart.

At the most unexpected moments, that little voice will faintly urge you to eat. It will fade with time but will never disappear entirely. You may notice it at times of anxiety, for instance. "Give me another chance," it will say. "I will make you feel good." Do not fall into the trap again. Prepare a list of the *dolores*—pains—she caused you when you weighed more. Review your list and stay resolute.

A Thinning Thought—
Un Pensamiento Esbelto

A weight-loss program that works like a vaccine would be ideal. Nobody would be fat. You could follow a reducing plan until you reach goal weight and then forget about watching your diet. That is not how things work, though. You must incorporate healthy habits into your everyday lifestyle. If you do not stick to good nutrition and an exercise program, you are bound to regain weight. To achieve permanent weight loss, set attainable goals, be patient, aim to lose no more than one pound a week. Remember, maintaining a slim, sexy figure is a lifelong endeavor.

REMINDER CARD—
Expectations

DON'T BE TEMPTED BY:

quick, "foolproof" **schemes**
programs that promise **extravagant results**
programs that promise weight loss **without exercise**
restrictive diets
diets that recommend **commercially prepared
foods, weight-loss pills or liquid drinks**
diets you would **not** want to **use the rest of your life**
nutritional **plans** that are **not medically tested**
"eat-all-you-want" diets
lotions or creams that are rubbed onto body parts
plastic wraps or sweat apparel
weight plans that are **mystical or supernatural**
diets that have you **lose more than three
to five pounds per week**
costly diets

DON'T EXPECT WEIGHT LOSS TO:

be effective until you are **ready to commit**
spot reduce specific areas of your body

solve all of your problems
be entirely **consistent**; it will vary from week to week
effective if you wander off the Latina Lite plan
be an easy project—you must **constantly work at it**

TO ESTABLISH YOUR GOAL WEIGHT:

use Table I in this chapter (page 284)
use Table I regardless of your **age**
consult with your physician if you are **pregnant** or
under his/her care.

....

Both the Quality and Quantity of What You Eat Count—Cuentan la Calidad y la Cantidad

Socrates, the Greek philosopher, said, "Other men live to eat, but I eat to live." To many of us *gordos*, Socrates' statement about our relationship with food will sound as if sensible eating habits and good nutrition take all the joy out of eating. The truth is that to be slim, you do not have to deprive yourself of the foods you like or of the pleasure of eating. By learning to select, prepare, and consume food healthfully, you can eat the tastiest dishes and slim down at the same time.

Food Enemies—*Demonios Engordadores*

There are three main culprits that, when consumed in excessive quantities, are responsible for weight gain:

FAT
SUGAR
SALT/SODIUM

We cannot live without these essential nutritional compo-
nents, and we cannot live with too much of them. When eaten
in excessive amounts, each plays a different physiological
role in converting food into body fat and water weight, thus
contributing to bulging obesity.

DIETARY FAT

I Don't Want to Burst Your Bubble,
Only Shrink It

Can you guess how many fat cells there are in your body,
hungrily waiting for you to swallow those *arepas, tostones,
tamales,* or *guanimes*? A woman over the age of twenty has
between thirty billion and fifty billion fat cells in her body.[1] The
main duty of fat cells is to reserve enough energy to see you
through periods of diminished food supplies. It does not take
much energy to keep them functioning, so they are able to
store up as much fat as you provide.

Fat cells are remarkably accommodating. If you weigh 130
pounds, your fat cells are probably about 0.2 *mg* (microgram
of lipid volume) in size. If you were to gain 70 pounds, they
would grow to 0.6 *mg*. At 260 pounds, your fat cells would be
an amazing 0.9 *mg*, four and a half times their original size.

It gets worse. If fat cells attain their maximum grandiose
size of 1.0 *mg*, they have the extraordinary capacity to split
into two identical cells. A slim woman weighing from 100 to
135 pounds has between 30 and 35 billion fat cells; an overweight woman of 150 to 200 pounds may have 75 billion. An

---

[1]W.C. Chumlea, *American Journal of Clinical Nutrition*, 1981.

extraordinarily obese woman could have up to 240 billion fat cells. Regardless of how many you have, Latina Lite can help you shrink the size of your fat cells. Unfortunately, they do not resemble old soldiers: They never fade away.

Fat Does Not Have to Be a Life Sentence

Do not be depressed. Your excess fat cells are not entirely your fault. Body structure and fat formation depend in large part on your mother's eating behavior while you were in the womb. Irma's mother, for instance, loved to eat and took full advantage of pregnancy to gorge herself. Irma was only a fetus when her fat cells began to multiply.

Born chubby, Irma was encouraged to suckle frequently and for long periods of time. Her mother's milk was supplemented with bottles of sweet, sticky cola. Still nursing after her first birthday, she weighed over thirty-five pounds. Irma did not begin to walk until she was seventeen months old. Her weight interfered with her balance. The pediatrician advised, "Change the type of food and reduce the calories." But her parents ignored these instructions and bragged about their gordita's eating capacity.

Irma's fat cells continued to multiply. At seven years old, she weighed almost 100 pounds and was estimated to carry more than 100 billion fat cells. Her fat-cell count had stabilized until she reached early adolescence, when her high-fat and high-calorie diet prompted them to increase to even greater numbers. Obese at sixteen, Irma carried an estimated 150 billion fat cells. Irma seemed doomed: She was born to an overweight mother and was fat during the critical stages of fat-cell development—gestation, birth to age six, and early adolescence.

Fortunately, biology is not destiny. At twenty-two, Irma was determined to overcome her fat legacy. She lost over ninety pounds and has kept it off by diligently following a sensible diet and walking half an hour a day, four times a week. It has been three years since Irma lost weight, and she is still wearing a size ten. If you were a fat child, you probably have more fat cells than the average, but you can assume ultimate responsibility for the shape of your adult body.

Fill It Up, and Up, and Up—
Llenarlo Más, Más y Más

It is too bad that we are not engineered like our cars. An automobile can only take in as much fuel as its gas tank can hold. If you try to put fifteen gallons in a tank that has a twelve-gallon capacity, the excess will simply spill out. Our bodies, on the other hand, are designed to conserve rather than waste consumed energy. When you overeat, your body does not discard the excess. Instead, the extra calories are converted to fat and stored in your fat cells. When fat cells reach their capacity, they do not burst. They adroitly duplicate themselves—in a process called *hyperplasia*—and continue to fill as long as you supply the fat calories.

In other words, you cannot have your cake and hide it, too. If you truly want to lose weight, you must declare war on your fat cells. Most of us have more fat cells than we really need. But do not despair. You can reduce the size of your enlarged fat cells by eating no more than the amount of fat prescribed in the Latina Lite plan and exercising regularly. The first few months after trimming down are the hardest. Your fat cells will miss the familiar, overstuffed feeling, at first. The longer you stay at your goal weight, the easier it will be to stay slim. After several months, your cells will develop a new "thin" memory.

Dietary Fats Are Absolutely Essential

Fats are the most concentrated source of dietary energy. They also provide essential fatty acids and carry fat-soluble vitamins required for proper growth and health. Aside from a few anorexic patients I have counseled, I have never met anyone who did not have enough fat in their diet. A healthy diet must include 15 to 25 percent fat, but not more. Typical Latino diets contain about 50 percent fat.

All Fats Have the Same Calories, But Some Are Better Than Others—*Unas Grasas Son Mejores Que Otras*

We must eat fat. However, we must not only limit the quantity but also select the healthier fats. Fats come in two varieties: **saturated** and **unsaturated**. Eating too much saturated fat stimulates the liver to produce the dangerous LDL cholesterol, which has been shown to cause heart disease. Unsaturated fat, on the other hand, encourages the liver to produce protective HDL cholesterol. We will talk more about the advantages of HDL and how to avoid heart disease a little later. For the time being, remember to select unsaturated fats over saturated ones.

How do you recognize the bad saturated fats? All saturated fats are solid at room temperature. Lard, bacon grease, animal fat, butter, palm and coconut oils, and hydrogenated vegetable oils are saturated. When you prepare *un sancocho* or *un guisado* and put it in the refrigerator, the white or yellow waxy fat crusting the top is saturated fat. Remove it all before serving. Lard, bacon, eggs, and most cheeses carry a lot of saturated fat.

Unsaturated fats are clear liquid at room temperature. All vegetable oils are unsaturated. Margarine is made of vegetable oil and would be liquid at room temperature, but its form is changed during manufacturing to make it solid at room temperature. Olive and safflower oils are unsaturated and especially important for good nutrition.

Fish oil carries a special fatty acid—Omega-3—which helps protect against heart disease. Some Omega-3 oil is found in all fish and shellfish, but it is especially abundant in fish used in many Latino *guisados*—*bacalao,* salmon, mackerel, *sardinas,* and anchovies—*anchoas.* The healthful oil is believed to produce an anticlotting agent in the blood, lowering both blood pressure and harmful blood cholesterol. Some reports suggest, however, that over-the-counter Omega-3 supplements may not be beneficial.

Every gram of fat equals nine calories. You should not eat more than thirty grams—approximately one ounce—of unsaturated fat daily. About half of this daily amount you get in your food, so you should not consume any more than one tablespoon—half ounce—of margarine, mayonnaise, or oil a day. The recommended amount of dietary fat is the same for men, women, and children: one tablespoon.

Check the following list of common ingredients and find out just how much saturated fat your favorite foods contain.

To be a prudent eater read the labels on food products before buying. Take a little calculator with you and if the product contains more than 25 percent fat, put it back. Be suspicious of the package of turkey ham that proclaims in bold print, "98 Percent Fat Free." When you calculate the weight of all the ingredients, the fat does represent less than 10 percent of total weight. But when you examine the total calories in the product, you will often find that about 70 to 90 percent of these calories are derived from fat.

Fat is a necessary component of good nutrition, but too much fat will surely make you put on weight and will take its toll on your health.

Table II:
SATURATED/UNSATURATED FAT

FOOD	AMOUNT	SATURATED FAT (GRAMS)	UNSATURATED FAT (GRAMS)
Butter	1 Tablespoon	7	4
Margarine* (Tub or squeeze bottle)	1 Tablespoon	2	9
Whipped Cream (evaporated whole milk)	1 Tablespoon	4	2
Lowfat Whipped Cream* (lowfat evaporated milk)	1 Tablespoon	2	2
Sour Cream	1 Tablespoon	2	1
Nonfat Sour Cream*	1 Tablespoon	0	0
2 Eggs Poached	2 Yolks	4	6
2 Eggs Fried (in 1 tsp. butter)	2 Yolks	5	8
2 or More Eggs*	1 Yolk	2	3
Whole Milk	8 Ounces	5	3
Lowfat Milk (2%)	8 Ounces	3	2
Nonfat Milk*	8 Ounces	<1	<1
Manteca, Lard	1 Tablespoon	5	8
Safflower Oil*	1 Tablespoon	1	12
Bacon	4 Strips	4	8
Fish*	4 Ounces	1	2
Whole Milk Cheese	1 Ounce	6	3
Lowfat Cheese (from part-skim milk)*	1 Ounce	2	1
Steak (New York cut)	4 Ounces	15	17
Trimmed Lean Sirloin Steak	4 Ounces	4	6
Ground Beef (Regular)	4 Ounces	9	11
Lean Ground (15 percent)	4 Ounces	7	9
Turkey, light* (without skin)	4 Ounces	2	3
Turkey, dark (without skin)	4 Ounces	3	6
Pork Loin or Chops	4 Ounces	11	18
Trimmed Pork Loin or Chops	4 Ounces	6	7

* The best choice

CARBOHYDRATES

Sugar Is as Sugar Does—Azúcar, La Dulce Energía

Sugar is more than just the white stuff you sprinkle on your cereal or put in your coffee. Carbohydrates are sugars, starches, and cellulose. Sugar and starch are digested into glucose, a more usable source of energy. Most foods contain a combination of sugar and protein, or protein and fat, or all three energy sources together, as in corn.

Every potato, ear of corn, *tortilla*, plate of pasta, piece of bread, bowl of rice, plate of *frijoles*, fruit or vegetable starts to be digested as soon as you begin to chew it. It then moves into your stomach and on to your small intestine, where all the carbohydrate foods are converted to glucose. The glucose is absorbed into the liver and from there it diffuses into the bloodstream. Blood glucose has no special destination in your body but is taken up by cells and organs where needed, as it circulates. If you have exercised, the glucose will be used to replenish the glucose used by the muscle cells during exercise. If you have not exercised or have eaten too much carbohydrate food, the glucose will be converted to fat and earmarked for transport to your hungrily awaiting fat cells.

Sugar, Take Away My Blues— Azúcar, Quítame La Tristeza

"*Endulzar tu vida*—sweeten your life," my grandmother would console me, offering cake, cookies, or *dulces*— sweets—whenever I was unhappy. I learned early that sugar made me feel good. Mimi learned the same lesson as I did. As a small child, every time she bruised herself, her mother was there with a *paleta*—lollipop—to take away the hurt. Her rewards for good behavior were *dulces*. She was conditioned like one of Pavlov's pooches to crave sweets in response to any unpleasantness—depression, anger, or boredom. With a "sugar fix," all pain disappeared, usually only to return half an hour later demanding another dose of sweets.

It is difficult to let go of the habits we learn as children. In her thirties, Mimi still responded to every challenging situation—even a disagreement over a bill the mechanic presented for car repair—by turning to her "remedy." She was overweight and unhappy. She knew sugar was fattening, knew she had to cut down, but did not know how.

Mimi needed to start by understanding how sugar is processed by her body. When she eats foods that contain refined sugar in the morning, she sets in motion an inexorable series of events. The sweet breakfast produces a temporary glucose lift. An hour or so later, her glucose level drops and she suddenly feels hungry, fatigued, and agitated. These feelings persist for the next hour or two and can only be satisfied by another infusion of sugar—her midmorning sweet roll and coffee. Two and a half hours later, at lunch, Mimi is eager for more sweets. By midafternoon, she is dying for a candy bar or anything sweet. That pretty much gets her through her eight-hour workday. On the way home, she grabs a little something sweet to tide her over until dinner.

The problem is that one sweet fix stimulates the need for another. Avoiding the first sugar temptation makes you stronger to resist the craving for the rest of the day. The first infusion of sugar gives you a very high blood glucose level, and you feel energized. Your body reacts quickly and tries to normalize the amount of glucose in your blood, but then there is a rebound effect, and your glucose level drops too far down. With low glucose, you feel hungry, tired, and agitated for the next two to three hours or until you sugar-up again. And so the cycle is repeated over and over, from morning till night.

My first recommendation to Mimi was to never skip breakfast but avoid all foods containing refined sugar and use sugar substitutes or natural fruit sugars from *papaya, guayabas, fresas*—strawberries. Then I counseled her to recognize that sweets never did "make it all better." It was just a conditioned response from her *mente gorda* that told her that another candy or piece of cake would still her fears, calm her down, or make the hurt go away. Finally, I suggested that while she was making the mental and emotional adjustment, she should prepare for her *mente gorda*'s attacks by carrying a small container of *jamoncillo*—fudge—*flan, batido,* or *gelatinas con leche* prepared the Latina Lite way.

In addition to turning her back on refined sugars, Mimi also began to exercise. She parks her car blocks away from her office, uses the stairs instead of the elevator, and works out at home. Exercise is another great way to keep your blood glucose at an optimum level. Toned, strong muscles burn more glucose than small, weak muscles, even during rest or sleep.

Sugar, Sugar Everywhere

We often consume sugar without even knowing it. Here are three examples of Latinas who were gaining weight from hidden sugar. Olivia took a popular antacid remedy, loaded with sugar, nightly. Mary regularly took her cough medicine; she liked the sweet taste. And Teresa, misled by television commercials, sipped a popular sports drink all day long. Sports drinks are healthful, when you are engaged in hard physical activity and are perspiring. You lose essential electrolytes—sodium, potassium, and chloride—in perspiration, and can replace them with sports drinks, whose formulas reproduce human sweat made palatable with added sugar. A cheaper and healthier method is to drink eight glasses of water a day and eat two or three pieces of fresh fruit.

Life Is Either Simple or Simply Complex—
La Vida Es Simple o Simplemente Compleja

Plant tissue is the main source of *hidratos de carbono*—carbohydrates—which provide the major part of your energy. The **simple** plant carbohydrates are called **sugar** and are found in all fruits, vegetables, leaves, roots of plants, and in foods that are made by man and animals from plants. Some examples include: papaya, *jícama, guava, nopales, calabaza,* spinach, lettuce, *caña* and refined sugar, *mermelada,* syrup, and honey.

The more **complex** carbohydrates are called **starch** and are found in grains, seeds, and root plants. They include bread, cereals, *tortillas, yautía,* corn, plantains, *yuca, boniatos, fideos,* rice, and pastas.

A third type of carbohydrate is called **cellulose**, or fiber. Fiber is found in the skin and husks of fruits and vegetables.

A small amount of carbohydrates is also found in meat, but meat should not be relied on as a significant source. The World Health Organization and the American Cancer Society recommend that 60 percent of your diet be energy-providing carbohydrates.

Rough Roughage and Ready Fiber— *El Salvage Salvado*

Cellulose fiber, sometimes called **bran**, is the main component in the cell walls of plants. It is the odd carbohydrate. It is not sweet, cannot be digested by humans, and yields almost no calories—less then three per teaspoon. Why bother eating it at all? Dietary fiber keeps us well and slim.

Here is how fiber works: The fat ingested in a typical meal passes from your mouth to your stomach, then through the rest of your digestive system. When the partially digested food reaches your large intestine, it is greeted by bile released by your gallbladder. The bile searches out the undigested fat still in the food, latches on to it, and escorts it to the liver. If you have eaten a lot of fat, the liver will not be able to cope with it and will pass the excess into your bloodstream and then into your fat cells.

Now let's add a little oat and wheat bran to that typical meal we just ate. The roughage gives you a double-barreled advantage. The cellulose fiber present in the food will bind with the bile and fat. Now, much of the fat cannot work its way out of the intestine into the liver. The other benefit derived from roughage is its ability to speedily push waste out of your digestive system. Fat combined with bile and roughage passes out of the body as soft stool. By the way, cellulose fiber from unprocessed carbohydrates is safer, less costly, and more effective than laxatives in speeding up elimination.

No Need to Suffer—*No Sufras Más*

One of the most common complaints people have at the beginning of their weight-loss programs is constipation. Constipation makes you feel uncomfortable, and if left unattended for years, can result in diverticulosis or even gastric cancer. The longer waste material stays in contact with the walls of the colon, the greater the exposure to cancer-producing toxins and gases. The fiber in carbohydrates stimulates the muscles in the intestinal lining to work more frequently, with stronger contractions, to push waste out faster. It is therefore especially important that you eat adequate amounts of carbohydrate fiber in the early stages of your weight-reduction program.

PROTEIN

David Ate Goliath's Lunch

Who do you think requires more protein, an active, growing six-year-old, a male construction worker, or a housewife? You are right if you answered that the man needs the most; he needs six to eight ounces of protein daily. Although I bet he eats more protein than he needs. The amount of protein necessary depends on your weight. The child, although he is growing, needs the least amount of protein.

The best sources of protein are meat, fowl, fish, and milk. Unfortunately, most protein-rich foods are also high in fat. Seventy-eight percent of the calories derived from most beef are from fat. Pork is even richer in fat. Most cheeses contain about 80 percent fat. An eight-ounce glass of regular milk yields two grams of pure protein, accompanied by eight grams of fat. The same serving of skim milk, on the other hand, has eight grams of protein and almost no fat.

To lose weight, you must choose your protein wisely. Lean, **skinned** chicken or turkey, fish, nonfat cottage cheese, nonfat yogurt, and skim-milk cheeses can supply all the protein you need, with minimal fat. Later you will learn to incorporate these lowfat, high-protein foods in all of your favorite dishes, preserving the *sabor rico*—rich taste—of traditional *comida sabrosa Latina*.

Animal, Mineral, or Vegetable?

Some *señoritas* become vegetarians in the hopes of controlling their weight. Raquel, seventeen, had for a year worked in a pizzeria, where she gained twenty-three extra pounds and a pimply complexion. She decided to lose weight, quit the pizzeria, got a job in a health-food restaurant, and became an avowed vegetarian.

When asked what she eats, Raquel replied proudly: "I am now a vegan and don't eat animal products or anything with eyes, except maybe potatoes. I shun anything made by man; I don't trust what they put into bread and such. My main diet consists of all green leafy vegetables, celery, radishes, tomatoes, mushrooms. And I make my own rice flakes. I also eat tons of nuts, avocados, papaya, bananas, apples, cantaloupe, all citrus, and water *batidos*, made with honey." A computer analysis of Raquel's diet showed that she was grossly undernourished, even though she was averaging 2,100 calories a day and was gaining weight. Her calcium level was 30 percent of what it should be, phosphorus was 52 percent, sodium 26 percent, zinc 42 percent, and her protein intake was half that recommended for healthy nutrition. She was missing several essential amino acids and was heading for serious health problems. The possible maladies could include organ failure, menstrual disorders, joint and muscle pain, osteoporosis, fatigue, mood swings, and psychotic symptoms of depression and even schizophrenia.

To be fair to legitimate vegetarians, Raquel's "diet" was far from well-considered vegetarian nutrition. She had to increase:

1. **Calcium**—Nonfat dairy products are plentiful, but for a vegetarian a calcium supplement might be suggested.
2. **Phosphorus**—Animal sources include fish, poultry, and eggs; plant sources include whole grains, seeds, and nuts.
3. **Sodium**—Normal diets are high in salt, while vegetarian diets are usually low in sodium.
4. **Zinc**—Animal protein is a source, as well as whole-grain products, brewer's yeast, wheat bran, wheat germ, and pumpkin seeds.

To ensure a supply of all the essential amino acids from vegetable protein, she must carefully mix vegetables like:

Frijoles + *tortillas* or whole-grain bread;
Rice + *garbanzos, habichuelas* or green peas;
Lentejas or beans + corn;
Soybeans + a whole-wheat product.

Today not many Latinos are vegetarians, but the practice may have an historical precedent. Meat was scarce in southern North America and Central America 900 to 2,000 years ago, yet the original inhabitants combined their carbohydrates in a way that provided them with a complete protein. Did they have a sophisticated knowledge of nutrition? Probably not, but they did discover the importance of combining rice, beans, and *tortillas*—the combination needed to replace animal protein—as the mainstays of their diet. If you are a vegetarian, consult with your physician and eat corn, or corn products, with beans, rice, or both, every day.

SODIUM AND SALT

Halt! Put Down the Salt!—*Alto! Basta de Sal!*

Salt is another diet demon. It causes water retention and raises your blood pressure. Too much salt makes weight loss almost impossible. It makes your limbs swell, your body bloat, and your sensual curves turn to displeasing bulges. When you wake up in the morning with puffy eyes and feel your rings constricting your fingers, salt is *embrujándote*—casting its tasty spell.

Most *comidas Latinas* are high in salt. Salt is made up of chlorine and sodium. Too much sodium can alter the normal functioning of your cells and organs. A cell is like a miniature engine that has a nerve attached to it. The nerve carries electricity to the cell so it can function normally. The electricity passes along the nerve with the aid of the minerals: potassium, chloride, and sodium. If your body has too much sodium and too little potassium, the electrical impulse may get blocked, leaving cell functions impaired. In extreme cases, dangerous cardiac irregularities can occur from a sodium-potassium imbalance. The best way to avoid these problems is to restrict salt intake and increase potassium by eating three to four fruits or vegetables every day.

Too much salt can also nibble away your bones. The more sodium you consume, the more calcium you lose. For every teaspoon of salt excreted in urine, you lose 23 milligrams of calcium. Exceeding recommended salt intake by only half a teaspoon daily results in bone loss of 1 percent in a single year. This puts you at great risk for developing osteoporosis in the future.

Immoderate salt use is also linked to gastric cancer. Sodium irritates the stomach lining, causing cancerous cells to multiply more frequently, and may make the cancer-causing chemicals more potent. If you abuse salt, you also raise your chances of developing kidney stones, asthma, congestive heart failure, and stroke. So, be careful what you shake!

You probably do not realize how much sodium you ingest every day. Take Clara, for example. Every time she sat down at the table, she reached for the *salero* and salted generously before tasting her food. Besides that, she never ate a banana, orange, melon, watermelon, pineapple, or one of her favorite sweets without a blizzard of salt. The principal ingredient in all of her *guisados*—stews—was *sofrito, caldo,* or granulated consommé—three high-salt offenders. To counteract the "*pica*"—hot sensation—of *chile,* Clara added even more salt to many dishes. She prepared other recipes with *salsa soya* and monosodium glutamate (MSG), also laden with sodium. She consumed lots of carbonated beverages, all of which contain sodium. Constantly watching her weight, she bought frozen diet dinners and lowfat foods, all of which disguise their bland flavors with lots of salt. Clara installed a home water softener for drinking water, adding more sodium. She used cough medicines, antacids, and bicarbonate-based laxatives that are all high in sodium. On average, Clara consumed no less than two to four teaspoons of salt daily. She needs no more than one teaspoon.

Once her puffy eyes were opened to the negative effects of salt on her health and her weight, Clara learned to wait to add salt to her cooking until after the dish was on the table. She filled her shakers with a mixture of half a tablespoon of salt and half a tablespoon of salt substitute. She also placed a shaker of flavorful grated herbs and another of pure garlic flakes on the table. She discovered that squeezing fresh lemon wedges over fruit enhanced their flavor more than sodium. Lemon also helped alleviate *la boca enchilada*—a mouth burning from chile. She purchased fewer prepared frozen dinners, began to use low-sodium soy sauce, and omitted MSG from her cooking. Blended fruit drinks—prepared with no-sodium bottled water—served as soda substitutes. Oat and wheat bran replaced sodium-filled laxatives. At first, Clara had a hard time cutting down, but after a short while she began to see the results of sensible salt consumption.

Safe Salt Summary

Salt regulates fluid balance, transmits nerve impulses, and allows muscles to contract. To maintain good health, you need about 2,400 milligrams, or one teaspoon, of salt/sodium daily. Here are some suggestions that will help you eat less sodium:

Do not add salt, consommé, *sofrito,* or *caldo* while cooking. Wait until the dish is cooked and add it just before serving.

Use fresh foods instead of canned or processed foods.

Rinse and drain all canned vegetables and fish.

Do not put the salt shaker on the table. If indispensable, use a half-and-half mixture of salt and salt substitute.

Check the label for sodium content before purchasing food. A serving that contains 35 to 140 mg is low-sodium, one that has 200 mg or more is high-sodium.

When eating out:

- Order your food cooked without salt or MSG.
- Do not order foods prepared with gravies or salty sauces. If you want to try the sauce ask for it on the side.
- Use soy sauce sparingly.
- When traveling by air, order low sodium meals in advance.
- You do not have to eat bland, tasteless food when you cut down on salt. Herbs, spices, garlic, and lemon can add delightful flavors.

IT ALL BOILS DOWN TO WATER

I Am Dying for a Drink—*Estoy Muriendo de Sed*

Most of us take water for granted. We drink it when nothing else is available and only when we are thirsty. If you wait until thirst persuades you to drink, you have waited too long. Thirst comes after your cells have started to run dry. Drink water five to ten times a day.

Did you know that your body loses about two quarts, or eight glasses, of water each day? Your body loses water through skin, respiratory organs, the gastrointestinal tract, and the urinary tract. It is very important to replace lost fluid. Eight glasses out, eight glasses in. Try to drink about one cup every hour or so, rather than trying to down two or three glasses at a time. Consider carrying a sixteen-ounce plastic water bottle as you go about daily activities. Increased water intake will temporarily increase frequency of urination. After a few weeks, your body will adjust, and you will urinate less frequently but will expel a greater amount at each "sitting."

One señora Venezolana credits her habit of drinking eight glasses of water a day with helping her maintain her optimal weight for seven years. "Water curbs my appetite," she explains. "Many times I feel hungry but don't know exactly what I want to eat. I am really more thirsty than hungry and the water takes away my thirst, dulls my hunger, and postpones any urge to snack."

Dr. Donald S. Robertson, M.D., M.Sc., a kidney expert, considers water one of the keys to fat metabolism, claiming that water makes your kidneys more efficient. Their job is to filter impurities and toxins from the blood. Denied sufficient *agua*, they will not work very well. Forced to assume part of the kidneys' function and detoxify the polluted blood, the liver is unable to metabolize as much stored fat into usable energy. Fat that is normally broken down and used up as energy remains deposited in your fat cells.

Water Weighs Me Down

Sometimes we use water as an excuse for our body weight. Adelina discreetly raised the baggy shirt that reached down to the tops of her thighs to reveal the open zipper of her pants. "I weigh more because I am retaining water. I can't even pull my pants up," she explained, stepping up to the scale.

Retained water bloats your body and makes you heavier. The best way to "unbloat" may seem illogical, but it is to drink more water! You must dilute the concentration of salt in your tissues, in the same way you fix a *caldo* or *sopa* that is too salty. This is how it works: If you consume too much salt or do not drink enough water, your blood becomes abnormally salty. To get the concentration of salt back to normal, your blood and other tissue hold on to more water, causing you to bloat. If you drink eight glasses of water a day, you will temporarily increase the amount of water in the blood. That will desalinate your blood to normal levels through increased urination. With lower levels of salt in the blood, the amount of water in the blood and other tissue will also return to normal. The bloat will be gone.

There are other good reasons to keep well hydrated. Supplying your body with adequate amounts of water helps produce a soft stool, protects you from becoming *extreñida*—constipated—and minimizes your chances of developing hemorrhoids. It also helps prevent kidney stones, which consist of mineral salts and uric acid. With enough *agua*, these substances are dissolved and removed. Drink enough water to help your body serve you better.

Another Gallon for the Road

"I figured that if eight glasses of water would improve my health, twice that much would make me even better," explained Mirna, a devoted follower of my program. "I've been drinking about two gallons a day." This was real cause for concern. Too much *agua* increases urination and can wash out your body's essential electrolytes—sodium, potassium, and chloride. The quantity and balance of the electrolytes is critical for normal transmission of impulses along your nerve cells. When nerve impulses are impaired, cell functions are disrupted and dangerous cardiac arrhythmias are apt to occur. At my suggestion, Mirna talked with her physician about the appropriate amount of water in her diet and returned to drinking eight glasses a day.

Dimples Are Cute, But Not on Your Thighs

Sagging skin is among dieters' biggest fears. Drinking adequate amounts of water can help reduce drooping. After weight loss, it customarily takes a few months for your skin to readjust. *Agua* plumps out all cells, including skin cells, that have lost fluid during the slimming process. The end result is you look more attractive sooner.

Cellulitis is not a medical term and cannot be found in medical books. It is an interesting word that probably describes the bumpy contour formed by unevenly packed fat cells that lie just under the skin. Uglier than ugly fat, it is an unwelcome condition. Regardless of who coined the term, it is a common reason for weight loss and a typical complaint after losing. Up to now, there is no surgical procedure, cream, or pill that will eliminate cellulitis. To get rid of the dimpling, maintain a steady rate of weight loss, exercise regularly, and drink your eight glasses of water each day. After about a year, the fat cells will shrink and appear more uniform, while other tissues that contain normal cellular fluid take up the slack and fill in the holes. With time, you will develop smoother, more attractive curves.

VITAMINS AND MINERALS

Vitamins are organic compounds that help break down energy nutrients: carbohydrates, proteins, and fats. There are approximately twenty recognized vitamins, and each plays a special role in digestion, absorption, metabolism, and generation or regeneration of cells. With few exceptions, vitamins are not manufactured in the body and must be obtained from food. There are fat-soluble and water-soluble vitamins. Your body may store excessive amounts of fat-soluble vitamins but expels unnecessary water-soluble vitamins in urine. Many Latinas take vitamin pills without knowing why. Unless you are ill, pregnant, or getting older, you may not need to supplement a balanced diet by taking vitamins. If you are uncertain of the nutritional quality of your diet, you can cover your bets by adding a daily vitamin and mineral supplement.

Fat-Soluble Vitamins

Lucrecia's mother had been blind since the age of forty, and Lucrecia did everything she could to protect her own eyesight. Aware that vitamin A plays an important part in safeguarding *la vista*, Lucrecia drank two large glasses of carrot juice daily and downed massive doses of vitamin A tablets. After following her self-prescribed regime for five months, she began to suffer constant headaches, accompanied by nausea, and her skin started to turn a sallow yellow. Lucrecia was poisoning herself with too much vitamin A. Only after she cut back to a half cup of carrot juice a day and reduced her intake of vitamin pills, did she regain her former color and health.

Proper amounts of vitamin A make bones, teeth, and body tissues healthy, enhance the immune system, and keep skin soft and supple. There is evidence that this vitamin inhibits the growth of tumors, giving some protection against cancer. Vitamin A abounds in liver, carrots, sweet potatoes, yellow squash, alfalfa, turnips, spinach, and cantaloupe.

Vitamin D is another fat-soluble vitamin. Unlike most of the other vitamins, it is manufactured by your body with the help of sunlight. Vitamin D's main function is to keep your teeth and bones strong. Milk fortified with vitamin D and fifteen minutes of sun enable you to manufacture all the vitamin D you need.

The rich and famous travel to Switzerland for rejuvenation treatments with vitamin E. Vitamin E is thought to increase sexual potency, smooth and fade skin scars, and prevent heart disease. There is, however, limited experimental evidence to prove these claims. Vitamin E does help to relieve the symptoms of fibrocystic breast disease and many delay the onset of Alzheimer's disease. The food sources for this very important vitamin are vegetable oils, grains, and cereals.

The final fat-soluble vitamin, vitamin K, is essential in the clotting of blood. A normal diet, consisting of dairy products, chicken, and fish, will provide double your needs of vitamin K.

Water-Soluble Vitamins

The vitamin B complex is made up of nine B vitamins, all containing nitrogen, carbon, hydrogen, and oxygen. Each one of the nine B vitamins is structured differently, and all are necessary for reproduction, cellular development, and nerve and brain functioning. Vegetables are so essential to your diet because during digestion beneficial intestinal bacteria consume parts of the vegetable matter to manufacture many of the B vitamins. A diet high in red meat inhibits the output of these B vitamins and slows the digestive process. Vitamin B–12 is very important in the proper functioning of your nervous system. Folacin or folic acid, another B vitamin, strengthens the genetic material in your cells. Among the best sources of folic acid are *garbanzo* beans—chickpeas. Other vitamin B–rich foods are: yeast, bran, soybeans, beans, fish, skinned chicken, dairy products, green vegetables, corn products, breads, whole-grain cereals, and pastas.

Collagen injections to smooth out wrinkles is a costly cosmetic surgical procedure. The collagen plumps out the skin and eliminates the dry prune look. Vitamin C maintains natural skin collagen, helps you look young and vital. A deficiency of this vitamin may prematurely weaken supportive skin tissue, causing your face to sag, adding years to your appearance. Insufficient levels of vitamin C lower your ability to combat infections. Although vitamin C is widely used as a remedy for the common cold, its effectiveness is controversial.

Vitamin C, once eaten, proceeds into the small intestine, and within three hours most of it is absorbed into the blood and used where needed for muscle cell repair. The major part of the excess is passed from the body as urine, with a small portion exhaled in breathing. Vitamin C should be consumed daily. And because it does not last long during storage or cooking, it is very important that fresh fruits be eaten soon after they are purchased. Fresh-squeezed orange juice can be left in a covered container for a day without any loss of vitamin C, but since the flavor changes very quickly, it is better to squeeze and drink right away. The best sources of vitamin C are: oranges, grapefruit, tangerines, *guanábanas, guavas, mandarinas,* papaya, *guayabas,* and strawberries.

A little-known vitamin seems to be important in strengthening the body's capillaries. If you suffer from bleeding gums, nosebleeds, skin disorders, or unusually prolific menstrual bleeding, you might want to be sure to include vitamin P, the bioflavonoids, in your diet. Frequent bruising might indicate that the capillaries are weak and need vitamin P. It is found along with vitamin C in citrus fruits.

Minerals

Minerals, like vitamins, are essential nutrients. Calcium, phosphorus, and magnesium are necessary in the body. Ninety-nine percent of the calcium found in your body is in your bones and teeth. A little is found in the muscle cells, and it is absolutely essential for muscle contraction. If your diet is deficient in calcium, your bones will give up calcium in order to supply the amount needed for muscle contraction. If you consume too much calcium, your body will eliminate it in urine. Calcium is found in milk and milk products and in green leafy vegetables. A single glass of nonfat milk, a half cup of nonfat plain yogurt, a half cup of canned salmon with the bone in, or a half cup of spinach or *acelgas* fulfills all of your daily calcium needs.

Phosphorus is an abundant mineral, which usually accompanies calcium in foods such as milk and most vegetables. Very seldom is a phosphorus deficiency found in humans. A deficiency may occur after severe bone fractures or if too many antacids are consumed.

Magnesium is essential because it allows the production of energy in the cell. It plays a part in the regulation of body temperature and neural transmission. A magnesium deficiency causes irritability, weakness, and possible heart damage. A lack of magnesium is associated with kidney stones, high blood pressure, and blood vessel disease. High sources of magnesium are soybeans, wheat germ, and raw spinach or *acelgas.*

You already know that the electrolytes—sodium, potassium, and chloride—are crucial for the transmission of electrical impulses from the brain to all the organs. Lowered levels of these minerals can cause severe heart arrhythmias, which can sometimes be fatal. Sodium and chloride are abundant in most ordinary diets; and potassium is plentiful in oranges, bananas, tomatoes, and other fruits.

In addition, there are thirteen elements that are essential to good nutrition in trace amounts—one grain daily (or the amount equal to a grain of sand). Iron leads the list. Anemia caused by iron deficiency is the most prevalent nutritional problem in both developed and developing countries. Physical signs of iron-deficiency anemia include pale skin, fatigue, difficult or labored breathing, heart palpitations, "spooning of the nails," or an inflamed red tongue. Yet too much iron can cause as many problems as too little. People who take excessive amounts of iron run the risk of serious damage to the liver, pancreas, heart, and other endocrine organs. Doctors recommend eating meat, fish, seafood, peas, and beans instead of downing iron pills.

Iron is toxic. Acute iron poisoning can threaten a child's life. It is imperative to keep all iron medications out of the reach of young children.

The Sexy Mineral

Here is the best reason for making sure you are getting enough zinc: It will keep your love life vital. The production of testosterone—the hormone that governs sexual drive in both men and women—depends on adequate amounts of zinc in your diet. So if you have been feeling apathetic toward sex or your male companion has had some erectile problems, it may be that one or both of you are low on zinc. You need only a minute daily amount. Seafood, peas, beans, and whole grains will provide you with all the zinc you need. Do not consume more than the recommended amount of zinc trying to be supersexy. Too much of any metal can be damaging.

Chromium, sold as Chromium Picolinate, has been promoted as the latest miracle "that melts the fat right off your body." The scientific community has serious doubts about how well it works. Chromium joins with insulin in your body to allow glucose to enter your muscle cells. Adults only need 250 micrograms—a tiny amount. Corn oil, brewer's yeast, and meats contain chromium.

Selenium is another trace element needed for good health. It is considered a powerful antioxidant, purported to slow aging and protect cellular membranes of the heart, lungs, and kidneys. There is also evidence that selenium is helpful as an anticancer agent. It is found in all seafood, meat, and grains.

GOOD EATING HABITS

Learning Self-control

It is often hard to control our eating. Not only does food seem sacred to us, but we harbor fears that we are not going to get enough. As a young child, Estela had to compete for food. Her parents and five brothers and sisters always ate together. Every dinner was a race. Estela learned early not to waste time chewing. She scarcely tasted her food. "If I needed to go to the bathroom I held it in, afraid to leave the table, since one of my brothers would steal the food right off my plate," Estela remembers. She still has moments when she wants to eat too much too fast, even though she has only two children and her comfortable income ensures plenty of food for the table. Whenever she feels the urge to "stuff it in," she must consciously stop and think, "No one is going to steal my food. I am not competing in a race."

No one is born with self-control. It must be learned. Your

willpower, like your muscles, needs exercise to develop. The only way to strengthen it is through purposeful training. Try a few mental exercises when the thought, sight, or smell of your favorite dishes awakens your *mente gorda* and makes your mouth water. Imagine yourself in a bathing suit when you are offered a helping of homemade *hojaldre*—rich, buttery brown-sugar cake. Put a small piece on your plate, recognizing that you never want to leave anything that finds its way there. Think of each spoonful turning into a lump of belly fat. Instead of stuffing your mouth and feeling guilty, imagine the compliments a slim person receives. Then think about how attractive you will be once you become lean.

Fina was known for her generosity and benevolence in everything except food. "When I see a table laden with delicious dishes, I think I'll never have the opportunity to eat again," she admitted. "I want to lie down on top of the food, saving every delectable morsel for me only." She usually succumbed to her desire and ate as much as she could fit in.

To develop self-control, Fina learned to repeat to herself, "All the food is not disappearing from the world today. A lot will be here tomorrow." She ate moderately, trying to remember that food would be with her for the rest of her life, and sensible consuming would afford her more years to enjoy it. With practice, Fina learned to take sufficient portions rather than excessive ones. Her initial reaction to cutting down was regret at leaving her favorite succulent morsels uneaten. But as she trimmed down, Fina began to enjoy the rewards of self-control. "I am strong enough to resist overeating," she says now. "I feel so good that I am helping myself to be slim."

I'll Stop Eating When the Food Is Gone— Cuando Se Termina la Comida Paro de Comer

How can you tell when you are full? You cannot while you are eating, especially if you are hastily gulping down your food. It takes ten to twenty minutes after the first morsel passes your lips for the message that you have had enough food to reach the satisfaction center in your brain. When you eat quickly, the satiety center does not have sufficient time to respond and relay the signal to stop eating. That is why you often feel that you have room for another helping or more dessert only to feel uncomfortably overstuffed minutes later.

Most of us who struggle with being overweight do eat too fast. Here are some hints to help you slow down your eating: Rest your knife and fork on your plate after every bite. Fill your plate from the pot. Omit putting the platter on the table. Chew every bite thoroughly and say a few words to your companions before taking the next bite. When your plate is empty, place your utensils on your empty plate and do not use them again until the next meal. Remove all food from your reach if you linger at the table after the meal.

At first, these changes will be difficult, and you have to think about the rules, but soon they will become habit. When you begin to eat more slowly, you will discover new tastes that previously passed unnoticed.

Why Not Overdo It

Thomas Jefferson, the third President of the United States, advised his cabinet, "Never be sorry that you ate just a little."

Aurora did not eat the wrong foods; she just ate too much of the right ones. She had lost twelve pounds to achieve her goal weight and intended to maintain it. In learning about good nutrition, Aurora had found out that fruits are a necessary daily component of a balanced diet. She had always adored mangos and tended several mango trees in the yard of her Key West, Florida, home. Faced with too many ripe mangos at the same time she opened a roadside stand. To avoid wasting the unsold mangos, she ate no less than eight every day. They ranged in size from *niños*—very small, at about 150 calories—to *petacones*—huge two-pounders, providing up to 450 calories each. Her scale registered a five-pound gain the following week. "It was only fruit," declared the stunned Aurora. "And fruit is good for you." True, but too much of a good thing can also make you put on weight. Aurora returned to the basic diet plan and in ten days took off the extra pounds.

A Calorie by Any Other Name Is Just as Sweet

Carbohydrates, fats, and proteins are the foods that fuel our bodies. Of course, food contains calories. If you eat more calories than you need, the extra energy is converted to body fat and makes you overweight.

In the Latina Lite plan, we do not count calories. However, you might want to know something about those pesky little critters. What is a calorie? Simple, a unit of energy. One calorie, in technical terms, is "the energy needed to raise the temperature of 1 gram of water 1 degree Centigrade." Obviously, you are not going to heat water within your body, but expressing food intake in terms of calories provides a convenient method of keeping track of how much energy you need.

How many calories does your body need to stay at its present weight? You can estimate this easily using Table III. To estimate how many calories you will need to hold steady at your present weight: 1. Select the proper age range. 2. Select the **Activity** column that best describes your level of daily movement and activity: If you generally do some walking, gardening, and shopping, select the **Average Activity** column. If you walk, garden, shop, **and** exercise, do aerobics, or dance weekly, select the **Busy Activity** column. And if you do all of the above **and vigorous exercise** four or more days a week, select the **Vigorous Activity** column. 3. Match your present weight to the four-digit number in the appropriate activity column. That is the number of calories you should consume per day.

Table III:
CALORIE REQUIREMENTS FOR WOMEN,
BY AGE GROUP AND ACTIVITY LEVEL

AGE 15 TO 40

WEIGHT POUNDS	AVERAGE ACTIVITY	BUSY ACTIVITY	VIGOROUS ACTIVITY
90	1120	1270	1420
100	1190	1340	1490
110	1260	1410	1560
120	1330	1480	1630
130	1400	1550	1700
140	1470	1620	1770
150	1540	1690	1840
160	1610	1760	1910
170	1680	1830	1980
180	1750	1900	2050
190	1820	1970	2120
200	1890	2040	2190
210	1960	2110	2260
220	2030	2180	2330
230	2100	2250	2400
240	2170	2320	2470
250	2240	2390	2540
260	2310	2460	2610
270	2380	2530	2680

AGE 41 AND OVER

WEIGHT POUNDS	AVERAGE ACTIVITY	BUSY ACTIVITY	VIGOROUS ACTIVITY
90	1052	1193	1334
100	1118	1259	1400
110	1184	1324	1466
120	1250	1390	1532
130	1316	1456	1597
140	1382	1522	1664
150	1448	1588	1729
160	1514	1654	1796
170	1580	1720	1861
180	1646	1786	1930
190	1712	1851	1993
200	1778	1918	2060
210	1844	1984	2126
220	1910	2049	2192
230	1976	2116	2258
240	2042	2182	2324
250	2108	2248	2390
260	2174	2314	2456
270	2240	2380	2522

If you wish to lose about two pounds a month, it is relatively easy. All you have to do is reduce your daily consumption by 300 calories. Most Latinas want to lose much faster than that and are willing to nearly starve themselves. It is unwise to diet drastically, and my program is designed to cut about 300 calories per day. If you want to lose about four to five pounds a month, you will need to add at least four days of exercise. The combination of fewer calories from food and increased energy consumption through exercise will generally produce a loss of one pound of fat per week. This is the most effective method to achieve permanent weight loss ever discovered.

The composition of your diet is also very important. Your body exhausts more energy digesting and using protein than fat, and even fewer calories are expended to process fatty foods into fat-cell storage. The lesson here is to reduce fatty food intake and be careful of protein foods that contain fat. Here is an example: One woman eats lean meat, fish, whole grains, fruits, and vegetables. The second prefers skinless chicken breast, fried foods, and rich desserts. They consume the same number of calories, yet the first is slimmer than the second, because her diet contains much less fat.

Choose wisely. You will feel fulfilled physically and emotionally when you eat to protect your health and stay trim.

REMINDER CARD

FOR HEALTHY EATING . . .

Avoid excess **Fat, Sugar,** and **Sodium/Salt**

Eat **nonfat dairy** products

Remove skin and **fat** from all meats

Avoid fatty ground meats

Select **fresh fruit not, sugary processed foods**

REMEMBER THAT . . .

Eating too much Fat, Protein, or Carbohydrate **will fatten you**

Adding **salt makes** good-tasting **food** taste **salty**

You can **avoid salt**—use spices, lemon, garlic, or salt substitute

Eating extra **protein** does **not improve** strength or athletic performance

All fats contain the same calories per gram

Vegetable oils are healthier than animal fats

Eating **sugar increases appetite** for more sweets

Eating **fresh fruit does not increase appetite** for more sweets

Your **brain functions** best with natural **carbohydrates**

Roughage protects against digestive ailments and colon cancer

A once-a-day **vitamin pill** should be given due consideration

TO BE SLIM YOU MUST . . .

Slightly **reduce** the **calories** in each meal

Reduce the size of your **fat cells**

Drink **eight glasses of water** a day

Control your **eating—If you don't, who will?**

La Grasa Insalubre— Too Much Body Fat Is Unhealthy

El Mal Más Viejo del Mundo— The World's Oldest-Known Malady

An obese Stone Age statue, an overweight Egyptian mummy, and a fat Greek god have all been unearthed. Throughout history, people have tended to become heavy when food was plentiful and life was leisurely. And throughout history, we have suffered the unhealthy consequences of excess body fat.

Evidence suggests that the overweight Egyptian whose mummy I mentioned had suffered from gallbladder disease. If you carry thirty to forty extra pounds, you have 600 percent greater risk of developing problems with your *vesícula*—gallbladder. In fact, one third of obese Latinas will face gallbladder removal before reaching age sixty.

Obesity is an ailment that is rarely caused by a glandular or hormonal imbalance, or eating disorder. Eating disorders are usually due to frustration and other emotional problems associated with obesity or fear of obesity. Overweight is not a psychological disorder. On the contrary, obesity may predispose humans to psychological or psychiatric disturbances.

People carrying excess weight are often malnourished, and because they eat a lot of the wrong foods, their resistance to disease is generally low. They are susceptible to a variety of diseases. According to some experts, if everyone achieved normal body weight, life expectancy would go up three years, and the incidence of heart disease and stroke would decrease by 25 and 35 percent, respectively.

The illnesses from which Latinos tend to suffer—cardiac problems, diabetes, hypertension, high cholesterol, orthopedic problems, digestive disorders, and cancer—are aggravated by obesity and for the most part can be ameliorated or fully controlled with a diet that stresses appropriate sugar, salt, and fat intake.

HEART DISEASE

Mi Corazón Está En Mis Manos— My Heart Is in My Hands

Can you protect yourself from heart disease? Yes, by defending yourself from the "risk factors" that cause heart disease. Some risk factors—such as **age, gender,** and **heredity**—cannot be controlled: The risk of heart disease increases with age; men are at greater risk than women; and people whose parents have heart disease are more susceptible. That is the bad news. The good news is that the major degenerative risk factors that cause heart disease can be completely controlled by you. You can maintain appropriate **cholesterol levels**; keep **blood pressure** low; remain **slim**; limit **saturated fat, salt,** and **sugar** in your diet; continue to **exercise**; set aside time for **relaxation**; quit **smoking**, if you do, and go out of your way to avoid **tobacco smoke**; and avoid situations that produce undue **stress** or **anger**.

By following the Latina Lite plan you will not only become thin but will automatically reduce many risk factors. Lowering them could lessen the likelihood of your developing heart disease in the future by an amazing 500 to 5,000 percent. *Buena suerte!*

CHOLESTEROL

Cholesterol is a soft waxy substance found in every cell of your body, especially in cell membrane. It is needed to manufacture vitamin D and many hormones, including sex hormones. Dietary cholesterol is found in all animal products but is not present in any foods of plant origin.

Cholesterol found in the blood is called serum cholesterol. It is always bound to protein, because if it were not attached, it would float like oil atop water. Cholesterol combined with protein is called a lipoprotein, such as HDL, LDL, VLDL, and so on. The amount of cholesterol in your blood is significantly influenced by diet and exercise. If you eat fatty foods, are overweight, and do not exercise, chances are your cholesterol levels are high. High cholesterol levels cause arteries to narrow, leading to potentially fatal heart disease or stroke.

Your liver produces different types of lipoproteins. The two major lipoproteins are: High-Density Lipoprotein (HDL)— "good cholesterol"—and Low-Density Lipoprotein (LDL)— "bad cholesterol." Consuming fatty foods, especially animal fats, causes your liver to produce LDL, while eating vegetables, fruits, and lowfat meats stimulates the production of HDL.

Apostaré Dos Dolares En HDL—
I'll Bet Two Dollars on HDL

HDL and LDL are like the proverbial twins—one is good, the other evil. When LDL enters the bloodstream, it rampages through the body, clogging blood vessels with dangerous cholesterol plaque. HDL, on the other hand, courses through the arteries, vigilantly cleaning out our blood vessels.

If it were not for HDL, the flow of blood would be dangerously obstructed by cholesterol, salt, and mineral deposits on arterial walls. Blood running through constricted vessels causes a rise in blood pressure—hypertension. When an artery becomes so narrow that a minute piece of tissue can completely block the passage of blood, a critical problem arises: If this happens in a coronary artery, it is called an *enfarto cardiaco*—heart attack, and in an artery in the brain, an *embolio*—stroke.

To prevent your arteries from clogging with cholesterol, you have to stimulate production of HDL in the liver and restrict production of LDL. Here is how you can help your liver manufacture more HDL and less LDL.

GO FOR	AVOID
Fruits and vegetables	*Fritangas* and fatty snacks
Whole-grain breads and cereals	Full-fat dairy products
Skinned and trimmed fish	Skin-on, fatty meats
Tasty, well-spiced, low-salt foods	Salty foods
Licuados and noncarbonated drinks	Too much soda
Daily exercise	Excuses not to be active
Staying lean	More than 4 egg yolks a week

Generally, *mujeres* have higher levels of HDL than men. This is especially true during the years that estrogen production is high. As Latinas age or become heavier, their bad cholesterol levels climb, so it is especially important to keep track of both HDL and LDL levels after menopause.

Health problems associated with high LDL levels are not limited to adults. After the age of two, millions of children have elevated levels of cholesterol, putting them at greater risk of heart disease later in life. Feed your *niños* fruits and vegetables, fat-free dairy products, and meat and whole grains to keep them healthy and lean.

HYPERTENSION

La Gordura Me Mantiene Presionada—
Obesity Keeps My Pressure Up

At forty-five, Susana was a heavy-hearted 175 pounds. Even *un día del campo*, a picnic was too much exertion for her overtaxed body. She suffered from hypertension and avoided most physical activity. Her family had written her off and no longer invited her to join them on their outings. Afraid to be far away from her physician, she had not taken a vacation for twenty-seven years. Imprisoned in her body she lived a sad, lonely life, totally dependent on her *pastillas*—pills—to control her condition. Anxiety about her health and the absence of pleasant diversions made her irritable and unhappy. Eating helped put depression and boredom out of her mind for a little while but made her blood pressure creep ever higher. Occasionally, Susana made feeble stabs at healthier eating, but circumstances supposedly beyond her control always interfered.

The saddest part is that Susana imposed this solitary life upon herself. One of the leading researchers of hypertension, Dr. William B. Kannel of the Boston University School of Medicine, found that 65 percent of women who have high blood pressure are overweight. He lists obesity as the foremost cause of high blood pressure. A weight-control program that includes more exercise and reduced salt intake could be the best medicine for high blood pressure.

Desde Joven Se Pueden Tener Buenos Hábitos—
Good Eating Habits Can't Start Too Soon

Claudia, fifty-seven, had neglected her health until her blood pressure hit 203/120 and her doctor insisted that she change her lifestyle immediately. Several of her adult brothers and sisters were obese, and all suffered from high cholesterol, hypertension, and heart disease. Three other siblings had passed away before the age of sixty.

Throughout Claudia's early life, the family had stretched the *presupuesto*—food money—by filling *los hijos* with inexpensive fatty foods. *Frijoles refritos*, refried beans, and *chicharrones*, pork cracklings, were served three to four times weekly. Everyone loved the greasy, salty taste. After they married and left their parents' home, the siblings continued to follow their favorite high-fat diets. They all suffered from high cholesterol and cardiac problems. The exceptions were Claudia's two youngest sisters, who had grown up away from home, at a relative's farm. Their diets were low in fat, and they were not obese and were in perfect health.

Claudia realized she was at high risk of a debilitating stroke or heart attack. She changed her lifelong eating habits and began a walking regimen. Her husband, a steak devotee, refused to relinquish his customary diet and continued to eat huge slabs of red meat whenever he could. Claudia had little support from her mate, but she was determined. She learned to prepare familiar *platillos* in new lowfat ways and began walking thirty-five minutes a day, five days a week. She lost thirty-eight pounds in six months and reduced her blood pressure dramatically, to 143/98.

DIABETES

Quiero Vivir Hasta La Muerte— I Want to Live Till I Die

A definite relationship exists between diabetes and diet. I will never forget the day fourteen years ago when twenty-three-year-old Renata and her sister Berta came to my office to talk about excess weight and diabetes. Both were thirty pounds overweight, and Renata was concerned about their family's history of diabetes. Two years before, their forty-six-year-old mother had passed away from diabetes complications. Their father was also wasting away from the same affliction.

Renata was anxious to trim down to reduce her chances of developing the illness. Berta, on the other hand, had a self-indulgent, fatalistic attitude. "I am going to get diabetes anyway when I am old," she reasoned. "So I want to *comer, tomar y disfrutar*—eat, drink, and be merry while I am young." Berta just would not hear that losing weight could prevent the onset of diabetes, in spite of her heredity.

In the fourteen years that have passed since, Berta, true to her promise, lived the "good life." She now has full-blown diabetes. Renata, who has maintained her goal weight, is healthy but worried about her sister.

If diabetes runs in your family, it is not inevitable that you will develop the ailment. You can defend yourself against diabetes by eating prudently and exercising regularly.

There are two kinds of diabetes: juvenile and adult-onset. Both can be controlled with physician-supervised medications, diet, and exercise.

Adult-onset diabetes is more easily controlled and can even be prevented. The problem starts with a malfunction of the pancreas, a large gland located to the side of your stomach. The pancreas has several functions. One is to release digestive secretions into the intestine. Another is to release insulin into the blood after carbohydrates have been digested. Insulin attaches to the outside membrane of all cells, except brain cells. When energy (glucose) is needed by the cell, insulin passes it through and helps convert it into usable energy. If there is leftover glucose in the blood, insulin helps convert it to fat and passes it into fat cells for storage. Exercise stabilizes and decreases the amount of glucose in the blood and reduces the quantity that is stored as fat.

People who have an impaired pancreas have diabetes. The pancreas of diabetics produces too little insulin or insulin that is not strong enough to pass glucose into cells. Without constant nourishment, their cells degenerate and waste away. They feel tired and sleepy; urinate frequently; experience constant gnawing hunger and thirst; undergo changes in vision;

experience impaired circulation; suffer frequent cramping and itching; and are constantly at risk of serious infections. In addition, insulin regulates the amount of glucose in their blood. If insulin is low, blood sugar level rises. This can cause mental confusion, profuse perspiration, fatigue, changes in vision, fainting, coma, and even death. If, on the other hand, carbohydrate intake is low or too much insulin is produced, the blood glucose level drops and symptoms of hypoglycemia occur. These can include weakness, fatigue, marked perspiration, faintness, coma, and even death.

If you think you may be at risk of having diabetes, see your doctor. Ask about the nutritional benefits of the Latina Lite program. It is important to protect yourself from this devastating disease.

DIGESTION

Heartburn is not usually serious but can be extremely discomforting. When you eat, food normally journeys down your esophagus to your stomach. If you eat too much fatty food, you may feel a burning sensation in the back of your throat. That is stomach acid that escapes from your stomach and backs up into your throat. When you eat too much, the muscles operating the valve between the top of the stomach and the esophagus are overwhelmed by the volume of food, cannot function normally, and digestive juices well up. In addition, carrying too much body fat puts pressure on the diaphragm, which pushes up against the stomach, making the problem more acute. To avoid heartburn, eat small meals, cut down on fatty foods, and reduce to your ideal weight.

Constipation is another digestive disorder that typically accompanies poor food habits. Defined as anything less than four bowel movements a week, constipation is caused by a diet lacking in natural fiber and high in fat, inadequate hydration, and a sedentary lifestyle. Laxative abuse, generally, causes the condition to become chronic.

A definite relationship exists between obesity and impaired health. In the forty-five to sixty-four age group, the incidence of gout goes up dramatically with every excess pound. Uric acid levels increase with overweight. Fat adds trauma to weight-supporting joints such as the knee. Osteoarthritis of the knee is markedly associated with excess poundage in middle-aged women. There is no benefit to carrying excess weight.

CANCER

Menos Peso, Más Seguridad— Less Weight, More Protection

Dietary fat seems to be public enemy number one. It is implicated in almost all of the ailments we have discussed. Dietary fat is thought to cause 35 percent of all cancer mortality in the United States. Overweight men are prone to colon and prostate cancer. Obese women have a three times greater incidence of breast, uterine, cervical, and ovarian cancer than thin females. Women with too much fat in their diets and on their bodies run seven times the risk of endometrial cancer—cancer of the lining of the uterus. Breast cancer is the third leading cause of death among women living in the United States. Women who carry excess fat in the upper abdomen, shoulders, and nape of the neck are thought to be at high risk of breast cancer.

Extra body fat sometimes makes discovering a cancer more difficult. A tiny tumor buried in layers of fat is hardly perceptible until it grows to a perilous size and metastasizes. All of this makes a great case for keeping your fat intake low and your body trim.

You are what you eat, but it is not only what you eat that counts—what you do not eat may count against you. Broccoli, broccoli sprouts, cabbage, brussels sprouts, bean sprouts, *acelgas,* soy, *romeritos, nopales,* and other dark-green vegetables seem to have an antitumor effect. For women the reason has to do with estrogen, the primary female hormone. Estrogen is processed by your body into either of two compounds—one harmless, the other carcinogenic (cancer-causing). Consuming dark-green vegetables helps your body to process estrogen into the safe compound. Being slim also aids this process.

ORTHOPEDIC AND SURGICAL

*"Un Cuerpo Sano Es un Huésped. Un Cuerpo Enfermo Es un Carcelero.—*A Healthy Body Is a Welcome Guest. A Sick One Is a Jailer."

Francis Bacon, the British philosopher, made that statement in the sixteenth century. He observed that years of extra weight resulted in more wear and tear on the body and every organ had to work harder to maintain the extra load. Today, strangely enough, we seem to take better care of the replaceable appliances in our houses than of our bodies. Rarely will we overload our washing machine. If we do, the agitator begins to grunt and groan about the abuse. Your body also complains about overload. Your joints ache; you have trouble breathing; you cannot sleep. Heed your body's signals before *se descompone*—it breaks.

Dificultades En Una Operación— Now Where Did That Scalpel Go?

Obesity provokes all kinds of complications. Surgeons hesitate to operate on overweight patients. Mariana desperately needed a fibroid tumor removed from her uterus, but her *médico* did not want to operate until she lost twenty pounds.

Not only do the layers of fat make the actual operation more cumbersome, but fat cells have few blood vessels and are slow to heal. Often, following an operation, a heavy person will need a drain tube to siphon liquid out of the surgical wound. Great risk of subsequent infection always accompanies surgery on the obese.

EMOTIONAL

La Verdad Incomoda—The Truth Sometimes Hurts

Obesity inhibits your agility. As your body expands, everyday activities become more and more burdensome. It is difficult to walk or climb stairs. Personal hygiene becomes more of a problem. Instead of being pleasurable, sex becomes an embarrassing, strenuous activity. If you carry 40 percent or more excess poundage, you may be unable to fit comfortably into the seats on airplanes or in movie theaters.

Take the case of Amelia. She was on her way to Denver, to visit her newborn first grandson. Having had to make last-minute reservations, she was assigned the middle seat in a bank of three. Amelia did her best to squeeze her oversized body in between her dismayed neighbors. But try as she might, she still ended up sitting on her fellow passengers, who called the flight attendant to complain. With few vacant seats on the plane, the attendant was forced to request that a volunteer seated in a space adjoining a single vacant seat exchange places with Amelia. Amelia felt humiliated as she stumbled down the aisle to the back of the plane, with the attendant loudly admonishing her, "Next time you travel, you will have to purchase two seats."

Emotional discomfort like Amelia's is among the most common consequences of being overweight. It often leads to depression, isolation, and serious physical ailments.

REMINDER CARD

CARRYING EXTRA WEIGHT INCREASES YOUR CHANCES OF DEVELOPING:

Diabetes

Gallbladder dysfunction

High uric acid levels, resulting in **gout**

Orthopedic (bone and joint) problems

Osteoarthritis

Digestive disorders

Stomach and bowel **cancer**

Respiratory difficulties

Emotional and psychological problems

Lower testosterone levels and **reduced libido**

Slow recovery after surgery

High levels of dangerous **cholesterol**

High blood pressure

Coronary heart disease

Stroke

Shortened life span by three to five years

Uno, Dos, Tres, Arranque—Ready, Set, Go! The Latina Lite Double-Track Permanent Weight-Loss Plans

La Palabra, "Dieta," Es Una Grosería—
Diet Is a Four-Letter Word

Carmen, wanting to rid herself of thirty-four ponderous pounds, planned to start her diet the following Monday. Before beginning her new *régimen*, she wanted to say "good-bye" to food in grand style. She invited her closest friends to a *despedida—Adios comida* party. In anticipation of months of deprivation, Carmen greedily feasted for the duration of the long weekend, gulping down mounds of food. By Monday, she had added another four pounds of fat that she would have to lose.

Most of us, like Carmen, tend to see *el régimen*—a diet—as a time of torture we must endure. When offered food, we announce in a tormented voice, "I can't, I'm on a diet." The person offering food immediately empathizes with our situation and attempts to help us by saying, "It's all right. Just this once you can break your diet." In restaurants, *la mesera* becomes our ally when we decline dessert because we are on a diet and says conspiratorially, "Don't worry. All of the *postres son dietéticos*—desserts are low-calorie."

To avoid feeling sorry for yourself and eliciting "well-meaning" pressure from others, do not announce that you are on a diet. If you have been on several diets, your friends and family are probably accustomed to your announcements. Do not give them another reason to say, "She is always on a diet and always fat." With Latina Lite you are not dieting, you are changing your eating habits for life.

You Are How You Were

Your body and how it currently looks is the end product of your former eating and exercise patterns. If you want to look better in the coming months, you must change your habits now. If you want to be slim and healthy from this point on, you will have to maintain proper eating and exercise from this moment on. Remember that permanent change is always gradual. You will have to consciously replace old habits for new ones. At first, breaking an old habit will seem difficult, but with success, subsequent changes will become easier.

Latina Lite is a two-phase plan. You will start with the highly motivational "Accelerated" plan. Then after four weeks, you will be ready to graduate to the basic Latina Lite Long-Term Plan.

Both Latina Lite plans will help you avoid turning weight loss into an ordeal. The first, Short-term Accelerated Program—"Lose One Dress Size in a Month"—will put you on the road to permanent slimness and improve your health in just four weeks. And since your *mente delgada* will begin to exert control over your *mente gorda*, you will be better prepared to resist unhealthy foods. The Long-Term Plan will help you take permanent control of your eating habits and your weight.

No Daré Paso Sin Linterna—I'll Never Step on Those Land Mines Again

Let's begin with the Golden Rules of Latina Lite. They will help you remain *siempre delgada*—always slim.

1. As you follow the four-week Accelerated eating plan, implement the following:
   - List the foods needed to complete the daily menu.
   - Purchase only the foods necessary for the meal plan.
   - To avoid temptation, do not shop for food when you are hungry.
   - Prepare all food according to the cooking instructions provided in Latina Lite.
   - Eat only the foods listed on your plan.
   - Never skip a meal. Skipping will tempt you to eat too much during the next meal.
2. Prepare the same meals for the whole family. Serve only the amount of food your family should eat during the meal. Do not *repetir*—take seconds. Place served plates on the table, rather than platters filled with food. Use medium-size plates instead of the largest ones, to give your "fat eyes" the impression of *mucha comida*—a lot of food.
3. Make dinner a pleasant, social experience, where every family member participates in leisurely conversation.
4. Chew every bite at least twenty times and rest your utensils on the table between bites.
5. If you know you are going to a *fiesta* or *reunión* where fattening food will be in abundance, you can either eat nonfat or lowfat bulky food before going, or take a "care package" of healthy food with you and eat it there.
6. When eating out, choose a restaurant that serves tasty foods allowed by your plan. Take time to read the menu and select only healthy items. If you need a motivating boost, look around and compare the food selections of those diners who are overweight with those of slimmer people.

7. Brush your teeth soon after eating. By removing the taste of food from your mouth, you will more easily forget about eating more.
8. Weigh yourself only once a week. It can be demoralizing when the indicator on the scale does not go down daily. Remember, you will not lose weight evenly from day to day.
9. Buy yourself a nonfood reward for good behavior. Use the money you would have formerly spent on snacks and fatty food. How about a reward fund for new clothes or entertainment?
10. Walk or do other aerobic exercise daily. Exercise helps to suppress your appetite and will ensure steady, faster weight loss.
11. After four weeks, graduate to the Basic Latina Lite eating plan.

Unos "Sí" y Unos "No" Antes de Empezar— Some Do's and Don'ts Before You Start

The Accelerated Program is designed specifically as a jump-start to stimulate the metabolism of healthy women and men over the age of sixteen. Children, pregnant women, the elderly, and the infirm should follow the regular long-term program, which will enable them to lose all of the weight they desire, but over a slightly longer period of time. Before embarking on any nutrition and exercise program, discuss the plan with your physician.

The Accelerated Plan assures quick weight loss but should not be used for more than four weeks at a time. Try to stick to the prescribed menu, without altering the meals. However, if an unavailable, unknown, disagreeable, or allergy-producing food appears on the menu, alternative foods listed at the end of this section can be used. For example, the breakfast for Day One (page 345) is: ½ cup orange juice, 1 cup cereal, 1 tablespoon of bran, ¾ cup fat-free milk, herb tea. Let's say you are allergic to orange juice and want to substitute. The fruit alternatives are found on page 384. You can select another fruit juice or a portion of papaya or mango, instead. If you are not in the mood for milk, say, the dairy alternatives on page 388 suggest fat-free yogurt.

The menus are not fixed and rigid; you can adapt them to your needs. You will find a variety of alternative proteins, dairy, fruits, vegetables, and breads at the end of this section. Take a moment and scan them before proceeding.

To ensure maximum results:

1. Always trim **fat** and **skin** from meat and fowl before cooking. If you are preparing a *mechado* or *caldo* for future use, refrigerate it soon after cooking, and remove the *capa de grasa* that forms. Meats and other protein selections are found on page 378.
2. All fish are good sources of protein—cold water fish such as salmon, mackerel, and cod are especially good because they contain more healthy Omega-3 oil. Any fish canned in oil should be rinsed with fresh water in a strainer, and excess oil should be squeezed out before cooking or eating. See page 379.
3. Fruits may be consumed raw, canned in their natural syrup without added sugar, or frozen without sugar. Select medium-sized fruits or half of a large fruit. See page 385.
4. Vegetables may be eaten raw, lightly steamed or cooked. Do not add salt or butter. See pages 382–384.
5. *Tortillas* should be corn unless otherwise indicated; bread may be any packaged bread, but avoid sweet breads and nut breads. If you prefer *arepas*, or *guanimes*, you can prepare them at home according to the Latina Lite recipes. See pages 200 and 201.
6. Margarine, any cooking oil, or mayonnaise may be used in prescribed amounts. Never use lard or animal fat. Avoid coconut milk, palm, and coconut products—all contain saturated fat. See pages 387 and 388.
7. All milk and milk products must be fat-free. Eggs and certain cheeses may be consumed according to the menu instructions. See pages 381 and 382.

8. Cereals may be bran flakes, corn flakes, wheat flakes, Rice Krispies, any unsweetened packaged whole grain cereal, or oatmeal.
9. For adequate roughage, mix ½ pound oat bran with ½ pound wheat bran in a storage container. When called for, sprinkle 1 tablespoon of the bran mixture over yogurt, in cereal, in soup, on fruit, or in a *licuado*. See page 387.
10. Liver is highly nutritious and should be eaten two to three times monthly. If your serum cholesterol levels present a health problem, eat chicken breast instead of liver. See page 380.
11. Drink eight glasses of water daily.
12. Limit your intake of coffee and tea to three cups a day. The caffeine in these beverages may stimulate hunger.
13. Eat all the lettuce, radishes, celery, *chiles* you want. All contain fiber, are rich in vitamins, and low in calories. Rinse and dry canned *chiles* to wash off oil.
14. Sugar substitute (NutraSweet or saccharine) may be used. Use sugar-free gelatin.

THE LATINA LITE ACCELERATED WEIGHT-LOSS PLAN

Mujeres, Comienzen a Comer— Ladies, Let the Eating Begin

Get started with the Latina Lite Accelerated Plan described below. Follow this planned program for four weeks. Then switch to the Latina Lite Long-Term Plan. After eight weeks on the basic plan, you may again use the Accelerated Plan. If you are impatient or have *estancada*—plateaued short of your goal weight—you may use the Accelerated Plan to quickly stimulate additional weight loss.

When you feel satisfied with your weight and dress size, use the Long-Term Plan as a guide to good eating. After a while, you will probably begin to formulate your own menus instead of following those described here.

FIRST WEEK

The only tools you need to prepare your food for cooking are a measuring cup and measuring spoons.

All food items written in capital letters are easy-to-follow recipes that start on page 3. Eat three meals every day, but you may wish to exchange DINNER for LUNCH, or BREAKFAST for LUNCH. If you work away from home, prepare your lunch as it appears in the menu the night before, bag it, and take it with you.

FIRST WEEK

Day 1

BREAKFAST: ½ cup orange juice, 1 cup cereal, 1 tablespoon bran, ¾ cup milk, herb tea.
Total calories: <u>219</u>

LUNCH: ⅓ cup **TUNA *CEVICHE***, 1 cup shredded cabbage, 4 salted crackers, 1 *guava* or *guayaba*, coffee, ¼ cup milk.
Total calories: <u>220</u>

DINNER: 2 **TURKEY MEAT BALLS IN TAMARIND SAUCE**, ½ cup cooked rice, 1 cup mushrooms, ½ cup peas, 1 cup watermelon, ½ cup sugar-free gelatin.
Total calories: <u>631</u>

Day 2

BREAKFAST: ¾ cup papaya, 1 cup cooked oatmeal, 1 table-spoon bran, ½ cup milk, tea.
Total calories: <u>239</u>

LUNCH: ⅓ cup sardines mixed with 1 teaspoon mayonnaise, ½ teaspoon mustard, spread on a small roll (1 to 1½ ounce), ½ cup alfalfa sprouts, 1 small tomato, ½ cup yogurt, ½ cup canned unsweetened pineapple, sugar substitute, herb tea.
Total calories: <u>440</u>

DINNER: ½ medium chicken breast in *SALSA VERDE ME-XICANA*, ½ cup baked *batata*, 1 teaspoon margarine, 1 cup Italian green squash (*calabacita*), ½ cup carrots, ½ mango, ½ cup sugar-free gelatin.
Total calories: <u>401</u>

Day 3

BREAKFAST: ½ grapefruit, *HUEVO RANCHERO,* coffee, ¼ cup milk.
Total calories: <u>295</u>

LUNCH: ¾ cup yogurt, 1 tablespoon bran, ½ cup strawber-ries, ½ cup papaya, sugar substitute, herb tea.
Total calories: <u>155</u>

DINNER: ½ cup tomato juice, 5 *FISH STICKS*, ½ cup broc-coli, ½ cup *yuca* or potato strips fried in 1 teaspoon oil with minced garlic, 1 cup peas and carrots, 1 cup shredded cab-bage with lemon and *chile*, gelatin.
Total calories: <u>537</u>

Day 4

BREAKFAST: ½ cup diced melon, ½ cup strawberries, ¼ cup diced papaya, ½ cup yogurt, 1 tablespoon bran, coffee, ¼ cup milk.
Total calories: <u>178</u>

LUNCH: Salad: ⅓ chicken breast, diced, ½ cup celery, diced, ½ tomato, ½ bell pepper, ½ cup shredded cabbage. Dressing: 1 teaspoon Japanese seasoned rice vinegar (optional), 2 teaspoons yogurt, and 2 teaspoons mayonnaise. 1 *tortilla* or bread, *JAMAICA* **WATER**.
Total calories: <u>227</u>

DINNER: **FISH SOUP**, 1 *tortilla*, 1 baked apple, gelatin, herb tea.
Total calories: <u>401</u>

Day 5

BREAKFAST: ½ cup orange juice, 1 cup cereal, 1 tablespoon bran, ½ cup milk, herb tea.
Total calories: <u>197</u>

LUNCH: ⅓ cup smoked or canned fish, ½ cup finely chopped celery, ½ sweet bell pepper minced, ½ tomato, lettuce. Dressing: 2 teaspoons mayonnaise, 1 teaspoon Japanese seasoned rice vinegar (optional), ½ cup carrots, 1 *tortilla* or bread, *BATIDO* with ½ cup milk and ¾ cup papaya.
Total calories: <u>390</u>

DINNER: *ARROZ CON POLLO* (½ chicken breast and ½ cup rice), 1 cup *chayotes*, ½ peeled sliced *jícama* with lemon and *chile*, iced tea.
Total calories: <u>492</u>

Day 6

BREAKFAST: 1 orange, **FRIED EGG**, 1 *GUANIME*, coffee, ½ cup milk.
Total calories: <u>313</u>

LUNCH: ⅓ roast chicken breast steamed in a corn husk with *AXIOTE MEXICANA*, 4 to 6 radishes, ½ cup carrot strips, 1 *tortilla* or bread, ½ recipe **COCONUT FUDGE**, lemonade.
Total calories: <u>266</u>

DINNER: ⅔ cup *BACALAO A LA VIZCAÍNA*, 1 cup *chayotes*, ½ tomato, ½ sweet bell pepper, lettuce, 1½-inch-thick slice of pineapple, 1 tablespoon bran, 1 cup watermelon, chamomile tea.
Total calories: <u>290</u>

Day 7

BREAKFAST: ½ cup orange juice, 1 *TOSTADA*, ⅓ cup **TUNA CEVICHE**, lemon, coffee, ½ cup milk.
Total calories: <u>206</u>

LUNCH: 1 cup consommé, ½ cup fish, ½ cup carrot sticks, 1 cup shredded cabbage, 2 teaspoons mayonnaise, 1 teaspoon Japanese seasoned rice vinegar (optional), ¾ cup yogurt, 1 tablespoon bran over 1 baked apple.
Total calories: <u>406</u>

DINNER: ½ chicken breast in *MOLE POBLANO*, *NOPALES* **SALAD**, *LICUADO* with ½ cup milk, 1 cup strawberries.
Total calories: <u>652</u>

Congratulations! You have completed your first week of proper eating. You should be proud of yourself for sticking to it. Success is within reach—failure is not an option. To reinforce your successful start, take a blank sheet of paper and at the top write *Auto-Estima* Register. Then record two or more things that happened this past week that made you feel good about yourself. Maybe you resisted the *frituras de plátano y mantecado* served at your weekly card game. Or perhaps you can now slide the ring off your finger without struggling. Next week, refer to these statements to strengthen your resolve. Keep the Register in a safe place. You will be making additional entries as you continue.

Do not allow yourself to hang on to your "fat eyes and mind" as Consuelo from Florida did. Depressed because she had not lost an ounce after the first week, she was ready to *hecharse por atrás*—call it quits. Luckily she asked for help. As it turned out, her family had an orange grove that produced the largest, sweetest, juiciest fruit. Each orange was the size of a grapefruit. Consuelo loved oranges and had substituted them for all other fruits included in the menus. The plan specifically calls for medium-size fruits and vegetables, but each one that Consuelo chose weighed more than a pound and a half. She had consumed over thirty pounds of oranges in the first week. Once Consuelo followed the instructions accurately, she easily reached her goal weight within seven weeks.

SECOND WEEK

Day 1

BREAKFAST: ½ cup orange juice, 1 cup cereal, 1 tablespoon bran, ½ cup milk, herb tea.
Total calories: 197

LUNCH: ⅓ cup cold shrimp or fish, ½ cup chopped celery, shredded lettuce, 1 teaspoon mayonnaise, ½ cup canned unsweetened applesauce.
Total calories: <u>179</u>

DINNER: 1 cup consommé, 2 soft *tacos* (*enchiladas*) prepared from 2 *tortillas*, ½ cup shredded chicken, 1 cup shredded cabbage, topping them with ½ cup **SALSA ROJA MEXICANA**, 1 tablespoon crumbled skim-milk cheese, ½ cup nonfat sour cream, 1 cup *chayotes*, 1 *guayaba*.
Total calories: <u>541</u>

Day 2

BREAKFAST: ½ grapefruit, 1 cup oatmeal, 1 tablespoon bran, 1 teaspoon margarine, ½ cup milk, coffee.
Total calories: <u>253</u>

LUNCH: ½ cup **CEVICHE ACAPULQUENO**, 1 **TOSTADA**, ½ cup shredded cabbage, ½ recipe **COCONUT FUDGE**, **BATIDO** with 1 cup water and 1 cup strawberries.
Total calories: <u>256</u>

DINNER: Turkey Vegetable Soup—1 cup consommé, ⅓ cup shredded turkey, ¼ cup diced onion, ½ cup diced celery, ½ cup carrots, ½ cup Italian squash (*calabacita*), ½ cup cubed *yuca*, 1 dried seeded *chile pasilla* simmered together; gelatin, 1 apple or pear, herb tea.
Total calories: <u>320</u>

Day 3

BREAKFAST: ¾ cup papaya, ½ cup yogurt, 1 tablespoon bran, herb tea.
Total calories: <u>115</u>

LUNCH: Mash ⅓ cup sardines with 1 teaspoon mayonnaise and ½ teaspoon mustard, ½ cucumber, ½ tomato, lettuce, 1 small roll, ½ cup canned unsweetened pineapple, ½ cup yogurt, herb tea.
Total calories: 466

DINNER: ½ cup grilled fish, **SALSA AJILIMOJILI**, ½ cup cooked rice, ½ cup Italian squash (*calabacita*), 1 cup raw spinach leaves, 2 teaspoons oil, vinegar, lemon, ½ banana, iced tea.
Total calories: 573

Day 4

BREAKFAST: 1 tangerine, 1 cup cereal, 1 tablespoon bran, ½ cup milk, herb tea.
Total calories: 179

LUNCH: 2 eggs less one yolk scrambled in 1 teaspoon margarine with 1 cup cooked diced Italian squash (*calabacita*), 1 *tortilla* or **AREPA**, 1 apple or pear.
Total calories: 310

DINNER: ½ chicken breast **ADOBADO**, 1 cup broccoli, 1 medium baked potato with ¼ cup yogurt mixed with ¼ cup nonfat sour cream, 1 teaspoon margarine, ½ cup green peas, gelatin.
Total calories: 371

Day 5

BREAKFAST: **LICUADO** with ¾ cup papaya, ¾ cup milk, 1 tablespoon bran, herb tea.
Total calories: 116

LUNCH: ½ cup tomato juice, ⅓ cup smoked or canned fish, ¼ cup diced celery, 2 teaspoons mayonnaise, 1 teaspoon Japanese seasoned rice vinegar, 1 cup cooked broccoli, 1 orange, gelatin.
Total calories: 259

DINNER: ½ cup chicken liver fried in 1 teaspoon oil, *SALSA VERDE MEXICANA*. ½ cup cooked rice, ½ cup cooked beans, 1 cup shredded cabbage, 1 teaspoon Japanese seasoned rice vinegar, 1 apple or pear, lemon tea.
Total calories: 622

Day 6

BREAKFAST: ½ cup orange juice, *HUEVO RANCHERO,* coffee, ¼ cup milk.
Total calories: 310

LUNCH: ⅓ cup nonfat cottage cheese with 1 cup strawberries, 1 tablespoon bran, gelatin, herb tea.
Total calories: 117

DINNER: ½ grilled chicken breast, 1½ tablespoons *AJILIMO-JILI,* ½ cup rice with ½ cup pigeon peas (*gandules*), ½ cup carrots, *LICUADO: CHAMPOLA DE GUANABANA* with ¾ cup milk.
Total calories: 553

Day 7

BREAKFAST: ½ grapefruit, 1 cup cereal, 1 tablespoon bran, ½ cup milk, herb tea.
Total calories: 161

LUNCH: ⅓ cup *TUNA CEVICHE*, 1 *TOSTADA*, 1 tomato, 1 cup shredded cabbage, 2 teaspoons mayonnaise, 1 teaspoon Japanese seasoned rice vinegar, ½ cup radishes, 1 baked apple.
Total calories: 344

DINNER: 1 cup consommé with lemon and *chile*, ¼ cup chicken or veal with 1 tablespoon **MOJITO DE AJO**, ½ cup beans, ½ cup green peas, **BATIDO** with ½ cup milk, ½ banana.
Total calories: <u>500</u>

Bravo! You're on your way to weight loss! You are beginning to feel more confident about yourself. People are starting to notice that you are slimmer. Add another two or three entries to your *Auto-Estima* Register. Refer to them during the next week.

During these first several weeks you probably have not thought about straying from your prescribed eating plan. But now that you are thinner, your *mente gorda* might make an effort to defend her *hogar*. She may try to convince you to *dejar de bajar*—quit losing. Her voice, "Lighten up a little. Relax. Sneak a candy or a little *galleta* between meals now and then. Everybody does it. No one will know." My advice: Do not give in to her.

It is all right to nibble part of any meal as a *tentempié*—snack. It is actually better to eat the same total amount of food in smaller quantities, at shorter intervals. Save the *licuados, jamoncillo*, bread, fruit, gelatin, carrot sticks, or radishes from the meals on your menu to eat between meals. The trick is to prepare snacks ahead of time and have them available when you feel hungry. Do not wait until your "fat mind" demands that you grab a candy bar. Try to remember: IT IS INFINITELY MORE SATISFYING TO NOURISH FAITH IN YOURSELF INSTEAD OF MERELY FILLING YOUR FAT CELLS. By the way, how are you doing on exercise?

THIRD WEEK

Day 1

BREAKFAST: ⅓ cup nonfat cottage cheese, ¾ cup papaya, 1 tablespoon bran, 1 toast, 1 teaspoon margarine, coffee, ¼ cup milk.
Total calories: <u>216</u>

LUNCH: 1 *California* or *poblano chile* (canned or fresh), stuffed with ⅓ cup cold small shrimp, ½ cup diced celery, 1 teaspoon mayonnaise, ½ tomato, ½ green bell pepper, ½ cup yogurt, ½ cup canned unsweetened pineapple.
Total calories: <u>297</u>

DINNER: **FISH IN A BAG,** ½ cup peas and carrots, ½ cup *camotes* or *boniatos* with ¼ cup milk, 1 tangerine, herb tea.
Total calories: <u>456</u>

Day 2

BREAKFAST: ½ grapefruit, 1 cup cereal, 1 tablespoon bran, ½ cup milk, 1 cup coffee.
Total calories: <u>164</u>

LUNCH: **SALPICON** with ⅓ cup imitation crabmeat. ½ tomato,½ green bell pepper, ½ sliced *jícama* with lemon and *chile*, herb tea.
Total calories: <u>325</u>

DINNER: 1 cup consommé, ⅓ cup roast turkey breast or tenders, 1 cup green beans, ½ cup carrots, 2 *tortillas* or 2 **GUANIMES** or 2 **AREPAS, BATIDO** with ½ mango and ¾ cup milk.
Total calories: <u>417</u>

Day 3

BREAKFAST: ½ cup orange juice, *HUEVO HABANERO*, 1 *tortilla*, coffee, ¼ cup milk.
Total calories: <u>232</u>

LUNCH: ⅓ cup shredded chicken, 1 cup shredded lettuce, ½ cup green peas, 1 tomato, 2 teaspoons mayonnaise, gelatin, herb tea.
Total calories: <u>295</u>

DINNER: **FISH SOUP**, 1 roll, *LICUADO* with ½ banana, ¾ cup milk, 1 tablespoon bran.
Total calories: <u>465</u>

Day 4

BREAKFAST: ¼ cup papaya, ½ cup yogurt, 1 tablespoon bran, herb tea.
Total calories: <u>115</u>

LUNCH: Salad with 2 slices cold turkey breast meat, 1 cup raw spinach leaves, ½ cup sliced radishes, ½ tomato, ½ green bell pepper. Dressing: 2 teaspoons mayonnaise, 1 teaspoon yogurt, 1 teaspoon Japanese seasoned rice vinegar. 1 bread, gelatin, 1 apple or pear.
Total calories: <u>321</u>

DINNER: 2 **TURKEY MEAT BALLS IN TAMARIND SAUCE**, ½ cup beans, ½ cup cooked rice with ½ cup pigeon peas (*gandules*), ½ recipe **COCONUT FUDGE**, herb tea.
Total calories: <u>693</u>

Day 5

BREAKFAST: 1 *guava* or 1 *guayaba*, ⅓ cup nonfat cottage cheese, 1 tablespoon bran, coffee, ½ cup milk.
Total calories: <u>149</u>

LUNCH: 1/3 cup **TUNA *CEVICHE***, 4 salt crackers, gelatin, 1 apple or pear.
Total calories: <u>198</u>

DINNER: ⅓ cup liver fried in two teaspoons oil with ½ cup onion, ½ cup mushrooms in ***ESCABECHE***, 1 *tortilla*, or 1 ***GUANIME*** or 1 ***AREPA***, 1 cup Italian squash (*calabacita*), 1 cup shredded cabbage, lemon, ½ cup nonfat sugar-free flavored yogurt.
Total calories: <u>522</u>

Day 6

BREAKFAST: ½ grapefruit, 1 cup cereal, 1 tablespoon bran, ½ cup milk, coffee.
Total calories: <u>164</u>

LUNCH: ½ sliced chicken breast with 1 teaspoon mayonnaise. 1 cup ***NOPALES*** **SALAD**, 1 *tortilla* or bread, ½ banana, gelatin.
Total calories: <u>430</u>

DINNER: ½ cup **VERACRUZ-STYLE FISH**, ½ cup carrots, ½ cup *chayotes*, ***LICUADO*** with ¾ cup papaya, ½ cup milk.
Total calories: <u>367</u>

Day 7

BREAKFAST: ½ cup orange juice, 2 eggs less one yolk scrambled with ⅛ cup chopped onion, ½ chopped tomato, *chile* (optional), in 1 teaspoon oil, 1 *tortilla*, coffee, ¼ cup milk.
Total calories: <u>302</u>

LUNCH: 1 slice diced melon (1½ inches thick), ½ cup strawberries, ¾ cup yogurt, 1 tablespoon bran, gelatin, herb tea.
Total calories: <u>176</u>

DINNER: ½ grilled chicken breast, **MOJITO DE AJO LAS BUGAMBILIAS**, 5 grilled scallions, ½ cup beans, 1 cup broccoli, gelatin.
Total calories: <u>515</u>

Good job! Aren't you feeling wonderful about yourself? You are on your way: Your belt is not as tight; your bra is not hurting as much; and the elastic in your pantyhose is not leaving deep red marks on your waist. Your clothes are beginning to feel looser. Make yourself feel even better. Take a pair of pants that you did not even dream of zipping up just a month ago out of the closet and try them on. Surprise, they fit or almost fit. Remember to write in your *Auto-Estima* Register. Review all of the entries during the fourth week to help you *superar*—overcome the weak moments. Keep exercising.

FOURTH WEEK

Day 1

BREAKFAST: ½ cup orange juice, 1 cup cereal, 1 tablespoon bran, ½ cup milk, coffee.
Total calories: <u>200</u>

LUNCH: 1 *QUESADILLA, SALSA ROJA MEXICANA,* 1 cup shredded cabbage with 1 teaspoon mayonnaise, 1 teaspoon Japanese seasoned rice vinegar, *BATIDO* with ½ cup milk, 1 cup strawberries.
Total calories: 377

DINNER: *CALDO DE PESCADO,* ½ cup beans, ½ mango, gelatin, herb tea.
Total calories: 496

Day 2

BREAKFAST: ½ cup yogurt, ¾ cup papaya, 1 tablespoon bran, coffee, ½ cup milk.
Total calories: 139

LUNCH: ⅓ cup tuna, ½ cup celery, 1 teaspoon mayonnaise, 1 bread, 1 apple or pear, coffee, ¼ cup milk.
Total calories: 291

DINNER: 1 cup consommé, 2 chicken livers with 2 table-spoons onion fried in 2 teaspoons oil, *SALSA VERDE MEXI-CANA,* ½ cup cooked rice, 1 cup spinach, 1 cup carrots, ½ banana, iced *JAMAICA* WATER.
Total calories: 619

Day 3

BREAKFAST: 1 *guava* or 2 *guayabas,* 1 cup cereal, 1 table-spoon bran, ½ cup milk, coffee with ¼ cup milk.
Total calories: 205

LUNCH: Salad with ⅓ cup shredded chicken breast, ½ cup shredded cabbage, ½ cup green peas, 1 sliced tomato, 1 tablespoon grated part-skim milk cheese, *chile,* 1 teaspoon olive oil, 1 roll, coffee, ¼ cup milk.
Total calories: 423

DINNER: 1 cup tomato juice, ⅓ cup baked fish, 1 tablespoon *MOJITO DE AJO*, 1 cup Italian squash (*calabacita*), ½ cup *yuca*, 1 baked apple, gelatin.
Total calories: 411

Day 4

BREAKFAST: 1 tangerine, 1 egg plus one egg white scrambled with ⅛ cup chopped onion, ½ chopped tomato, *chile* (optional), in 1 teaspoon oil, 1 *tortilla*, coffee, ¼ cup milk.
Total calories: 282

LUNCH: 2 long, green, fresh *chiles* (*Californias* or *poblanos*), stuffed with ⅓ cup tuna, ½ cup diced celery, ¼ cup diced onion, 1 teaspoon mayonnaise, *LICUADO* with ¾ cup milk, ½ cup strawberries, 1 tablespoon bran.
Total calories: 251

DINNER: 2 slices turkey breast in 2 tablespoons *MOLE POBLANO*, ½ cup beans and rice, 1 cup broccoli, herb tea.
Total calories: 649

Day 5

BREAKFAST: 1 orange, 1 cup oatmeal, 1 tablespoon bran, ½ cup milk, coffee.
Total calories: 262

LUNCH: ½ roasted chicken breast, ½ tomato, ½ green bell pepper, 1 *tortilla*, 1 *GUANIME* or 1 *AREPA*, 1 apple or pear, gelatin, herb tea.
Total calories: 349

DINNER: ¼ cup grated part-skim milk cheese melted over 1 cup Italian squash (*calabacita*), *SALSA ROJA MEXICANA*, ½ cup green peas, 1 *tortilla*, *BATIDO* with ½ banana and ½ cup milk.
Total calories: 502

Day 6

BREAKFAST: ¾ cup papaya, ½ cup yogurt, 1 tablespoon bran, 1 toast, coffee, ¼ cup milk.
Total calories: <u>192</u>

LUNCH: Mix ⅓ cup sardines with 1 teaspoon mayonnaise, ½ teaspoon mustard, lemon. 1 tomato, ½ cup carrot sticks, lettuce, 4 salted crackers, ½ mango.
Total calories: <u>396</u>

DINNER: 1 cup tomato juice, 1 cup *ALBONDIGAS DE CAMERON*, ½ cup *yuca*, *ENSALADA DE CALABACITA Y JITOMATE,* gelatin, herb tea.
Total calories: <u>357</u>

Day 7

BREAKFAST: ⅓ cup nonfat cottage cheese, ½ cup strawberries, ½ cup papaya, 1 tablespoon bran, coffee, ¼ cup milk.
Total calories: <u>138</u>

LUNCH: 1 cup *AJIACO*, 1 *tortilla*, ½ cucumber, ½ cup carrot sticks, *LICUADO* with ¾ cup milk and ½ banana.
Total calories: <u>482</u>

DINNER: 1 cup *CUBAN CHICKEN WITH RICE*, 1 cup green beans, ½ cup beets, 1 plum, gelatin.
Total calories: <u>360</u>

You have done it! You are—most likely—at least one size smaller. You probably have not lost all your excess weight. To reach your goal weight, now change to the Long-Term Plan. If you began just a little *llenita* and have already reached your *meta* at the end of these four weeks, go on the Long-Term Program for the next month to continue to balance your meals. Bear in mind that your fat cells still are thinking about the good old days and want, very much, to return to their former size. They need at least a month more to adjust to their new size. Do not be afraid of losing every pound of excess fat. In twenty-five years of helping Latinas lose weight, I have seen over ten quintillion (10,700,000,000,000,000,000) fat cells shrink but have never seen one person harmed by proper weight loss. Continue exercising while you follow the Long-Term Plan.

BAJAR DE PESO: THE LATINA LITE LONG-TERM WEIGHT-LOSS PLAN

Here it is, the program used by more than a quarter of a million Latino *mujeres* and *hombres* to take off excess weight for keeps. The Latina Lite Long-Term Plan facilitates controlled, gradual, permanent weight loss. The menus are scientifically formulated to provide excellent nutrition for an unlimited period of time. The following is a whole month of helpful meal plans that will provide a structured eating schedule and ensure real weight loss.

Antes de Empezar—Before You Start

The Long-Term Plan is designed for slow, steady weight loss and offers substantially more food than the Accelerated Plan. Each meal plan contains foods that are necessary. If a specific food is distasteful to you, unavailable, or provokes a disagreeable reaction, exchange it for one of the alternatives offered at the end of this chapter.

1. Review the general instructions for the Latina Lite Accelerated Plan on page 344.
2. Each day, eat the REQUIRED FOODS or their substitutes (listed at the end of this section) in the amounts indicated.
3. This is a complete, nutritious eating plan, so prepare the same meals for the whole family including children over

five, pregnant women, lactating mothers, and the elderly.

4. Portion sizes vary for women, men, and children. Check the instructions for each food group at the end of this chapter.
5. As with the Latina Lite Accelerated Program, regular exercise is necessary for maximum weight loss.
6. Measure and weigh yourself no more than once weekly. Always get on the scale at approximately the same time of day, wearing clothes of the same weight.
7. Continue writing in your *Auto-Estima* Register. Reinforce your conviction to lose weight by reviewing your entries every time you are feeling low.

THE LATINA LITE LONG-TERM WEIGHT-LOSS PLAN AT A GLANCE

REQUIRED FOODS	AMOUNT		
	WOMEN	MEN	CHILDREN
WATER	8- 8 oz. glasses/day	8- 8 oz. glasses/day	8- 4 oz. glasses/day
PROTEIN	1 cup/day	1½ cups/day	1 cup/day
Chicken	Up to 10 meals/week	Up to 10 meals/week	Up to 10 meals/week
Fish	4 or more meals/week	4 or more meals/week	4 or more meals/week
Liver	Once every other week	Once every other week	Once every other week
VEGETABLES	3 cups/day	3 to 4 cups/day	3 cups/day
FRUITS	3 pieces/day	5 pieces/day	5 pieces/day
BREAD AND TORTILLA	3 pieces/day	4 pieces/day	4 pieces/day
FATS	3 teaspoons/day	3 teaspoons/day	3 teaspoons/day
MILK AND MILK PRODUCTS	1- 8 oz. cup/day	1- 8 oz. cup/day	2- 8 oz. cups/day

FOUR WEEKS OF LATINA LITE LONG-TERM WEIGHT-LOSS MENUS

An index of recipes for all the dishes that appear in **CAPITAL LETTERS** can be found on page 401. Exercising regularly will make you reduce more than twice as fast.

FIRST WEEK

Day 1

BREAKFAST: ½ cup tomato juice, 1 hard-boiled egg, ½ diced tomato, ½ green bell pepper, 1 teaspoon onion, cilantro, and *chile* to taste, 1 teaspoon mayonnaise, 1 *tortilla*, 1 cup strawberries, ½ cup yogurt, 1 tablespoon bran, herb tea.
Total calories: <u>307</u>

LUNCH: ½ cup chopped chicken breast, ½ cup *gandules*, ½ cup carrots, ½ bell pepper, lettuce, 1 teaspoon mayonnaise, *chile chipotle* to taste, 1 **AREPA**, 1½-inch slice pineapple, **JAMAICA WATER.**
Total calories: <u>796</u>

DINNER: 1 cup consommé, 1 serving **PESCADO VERA-CRUZANO**, ½ cup cooked rice, 1 cup broccoli, **BATIDO** with ¾ cup papaya, ½ cup milk.
Total calories: <u>515</u>

Day 2

BREAKFAST: ½ cup orange juice, **PAN DULCE,** coffee, ¼ cup milk.
Total calories: <u>359</u>

LUNCH: 1 *TOSTADA*, ½ cup shredded chicken, shredded let-tuce, ¼ cup *GUACAMOLE*, 1 cup carrot sticks, *JAMAICA WATER.*
Total calories: 319

DINNER: 2 long green *chiles* stuffed with ¼ cup part-skim milk grated cheese baked in 1 cup tomato sauce, 1 cup *ca-labacitas*, ½ cup beans, *LICUADO* with ¾ cup papaya, ¾ cup milk, 1 tablespoon bran.
Total calories: 571

Day 3

BREAKFAST: ½ cup papaya, ½ banana, ½ orange, ½ cup nonfat cottage cheese, 1 tablespoon bran, ½ cup sugar-free gelatin, coffee, ¼ cup milk.
Total calories: 259

LUNCH: 1 bread, ½ cup tuna, ½ cup peas, ½ cup carrot strips, 1½ teaspoons mayonnaise, 1 apple, coffee, ¼ cup milk.
Total calories: 439

DINNER: 1 serving *PALITOS DE PESCADO*, ½ cup rice, ½ cup beans, ½ cup *chayotes*, 1 tomato, lettuce, 1 teaspoon oil, vinegar, ½ recipe **COCONUT FUDGE**.
Total calories: 654

Day 4

BREAKFAST: ½ grapefruit, *HUEVO RANCHERO,* coffee, ¼ cup milk.
Total calories: 449

LUNCH: *TORTA*—1 roll, ½ cup turkey breast, ½ tomato, ½ sweet bell pepper, lettuce, 2 teaspoons mayonnaise; ½ cup carrot strips, ½ cup sugar-free applesauce, diet soda.
Total calories: 380

DINNER: 1 serving *ROPA VIEJA DE POLLO*, 1 cup cauliflower, ½ cup peas, *LICUADO* with ½ mango, ¾ cup milk, 1
tablespoon bran.
Total calories: 598

Day 5

BREAKFAST: ½ cup orange juice, 1 cup oatmeal, 1 tablespoon bran, ½ cup milk, herb tea.
Total calories: 254

LUNCH: 1 cup tomato juice, 2 *TAMALES DE POLLO*, *SALSA
VERDE O ROJA MEXICANA*. 1 *jícama* cut into strips, mari-
nated in lemon juice, soy sauce, and Tabasco, iced tea.
Total calories: 529

DINNER: ½ cup baked or grilled fish, 1 medium baked potato,
½ cup carrots, 1 cup green beans. Salad—1 cup spinach
leaves, ¼ sliced medium red onion, 1 tablespoon crumbled
part-skim milk white cheese, *chile,* 2 teaspoons mayonnaise,
2 teaspoons yogurt, 1 teaspoon Japanese seasoned rice
vinegar. Gelatin, 1 peach.
Total calories: 481

Day 6

BREAKFAST: ½ cup cottage cheese, ¾ cup papaya, 1 tablespoon bran, herb tea.
Total calories: 133

LUNCH: 1 *TOSTADA* with 1 serving *FRIJOLES REFRITOS*, 1
slice melted American cheese, ⅓ avocado, ½ cucumber, lettuce, *SALSA ROJA MEXICANA,* ½ cup canned sugar-free
pineapple.
Total calories: 725

DINNER: *CALDO SANTO,* ½ cup *gandules*, ½ cup grapes.
Total calories: 350

Day 7

BREAKFAST: 1 cup cereal, ½ cup milk, *BATIDO* with ½ banana, ½ cup milk, 1 tablespoon bran.
Total calories: 286

LUNCH: 1 roll, ½ cup tuna fish, ¼ cup diced celery, 1 tablespoon diced onion, 1 teaspoon mayonnaise, 1 tomato, lettuce, 1 cup carrot strips, ½ cup canned sugar-free pineapple.
Total calories: 445

DINNER: 1 serving *PICADILLO CUBANO*, ½ cup beans, 1 cup spinach, gelatin, 1 apple, iced tea.
Total calories: 591

Now do you believe that losing weight is easy with the Latina Lite Plan? Your family and friends hardly believe that you are on a diet. Do not be surprised that you have more energy and are eating a more varied, tastier menu than ever before.

You can really enjoy food when you decide to eat the right amount of the right foods. Remind yourself that real pleasure is not in how much you can stuff in quickly but in how long you can make the enjoyment last. Continue to eat more slowly, delight in every bite, and know that good eating habits lead to a leaner body.

SECOND WEEK

Day 1

BREAKFAST: 1 orange, 1 cup cereal, 1 tablespoon bran, ½ cup milk, herb tea.
Total calories: 203

LUNCH: *QUESADILLA* with 1 *tortilla*, ¼ cup part-skim milk mozzarella cheese, *SALSA ROJA MEXICANA,* shredded lettuce, ½ bell pepper, ½ cucumber, 1 cup strawberries in ½ cup yogurt, diet soda.
Total calories: 427

DINNER: **BACALAO A LA VIZCAINA,** ½ cup rice, ½ cup **FRI-JOLES REFRITOS,** 1 cup *chayotes*, 1 teaspoon margarine, 1 cup peas and carrots, 1 cup watermelon.
Total calories: 733

Day 2

BREAKFAST: ½ cup orange juice, 1 egg plus 1 egg white scrambled, 1 teaspoon margarine, 1 *tortilla*, coffee, ¼ cup milk.
Total calories: 273

LUNCH: 1 bread, ½ cup tuna, ½ cup diced celery, ½ tomato, 1 teaspoon mayonnaise, 1 teaspoon Japanese seasoned rice vinegar (optional), **LICUADO** with ½ banana, ¾ cup milk, 1 tablespoon bran.
Total calories: 392

DINNER: 1 cup **CREMA DE PLATANOS VERDES**, lemon, *chile,* ½ cup chicken liver, ½ cup onion, 1 bell pepper, 1 tomato, 1 teaspoon oil, melon, iced tea.
Total calories: 427

Day 3

BREAKFAST: 1 cup strawberries, ½ cup nonfat cottage cheese, 1 tablespoon bran, 1 **AREPA**, coffee, ¼ cup milk.
Total calories: 262

LUNCH: 1 cup Clamato juice, 1 bell pepper stuffed with ½ cup canned salmon, ½ cup diced celery, ½ cup shredded lettuce, 1 cup peas, 1 teaspoon mayonnaise, 1 bread, ½ banana, ½ cup yogurt, 1 tablespoon bran.
Total calories: 594

DINNER: 1 roast chicken breast in *MOJITO DE AJO*, 1 cup green beans, 1 serving *COMPOTA DE FRUTAS*, coffee, ¼ cup milk.
Total calories: <u>450</u>

Day 4

BREAKFAST: ¾ cup papaya, 1 scrambled egg plus 1 egg white with ½ diced tomato, 1 tablespoon chopped onion, *chile,* cilantro, ½ teaspoon margarine, coffee, ¼ cup milk.
Total calories: <u>179</u>

LUNCH: Sandwich—1 *birote* (roll), ½ cup turkey breast, 1 tomato, lettuce, *chile* in *escabeche,* 1 teaspoon mayonnaise; 1 apple or pear, 1 tablespoon bran, gelatin, orangeade with ½ cup orange juice.
Total calories: <u>399</u>

DINNER: 1 cup Clamato juice, 1 serving *PALITOS DE PESCADO,* 1 cup broccoli, 1 cup carrots, **PUERTO RICAN RICE PUDDING,** herb tea.
Total calories: <u>578</u>

Day 5

BREAKFAST: ½ cup orange juice, 1 cup oatmeal, 1 tablespoon bran, ½ cup milk, coffee.
Total calories: <u>257</u>

LUNCH: ½ cup cottage cheese, celery, radishes, 1 tomato, 1 bread, ½ cup carrot juice, melon, iced tea.
Total calories: <u>280</u>

DINNER: 1 cup consommé with lemon, *CHILES RELLENOS CON FRIJOLES,* 1 cup spinach, *BONIATO* PIE.
Total calories: <u>577</u>

Day 6

BREAKFAST: *LICUADO* with ¾ cup papaya, ½ cup milk, 1 tablespoon bran, herb tea.
Total calories: <u>94</u>

LUNCH: ½ cup **TUNA CEVICHE**, 1 **TOSTADA**, 1 cup shredded cabbage, 1 teaspoon yogurt mixed with 2 teaspoons mayonnaise and ½ teaspoon Japanese seasoned rice vinegar. 1 baked apple, ½ cup frozen nonfat sugar-free yogurt.
Total calories: <u>448</u>

DINNER: 1 breast of chicken in *MOLE*, ½ cup rice, 1 cup broccoli, 1 cup *chayote,* ½ mango, gelatin, iced tea.
Total calories: <u>707</u>

Day 7

BREAKFAST: ½ grapefruit, 1 cup cereal, 1 tablespoon bran, ½ cup milk, coffee.
Total calories: <u>164</u>

LUNCH: 1 slice of melted white cheese over 1 cup of Italian squash (*calabacita*), 1 cup tomato sauce, *chile jalapeño* in strips, 1 tomato, 1 *tortilla*, **BATIDO** with 1 cup strawberries, ½ cup milk.
Total calories: <u>363</u>

DINNER: 1 serving **ROPA VIEJA DE POLLO**, ½ cup *yautía*, ⅓ avocado, 1 cup green beans, gelatin, 1 *guayaba*.
Total calories: <u>632</u>

You are slimming down and have few excuses left. There are hardly any *privaciones*—deprivations. You have eaten refried beans, *mole, picadillo,* fried *yuca,* coconut fudge, butter-rum plantains, and rice pudding, and you have still lost weight.

This diet is really a way of life, where nothing is fattening. You will never have to cheat in order to savor cherished foods, because you can now make them with substantially fewer calories. You may not cook exactly the way your *abuelita* did, but then you're not toting water home and you don't grind corn by hand, either. This program makes it easy to stay *siempre delgada*.

At this point, you are ready to acknowledge and let go of your weight problems. Try telling some of the people *a tu alrededor*: "I hate being fat, and I don't have to be that way. I'll never get fat again!" One by one, strip away all of your *pretextos*—pretenses—for being heavy. After you reveal your intentions to those around you, write down in your Register how it makes you feel. Keep saying to yourself: "Soon I will be able to choose clothes *que me gusta*—I like—instead of settling for those *que me queda*—that fit me."

THIRD WEEK

Day 1

BREAKFAST: ½ grapefruit, 1 cup cereal, ½ banana, 1 tablespoon bran, ½ cup milk, coffee.
Total calories: 242

LUNCH: ½ cup tuna, ½ cup peas, 1 teaspoon mayonnaise mixed with 1 teaspoon yogurt and ¼ teaspoon Japanese rice vinegar, ½ tomato, ½ sweet bell pepper, lettuce, 2 plums, iced tea.
Total calories: 336

DINNER: 1 serving *FRICASE ESPANOL DE POLLO*, 1 serving *NOPALES* SALAD, 1 *tortilla*, ½ recipe *COCONUT FUDGE*, herb tea.
Total calories: 523

Day 2

BREAKFAST: ⅓ cup papaya, ½ cup strawberries, ½ cup cottage cheese, 1 tablespoon bran, gelatin, 1 toast, ½ teaspoon margarine, coffee, ½ cup milk.
Total calories: 255

LUNCH: *Torta* with 1 roll, ½ cup turkey breast, ½ tomato, ½ sweet bell pepper, lettuce, 1 teaspoon mayonnaise, ½ cup **CARROTS IN *ESCABECHE***, ½ cup sugar-free apple sauce, ½ cup yogurt, diet soda.
Total calories: 421

DINNER: 1 serving **CHAYOTE SALAD**, 1 cup **PESCADO VERACRUZANO**, ½ cup rice, ½ cup asparagus, 1½-inch slice of pineapple.
Total calories: 432

Day 3

BREAKFAST: ½ cup tomato juice, **HUEVOS RANCHEROS**, coffee, ¼ cup milk.
Total calories: 275

LUNCH: ½ cup nonfat sugar-free flavored yogurt, ½ banana, ½ cup strawberries, ¾-inch slice pineapple, 1 tablespoon bran, 6 lightly salted crackers, **JAMAICA WATER**.
Total calories: 252

DINNER: 1 cup consommé with 1 cup mixed vegetables, 1 serving **PALITOS DE PESCADO**, ½ cup *yuca* fried in 1½ teaspoons **MOJITO DE AJO**, 1 cup broccoli, 1 cup beets, ½ mango, coffee, ¼ cup milk.
Total calories: 643

Day 4

BREAKFAST: ½ cup orange juice, 1 cup oatmeal, 1 table-spoon bran, ½ cup milk, coffee.
Total calories: <u>257</u>

LUNCH: 1 serving *SALPICON*, 1 tomato, 1 *TOSTADA*, 1 apple, diet soda.
Total calories: <u>406</u>

DINNER: 1 serving **TURKEY MEAT BALLS IN TAMARIND SAUCE**, ½ cup rice, 1 cup *chayotes*, ½ cup carrots, *BATIDO* with ¾ cup papaya, ½ cup milk.
Total calories: <u>697</u>

Day 5

BREAKFAST: 1 tangerine, **FRIED EGG**, 1 *AREPA*, coffee, ¼ cup milk.
Total calories: <u>303</u>

LUNCH: 1 serving **TUNA** *CEVICHE*, ½ cup shredded cab-bage, ½ cup carrot juice, 1 *jícama* in strips, 1 *tostada*, herb tea.
Total calories: <u>276</u>

DINNER: 1 serving *PESCADO VERACRUZANO*, ½ cup *TOSTONES*, ½ cup sweet peas, 1 cup spinach, 3 tablespoons raisins, 1 tablespoon bran over **PUERTO RICAN RICE PUD-DING**.
Total calories: <u>749</u>

Day 6

BREAKFAST: ½ cup orange juice, *PAN DULCE,* coffee, ½ cup milk.
Total calories: <u>380</u>

LUNCH: ½ cup sardines, 1 teaspoon mayonnaise, ½ teaspoon mustard (optional), 1 tomato, 1 sweet bell pepper, lettuce, ½ recipe **COCONUT FUDGE**, iced tea.
Total calories: <u>365</u>

DINNER: 1 cup Clamato, ½ cup broiled beef, ½ cup *FRI-JOLES REFRITOS*, 1 cup Italian squash in tomato sauce, 1 *tortilla*, 1 baked apple, 1 tablespoon bran.
Total calories: <u>567</u>

Day 7

BREAKFAST: 3/4 cup papaya, 1 cup cereal, 1 tablespoon bran, ½ cup milk, coffee.
Total calories: <u>185</u>

LUNCH: 1 *California* or *poblano chile* (canned or fresh) stuffed with ½ cup cold small shrimp, ½ cup diced celery, 1 teaspoon mayonnaise, 1 tomato, lettuce, ½ cup carrot strips, 1 roll, ½ mango, **CHIA WATER.**
Total calories: <u>400</u>

DINNER: 1 serving **ARROZ CON POLLO**, ½ cup black beans, 1 cup yellow squash, ½ cup frozen nonfat sugar-free yogurt with 1 cup strawberries.
Total calories: <u>603</u>

Felicidades are in order! You are becoming *delgada* and learning not to be a food victim. This is your nutrition and your body, and you have control of both. Make healthy eating and exercise your top priorities. Invest in yourself—it is the only way to get slim and stay that way. Put aside the time necessary to prepare your lunch, a snack for the road, a satisfying dinner, and thirty-five minutes of exercise. *Querer es poder!* Now that you truly want to be slim, you will find time to do it.

FOURTH WEEK

Day 1

BREAKFAST: ½ cup nonfat cottage cheese, ½ orange, ¾-inch slice of pineapple, ½ cup papaya, 1 tablespoon bran, coffee, ¼ cup milk.
Total calories: <u>202</u>

LUNCH: ½ cup canned salmon, ½ cup peas, ¼ cup onion, 2 teaspoons mayonnaise, ½ tomato, lettuce, 1 *birote* (Mexican roll), ½ cup yogurt with ½ cup strawberries.
Total calories: <u>505</u>

DINNER: 1 cup **SOPA DE YAUTIA-CHAYOTE-PORO**, 1 roasted medium chicken breast, ½ cup **CARROTS IN *ESCABECHE***, 1 cup asparagus, 1 baked apple, coffee, ½ cup **CREMA CHANTILLY**.
Total calories: <u>473</u>

Day 2

BREAKFAST: 1 cup bran flakes in ¾ cup yogurt with 1 cup strawberries, 1 tablespoon bran, coffee, ¼ cup milk.
Total calories: <u>301</u>

LUNCH: 1 *California* or *poblano chile* (canned or fresh) stuffed with ½ cup tuna, ½ cup diced celery, ½ cup peas, 1 tomato, 1 teaspoon mayonnaise, 1 bread, 1 pear, iced tea.
Total calories: <u>433</u>

DINNER: 1 serving **MOLE POBLANO**, ½ cup rice, 1 cup green beans, 1 *tortilla*, 1 cup watermelon.
Total calories: <u>690</u>

Day 3

BREAKFAST: *BATIDO* with ¾ cup papaya, ¾ cup milk, 1 tablespoon bran, herb tea.
Total calories: 113

LUNCH: ½ cup **FISH *CEVICHE***, lettuce, ½ cup carrot strips, ***ARROZ CON LECHE PUERTORRIQUENO,*** coffee, ¼ cup milk.
Total calories: 535

DINNER: 1 cup consommé, 4 chicken livers, ½ tomato, ½ bell pepper, ½ cup onion fried in 2 teaspoons oil, ½ cup *yuca* fried in 1 teaspoon oil, ½ cup *gandules*, 1 cup *chayotes*, gelatin, diet soda.
Total calories: 465

Day 4

BREAKFAST: ½ cup orange juice, *HUEVOS RANCHEROS,* coffee, ¼ cup milk.
Total calories: 310

LUNCH: 1 ***QUESADILLA, SALSA VERDE MEXICANA,*** 1 cup ***NOPALES*** **SALAD**, ½ mango, iced tea.
Total calories: 371

DINNER: 1 cup ***CREMA DE VERDURA, PICADILLO CUBANO,*** ½ cup Italian squash (*calabacita*), ½ cup strawberries, ¼ banana sprinkled with 1 tablespoon bran, sugar substitute, cinnamon.
Total calories: 528

Day 5

BREAKFAST: ½ grapefruit, 1 cup cereal, 1 tablespoon bran, ½ cup milk, coffee.
Total calories: <u>164</u>

LUNCH: 1 serving **SALPICON**, 1 bell pepper, 1 cup carrot strips, 3-inch slice melon, iced tea.
Total calories: <u>396</u>

DINNER: 1 cup Clamato juice, 1 serving **ROPA VIEJA DE POLLO**, ½ cup beans, 1 cup shredded cabbage, 1 teaspoon Japanese seasoned rice vinegar, 2 teaspoons mayonnaise, 1 cup strawberries, ½ cup yogurt, gelatin.
Total calories: <u>711</u>

Day 6

BREAKFAST: ½ grapefruit, **FRIED EGG,** 1 **AREPA**, coffee, ½ cup milk.
Total calories: <u>276</u>

LUNCH: ½ cup tuna, ½ cup diced celery, ½ cup peas, 1 teaspoon mayonnaise mixed with 1 teaspoon yogurt and ½ teaspoon Japanese seasoned rice vinegar, ½ tomato, lettuce, 1 bread, **BATIDO** prepared with ½ banana, ½ cup orange juice, 1 tablespoon bran.
Total calories: <u>457</u>

DINNER: 1 roast chicken breast, 1 cup *chayotes*, 1 cup spinach, **BONIATO PIE**, coffee, ½ cup milk.
Total calories: <u>504</u>

Day 7

BREAKFAST: ½ cup orange juice, 1 cup oatmeal, 1 tablespoon bran, ½ cup milk, coffee.
Total calories: <u>257</u>

LUNCH: 1 **CHICKEN** *TAMAL*, ¼ cup *GUACAMOLE*, salad with ½ tomato, ½ bell pepper, lettuce, 1 teaspoon mayonnaise, 1 teaspoon yogurt, ½ teaspoon Japanese seasoned rice vinegar, 1 cup watermelon, gelatin.
Total calories: <u>491</u>

DINNER: 1 serving **VERACRUZ-STYLE FISH**, ½ cup rice, 1 cup carrots, ½ cup broccoli, 1 *FLAN, JAMAICA* **WATER**.
Total calories: <u>629</u>

¡Qué padre! You are getting leaner. But it is not always effortless. Nobody ever said that fat gives up without a fight. After years of settling in and staking you out as its property, it does not want to be run off easily. It will use every resource at its disposal to stay inside. But fat can only exist if you nourish it.

As you continue to become *delgada* and remain *esbelta*, you are going to have to keep strengthening your inner "thin voice." It has been a weak little whisper: "Don't eat too many fattening *empanadas*." Your *mente gorda*, on the other hand, ordered loudly, "Down everything in sight!" Persist in thinking thin and you will further empower your *alma delgada*—skinny soul.

Be careful of the traps that await us. It seems as though the world is filled with food: Commercials on TV *te hace baba*—make you salivate. At the movies you embrace tubs of popcorn large enough to bathe in. *Tacos, tostones, empanadas,* and *nachos* are lurking on every corner. Be especially aware of tempting food offered by friends and associates. They are the most dangerous. Since you cannot hide, learn to deal with the pitfalls.

One 4' 11" Latina went from a size sixteen to a petite, shapely, graceful size two. It has been three years, but her friends and family still say to her with astonishment, "What's wrong? You haven't gained an ounce!" Do not count on a lot of positive support. As you slim down, some people will feel intimidated and envious. You may even find that your slim friends resent competing with your emerging beauty. Take pleasure in your own appearance and do not pay attention to such bothersome comments as:

"All that food, and you expect to stay slim?"

"You're getting too lean, stop!"

"Are you ill? You don't look well."

"You'll gain the weight back when you stop dieting."

"A little cake isn't going to hurt you."

Be especially careful when you reach a plateau. Plateaus are normal. These seem to be periods when the body pauses and adjusts to its new weight. Measure yourself during these times—you will feel better knowing that your hips are getting smaller even when the scale does not reflect it. Let go of your fat image and adopt a new, slimmer you.

ESSENTIAL FOOD GROUPS

Proteins:

Fish, Fowl, Meat, Cheese, Eggs

Proteins must be consumed daily to ensure cell growth and replacement. **Women** and **children** need **1 cup daily**, and **men, 1½ cups per Day**.

Remember:
- When estimating the volume of cooked fish or meat, a piece the size of 2 of your fingers approximates ¼ cup, 3 fingers, ⅓ cup, and 4 fingers, ½ cup.
- All **fat** and **skin** must be removed from meat and fowl before cooking.
- *Mechados, asopaos, caldos*, or meat broth should be refrigerated, fat should be skimmed off the top and discarded before the food is reheated or served.

Any protein listed below can be used instead of the protein suggested in the menus. Proteins marked with an asterisk

(*) are the most healthy and should be among your first choices.

Fish*—All fresh, frozen, canned (rinsed and drained), smoked, and dried fish are permitted, including squid, octopus, imitation crabmeat, and imitation shrimp.

Poultry and Other White Meat—Can be eaten almost every day of the week. The white meat of chicken or turkey contains 50 percent less fat and 25 percent less cholesterol than dark meat. Wings and feet should not be eaten—they contain 42 percent more calories and 80 percent more fat than breast meat. Acceptable poultry alternatives include:

> *Cabrito** (Baby Goat)
> Capons
> Chicken
> Chicken Breast*
> Cornish Game Hen
> Deer*
> Frogs Legs*
> Game Birds
> Goat
> Rabbit*
> Smoked Chicken*
> Smoked Turkey*
> Turkey
> Turkey Breast*
> Veal*

You can substitute one of the following selections for a Poultry, Veal, or Other White-Meat choice once a week:

> Beef
> Beef Tongue
> *Carnitas*
> Chicken Franks
> Chicken Gizzards and Hearts

Chicken Ham
Chorizo
Ham
Kidneys
Lamb
Machaca
Mutton
Pork
Shellfish—crab, lobster, oysters, mussels, scallops, shrimp
Soy-Beef Combination
Soy *Chorizo*
Turkey Frankfurters
Turkey Ham
Turtle or *Cahuamanta*

Liver—Chicken, beef, or calf's liver should be eaten once every other week.

Vegetarian Substitutes—If you are a vegetarian, consult with your physician, but we are told that the following combinations **must** be consumed together every day to assure that you are getting the essential amino acids. Combine ½ cup from each column as a substitute protein serving.

DICOTYLEDONS	MONOCOTYLEDONS
Beans (All varieties)	Barley
Cereals (Whole Grain)	Bread (Whole Grain), ½ slice
Chickpeas	Corn
Dried Green peas	Oats
Green peas	Pasta (Whole Grain)
Lentils	Rice
Pigeon Peas or	Soy
Gandules	
Soy Products	Tofu and Tofu Products

Cheese

Cheese may be substituted for protein, but because most cheeses are very high in fat, calories, and cholesterol you should eat a smaller portion. For example, if the menu calls for ½ cup chicken breast and you want to eat cheese instead, replace the ½ cup of meat with only ¼ cup of cheese. **Two slices** or **¼ cup** is a serving, and you should not eat more than two servings of cheese per week.

You can mix two proteins for any meal, just use half as much of each. For example, if your meal calls for ½ cup of turkey breast, you can make a turkey melt by using **one slice** (⅛ cup) of *Manchego* cheese over **¼ cup** of cooked turkey.

If your favorite cheese is not on the following list, before buying, check the ingredients to see if it contains whole or skim milk. Skim milk cheeses usually contain 40 percent fewer calories, about ½ the grams of fat, and 50 percent less cholesterol. You may eat **four** slices or **½ cup** of **part-skim milk cheese, up to three times weekly,** in place of any protein. If your favorite part-skim milk cheese is not on the following list, add it. Lowfat cheeses include:

Cotija*	Muenster*
Cottage (non or lowfat)*	Panela*
Cream Cheese (nonfat)*	Parmesan*
Enchilada Cheese*	Ranchero*
Farmer*	Requesón*
Feta*	Requesón (skim milk)
Goat Cheese (soft)*	Ricotta*
Jarlsberg (lowfat)*	Romano*
Mormon*	String Cheese*
Mozzarella (low or nonfat)*	White Cheese*

You may eat **¼ cup** of **regular cheeses** up to **twice weekly.** High-fat cheeses have been ranked below. Those listed first are lowest in combined calories, fat, and cholesterol content. Those cheeses at the bottom of the list are the most fatty.

Requesón (whole milk)
Mozzarella (whole milk)
Jarlsberg (whole milk)

Brie
Swiss (pasteurized)
Asadero
Oaxaca
Manchego
Provolone

American Yellow (processed)
Monterey Jack
Chihuahua
Colby
Swiss

Añejo
Camembert
Cheddar
Parmesan
Goat (hard)

Eggs

Four egg yolks a week may be eaten. An egg yolk contains 6 grams of fat, and the egg white is pure protein accompanied by 88 percent water. You may continue substituting omelets, scrambled eggs, and other egg dishes for protein, but instead of using three whole eggs, use one yolk and three whites. The taste difference is minimal, and this counts as only one egg.

VEGETABLES

Vegetables are nutritionally important. **Three cups** of raw, cooked, frozen, or canned and rinsed vegetables must be eaten every day. However, several vegetables can be eaten in addition to the required three cups: celery, lettuce (any variety), radishes, watercress (*berro*), all herbs and spices, and *chiles* (hot varieties). Rinse all canned *chiles* to remove the oil. You are encouraged to eat as much as you want of these low-calorie vegetables at any time, especially for snacks.

You may mix and match *verduras* as desired. For example, one cup may contain ½ cup of canned mushrooms combined with ½ cup of frozen cooked green beans. To ensure maximum nutritional value from all vegetables: Cook them briefly in a steamer or in a small amount of boiling water—most vegetables lose vitamin content when overcooked. If you are not familiar with a certain vegetable or do not know where to get it, select a substitute from the following list:

Acelgas
Alfalfa
Artichoke (one = ½ cup)
Asparagus
Bamboo
Bean Sprouts
  (all varieties)
Beets (white or red)
Broccoli
Brussels Sprouts
Cabbage
Calabacita (Italian squash)
Carrot Juice (½ cup)
Carrots
Cauliflower
Chayote
Chinese Vegetables
  (canned)
Cucumber
  (1 medium = 1 cup)
Eggplant
Gandules (pigeon peas)
Green Beans
Green Peas
Green Tomatoes
Heart of Palm

Huitlacoche
  (black mushrooms)
Leeks
Llerenes
Mushrooms (all varieties)
Nopales (cactus leaves)
Okra (*quimbobo*)
Onions (all varieties)
Pumpkin Flowers
  (*flor de calabaza*)
Romeritos (large
  leaf rosemary)
Sauerkraut
Scallions
  (green onions)
Snow Pea Pods
Spinach
Squash (acorn,
  butternut, pumpkin,
  turban, etc.)
Sweet Bell Pepper
  (1 medium = 1 cup)
Tomato
  (1 medium = 1 cup)
Verdolagas (purslane)
Turnip

Starchy Vegetables

The following *hortalizas* are excellent foods but are a little high in calories. For these vegetables **½ cup = one serving**.

Batata or *Boniato* (½ cup)
Beans, dried (any variety—
   ½ cup cooked)
Corn (1 medium ear or
   ½ cup kernels)
Ñame or *Yam*
   (½ cup cooked)

Plantains (½ cup cooked)
Potato (1 medium
   or ½ cup)
Yautía (½ cup cooked)
Yuca (½ cup cooked)

Vegetable Juice

Additionally, you may add 1 cup of tomato or Clamato juice to your menu daily, or if you wish, you may cook with 1 cup of tomato sauce.

FRUITS

Fresh, cooked, dried, frozen, or sugar-free canned fruits are permitted. One-half cup of canned fruit, excluding the juice, equals one fruit. **Women** should eat **3 fruits daily**, one must be from the vitamin C fruits. **Men and children** are permitted **5 fruits a Day**, including at least one choice from the vitamin C fruits.

Vitamin C Fruits

You may choose all of your fruits from this group, or at least one every day. You can use up to two lemons daily—they do not count as a fruit serving. This bonus serving may be used for flavoring foods or to make lemonade sweetened with sugar substitute. Select medium-size fruits from the following:

Acerolas (Granada cherries, ½ cup)
Chironja (orange-grapefruit)
Grapefruit (½)
Guava or *Guayaba*
Juice: Orange, Grapefruit (½ cup)

Kumquats (2)
Loquats (2)
Orange (any variety)
Papaya (¾ cup)
Strawberries (1 cup)

Low-Sugar Fruits

After selecting your vitamin C fruit, you may choose the remaining fruits—either fresh, frozen, dried, or canned and unsweetened—to complete your daily fruit allotment. One-half cup of canned unsweetened fruit is the same as one medium natural fruit.

Apple
Apple Sauce (½ cup)
Blackberries (1 cup)
Blueberries (1 cup)
Breadfruit (*pana*, ¾ cup)
Carambola (starfruit)
Chirimoya (¾ cup)
Cranberries (1 cup)
Figs (2)
Granada (all varieties)
Guanábana (1 cup)
Jícama (3 cups)
Juice: Apple, Pineapple, Pear (¾ cup)

Kiwi Fruit (2)
Lychees (3)
Mamey (½)
Mango (½)
Melon (any variety, 3" slice)
Membrillo (quince)
Nectarine
Passion Fruit (*grenadilla*)
Peach
Pear
Persimmon
Pineapple (1½" slice)
Plums (2)

Quenada
Raspberries (1 cup)
Tamarind (4 complete
   pods)

Tejocotes (sloes, 3)
Tuna (prickly pear)
Watermelon (2" slice)
Zapote (all varieties)

High-Sugar Optional Fruits

One selection is permitted from this group daily. It is not imperative to choose any.

Capulines (½ cup)
Cherries (½ cup)
Dates (3)

Grapes (½ cup)
Raisins (¼ cup)

Seeds and Blossoms

If you desire, you may prepare Agua Fresca by boiling the following seeds or blossoms in water for at least 20 minutes and then straining the liquid. Drink hot or cold.

You may use an unlimited amount of these seeds and blossoms.

Chia Seeds   Jamaica—Red Hibiscus Blossoms

Sweeten these drinks with sugar substitute.

STARCHES

Bread, Tortillas, Grains, Beans, Etc.

Included are **3 daily bread** choices for women and **4** for men and children. A bread serving can be one slice of any packaged bread, except those high in fat, sweetened, or nut breads. Tortillas should be **corn**. Flour tortillas, made with vegetable oil (not lard), should be limited—they are usually larger in size and have twice the calories. One flour *tortilla* counts for two corn.

Every Day **one bread or corn** *tortilla* may be **substituted** for **one of the following selections**.

Arepa	Hamburger Roll
Bagel	Hot Dog Roll
Barley (½ cup cooked)	Melba Toast (6)
Birote (bolillo)	Pasta (½ cup cooked)
Bread Sticks (6)	Popcorn (1 cup)
Cornstarch (⅓ cup)	Rice (½ cup cooked)
Couscous (½ cup cooked)	Roll
English Muffin	Salt Crackers (6)
Flour (½ cup)	Waffle
Guanime	

BRAN

Roughage is essential. Consume **1 to 2 Tablespoons of bran daily. Mix** ½ pound of oat bran with ½ pound of wheat bran in a container and keep it handy.

FATS

Fats are an essential part of your daily diet, but they must be limited. You should eat the same amount of fat daily—**1 Tablespoon** or **3 Teaspoons** (1 pat of margarine = 1 teaspoon). You may choose: Margarine; Mayonnaise; Any Vegetable Oil.

When you use oil or margarine to fry, you must deduct the amount used from your daily total. For example, if you use 3 Tablespoons of oil to fry chicken or fish for 4 people, subtract 2 Teaspoons from the daily ration of each person, leaving each person only one more teaspoon for that day.

Fat Substitutes

Once a week, you may substitute either Avocado (½ medium) or 1 Tablespoon Peanut Butter for your total fat for a single Day. You may use fat-free liquid margarine whenever you wish, without counting it as part of your daily fat ration. (It may cause digestive upset in some people).

MILK AND MILK PRODUCTS

Almost everyone should drink milk daily. **Women and men need at least 1 cup** of **fat-free milk,** and **growing children, 2 to 3 cups of fat-free milk** daily. **Children from 3 to 6** years of age should drink **lowfat milk.** If fresh milk is not available, good alternatives are fat-free evaporated milk and fat-free powdered milk. One cup of fat-free yogurt, or frozen fat-free, sugar-free yogurt, or fat-free sour cream can be substituted for milk. To make milk more interesting, try adding 1 to 2 tablespoons of unsweetened powdered cocoa and a sugar substitute. (Do not use powdered hot chocolate mix).

OPTIONAL EXTRAS

Alcohol

Most of us know ahead of time when we are going to have an alcoholic beverage. Learning to balance means planning. One drink equals one bread, so if you expect to *tomar una copa*, save a piece of daily bread for each drink. Do not exceed three drinks in a single Day. Do not be like the lady in Los Angeles who did not eat any bread all week long so she could party with her friends on Saturday night. Alcohol does not contain either fiber or vitamins, but in moderation may be consumed occasionally.

EACH DRINK EQUALS ONE BREAD: 12 ounces beer; 1 ounce hard liquor; 3½ ounces wine.

CEREAL

One cup of cereal three times a week is permitted. You may use your favorite unsweetened whole-grain cereal without nuts. Measure the cereal dry, before cooking or pouring on the milk. One lady complained that she could not swallow her oatmeal—having misunderstood this instruction, she was trying to eat dry oatmeal.

COFFEE AND TEA

You may drink two to three cups of coffee or tea every Day. The use of caffeine-free herbal tea is unlimited.

BROTH

You may consume one cup of broth daily—prepared from *caldo natural*—without the fat—a fat-free bouillon cube, or a teaspoon of granulated instant nonfat consommé.

DIET SODA

If you must, you may drink 2 eight-ounce glasses of diet soda each day, but since the sodium content is high, the consumption of soda is not recommended.

GELATIN

Six cups of sugar-free gelatin may be eaten daily.

REMINDER CARD

....

How To Improve Your Eating I.Q. . . .

Purchase only the food items on your meal plan

Do not shop for food when you are hungry

Prepare the food according to the cooking instructions

Always trim fat and skin from meat and fowl
before cooking

Prepare the same meals for the whole family

Eat only the food listed in your plan

Rest your utensils on the table between bites

When eating out, read the menu and select only
healthy items

Drink eight glasses of water a Day

Never skip a meal

....

GLOSSARY

Terms in Spanish vary from country to country. Corn may be *masorca*, corn on the cob, in Guatemala, *choclo* in Chile and Argentina, and *maíz* or *elote* in most other Spanish-speaking countries. Often, the ingredients in recipes from Ecuador confound Mexicans, and the names for Mexican foods confuse Spaniards. To help identify many common foods, spices, and cooking terms, this glossary contains many of their English and Latin equivalents.

Aceitunas—olives
Acelgas—Swiss Chard
Acerolas—Barbados cherries
Achicoria—*escarola, endivia, endibia,* endive
Achiote—*axiote,* annato seeds
Aguacate—*palta,* avocado
Ají cachucha—*rocatillo,* small round hot *chile* pepper
Ají dulce—*pimiento dulce, pimiento morrón,* sweet bell pepper
Ají dulce—sweet *chile* pepper
Ají picante—*chile pequín,* Tabasco
Ajo—garlic
Ajo puerro—*cebollín, puerro,* chives
Ajonjolí—*sésamo, alegría,* sesame seeds
Albahaca—basil
Albaricoque—*chabacano, damasco,* apricot
Alcachofa—*alcaucil,* artichoke
Alcaparra—caper
Alcaparrado—a mixture of olives, red pimientos, and capers
Alcaravea—caraway

Alcaucil—Alcachofa, artichoke
Alegría—sésamo, ajonjolí, sesame seeds
Alubias—frijoles, fríjoles, frejoles, judías, habichuelas, granos, porotos en vaina, beans
Amarillo—plátano maduro, ripe banana
Ananás—piña, pineapple
Anchoas—anchovies
Anchovies—anchoas
Aní en semilla—aniseed
Aniseed—aní en semilla
Annato seeds—achiote, axiote
Anona chirimoya—chirimoya, catuche, anona or cherimolia
Anona or cherimolia—Anona chirimoya, chirimoya, catuche
Apio—arracacha, celery in Mexico, a brown-skinned yellow root vegetable in Puerto Rico
Apricot—albaricoque, chabacano, damasco
Arracacha—apio, celery in Mexico, a brown-skinned yellow root vegetable in Puerto Rico
Arroz—rice
Artichoke—alcachofa, alcaucil
Arvejas—guisantes, chícharos, pitipuá, garbanzos verdes, green peas
Asopao—guisado, sopón, thick soupy stew
Atún—tuna fish
Auyama—calabaza, zapallo, squash
Avena—oats, oatmeal
Avocado—aguacate, palta
Axiote—achiote, annato seeds
Azafrán—saffron
Bacalao—codfish (dried and salted)
Banana—banana, plátano, guineo, cambur, cambure
Banana—plátano, guineo, cambur, cambure, banana
Barbados cherries—acerolas
Barley—cebada
Basil—albahaca
Batata—papa, patata, potato
Batatas dulces—camotes, yams
Bay leaf—hoja de laurel

Beans—*alubias, frijoles, granos, fríjoles, frejoles, judías, habichuelas, porotos en vaina*
Beef—*carne de res*
Bell pepper—*pimiento dulce, ají dulce, pimiento morrón*
Bell pepper in Mexico—*pimiento morrón*
Bell pepper in Puerto Rico and Cuba—*pimiento*
Berenjena—eggplant
Berro—watercress
Berza—collard greens
Bianda—Puerto Rican native root plants such as *yautía, ñame, yuca,* cassava, etc.
Boniato—Florida yam (white sweet potato)
Bran—*salvado*
Breadfruit—*pana* or *panapén*
Brécol—*bróculi,* broccoli
Brécol de cabeza—*coliflor,* cauliflower
Broccoli—*brécol, bróculi*
Bróculi—*brécol,* broccoli
Cabbage—*col, repollo*
Calabaza—*auyama, zapallo,* squash
Calamar—squid
Camarones—shrimp
Cambur—*banana, plátano, guineo, cambure,* banana
Camotes—*batatas dulces,* yams
Canela—cinnamon
Caper—*alcaparra*
Capulines—Mexican yellow cherries
Caraway—*alcaravea*
Carne de res—beef
Carne estofada—*carne mechada,* pot roast
Carne mechada—*carne estofada,* pot roast
Carrots—*zanahorias*
Cártamo—safflower
Cassava root—*yuca*
Catuche—*anona chirimoya, chirimoya,* anona or cherimolia
Cauliflower—*brécol de cabeza, coliflor*
Cebada—barley
Cebollín—*ajo puerro, puerro,* chives

Celery—*apio, arracacha,* a brown-skinned yellow root vegetable in Puerto Rico

Chabacano—albaricoque, damasco, apricot

Champiñones—hongos blancos, hongos franceses, cultivated white button mushrooms

Chayote—tayote, water pear or christophine (pale green pear-shaped squash)

Chícharos—arvejas, guisantes, pitipuá, garbanzos verdes, green peas

Chickpeas—*garbanzos*

Chile pepper (small round hot)—*ají cachucha, rocatillo*

Chile pequín—ají picante, Tabasco

China—naranja, orange

Chinese parsley—*cilantro, culantro,* coriander

Chirimoya—anona chirimoya, catuche, anona or cherimolia

Chironja—orange-grapefruit hybrid

Chives—*cebollín, ajo puerro, puerro*

Choclo—maíz, maíz tierno, elote, masorca, corn

Cilantro—culantro, cilantro, Chinese parsley, coriander

Cinnamon—*canela*

Coco plum—*hicaco*

Codfish (dried and salted)—*bacalao*

Cohombro—pepino, cucumber

Col—repollo, cabbage

Coliflor—brécol de cabeza, cauliflower

Collard greens—*berza*

Comino—cumin

Coriander—Chinese parsley, *cilantro, culantro*

Corn—*choclo—maíz, maíz tierno, elote, milpa*

Crab—*juey, jaiba*

Cuchifritos—frituras, fritangas, fried foods (fritters), fried pork

Cucumber—*cohombro, pepino*

Culantro—cilantro, cilantro, Chinese parsley, coriander

Cultivated white button mushrooms—*champiñones, hongos blancos, hongos franceses*

Cumin—*comino*

Damasco—albaricoque, chabacano, apricot

Dill—*eneldo*

Dominicos—guineítos, ladyfinger bananas (small bananas)

Durazno—*melocotón,* peach
Eggplant—*berenjena*
Ejotes—*porotos verdes,* green beans
Elote—*choclo, maíz, maíz tierno, masorca,* corn
Endive—*endivia, escarola*—*achicoria, endibia*
Endivia—*escarola, achicoria, endibia,* endive
Eneldo—dill
Escarola—*achicoria, endivia, endibia,* endive
Estragón—tarragon
Florida yam (white sweet potato)—*boniato*
Frejoles—*alubias, frijoles, fríjoles, judías, habichuelas, granos, porotos en vaina,* beans
Fried foods (fritters)—*cuchifritos* (pork), *frituras, fritangas*
Frijoles—*alubias, fríjoles, frejoles, judías, habichuelas, granos, porotos en vaina,* beans
Fritangas—*cuchifritos* (pork), *frituras,* fried foods (fritters)
Frituras—*cuchifritos* (pork), *fritangas,* fried foods (fritters)
Fruta bomba—*lechosa, papaya,* papaya
Gandules—pigeon peas
Garbanzos—chickpeas
Garbanzos verdes—*arvejas, chícharos, guisantes, pitipuá,* green peas
Garlic—*ajo*
Girasol—sunflower
Granada—pomegranate
Granos—*alubias, frijoles, fríjoles, frejoles, judías, porotos en vaina,* beans
Green beans—*ejotes, porotos verdes*
Green peas—*arvejas, guisantes, chícharos, pitipuá, garbanzos verdes*
Guanábana—soursop
Guineítos—*dominicos,* ladyfinger bananas (small bananas)
Guineo—*banana, plátano, cambur, cambure,* banana
Guineo—*plátano macho,* plantain
Guingambó—*quimbombó,* okra
Guisado—*asopao, sopón,* thick soupy stew
Guisado—*sancocho,* stew
Guisantes—*arvejas, chícharos, pitipuá, garbanzos verdes,* green peas

Habas—lima beans
Habichuelas—*alubias, frijoles, fríjoles, frejoles, judías, granos, porotos en vaina,* beans
Habichuelas rojas—kidney beans
Hicaco—coco plum
Hoja de laurel—bay leaf
Hominy (large white kernel corn)—*nixtamal, huazontle*
Hongos—*setas,* all mushrooms except white cultivated button mushrooms
Hongos blancos—*champiñones, hongos franceses,* cultivated white button mushrooms
Hongos franceses—*champiñones, hongos blancos,* cultivated white button mushrooms
Hortalizas—*verduras, legumbres, vegetales,* vegetables
Huazontle—*nixtamal,* hominy (large white kernel corn)
Jaiba—*juey,* crab
Judías—*alubias, frijoles, fríjoles, frejoles, habichuelas, granos, porotos en vaina,* beans
Juey—*jaiba,* crab
Kidney beans—*habichuelas rojas*
Ladyfinger bananas (small bananas)—*guineítos, dominicos*
Langosta—lobster
Lechosa—*fruta bomba, papaya*
Leeks—*poros*
Legumbres—*verduras, hortalizas, vegetales,* vegetables
Lima beans—*habas*
Lobster—*langosta*
Loquat—*níspero, sapodilla*
Maíz—*choclo, maíz tierno, elote, mazorca,* corn
Malanga—*yautía,* taro, tanier, or dasheen, white starchy root plant
Mamey—mammee apple (avocado's cousin, fruit with large pit and sweet yellow to red flesh)
Marjoram—*mejorana*
Masorca—*choclo, maíz, maíz tierno, elote,* corn
Mejorana—marjoram
Melocotón—*durazno,* peach
Membrillo—quince
Mexican yellow cherries—*capulines*

Molcajete—*pilón,* mortar and pestle
Mortar and pestle—*molcajete, pilón*
Mushrooms (all except white cultivated button
    mushrooms)—*hongos, setas*
Ñame—large yam
Naranja—*china,* orange
Níspero—*sapodilla,* loquat
Nixtamal—*huazontle,* hominy (large white kernel corn)
Nuez moscada—nutmeg
Nutmeg—*nuez moscada*
Oats, oatmeal—*avena*
Octopus—*pulpo*
Okra—*guingambó, quimbombó*
Olives—*aceitunas*
Orange—*china, naranja*
Orange-grapefruit hybrid—*chironja*
Oregano—*orégano*
Orégano—oregano
Palta—*aguacate,* avocado
Pana or *panapén*—breadfruit
Papa—*patata, batata,* potato
Papaya—*fruta bomba, lechosa*
Parsley—*perejil*
Patata—*papa,* potato, *batata*
Peach—*melocotón, durazno*
Peas—*arvejas, guisantes, chícharos, pitipuá, garbanzos
    verdes*
Pepino—*cohombro,* cucumber
Perejil—parsley
Pigeon peas—*gandules*
Pilón—*molcajete,* mortar and pestle
Pimiento—bell pepper in Puerto Rico and Cuba, pepper in
    Mexico
Pimiento dulce—*ají dulce, pimiento morrón,* sweet bell
    pepper
Pimiento morrón—*ají dulce, pimiento dulce,* sweet bell
    pepper, roasted red pepper in Puerto Rico and Cuba
Piña—*ananás,* pineapple
Pineapple—*ananás, piña*

Pitipuá—*arvejas, guisantes, chícharos, garbanzos verdes,* green peas
Plantain—*plátano macho, guineo*
Plátano—*banana, guineo, cambur, cambure,* banana
Plátano macho—*guineo,* plantain
Plátano maduro—*amarillo,* ripe banana
Pomegranate—*granada*
Poros—leeks
Porotos en vaina—*alubias, frijoles, fríjoles, frejoles, judías, habichuelas,* beans
Porotos verdes—*ejotes,* green beans
Potato—*patata, batata, papa*
Prickly pear—*tuna*
Puerro—*cebollín, ajo puerro,* chives
Pulpo—octopus
Quimbombó—*guingambó,* okra
Quince—*membrillo*
Repollo—*col,* cabbage
Rice—*arroz*
Ripe banana—*amarillo, plátano maduro*
Rocatillo—*ají cachucha,* small round hot *chile* pepper
Romeritos—rosemary
Rosemary—*romeritos*
Safflower—*cártamo*
Saffron—*azafrán*
Sage—*salvia*
Salvado—bran
Salvia—sage
Sancocho—*guisado,* stew
Sapodilla—*níspero,* loquat
Sesame—*ajonjolí*
Sésamo—*ajonjolí, alegría,* sesame seeds
Setas—*hongos,* all mushrooms except white cultivated button mushrooms
Shrimp—*camarones*
Sopón—*asopao, guisado,* thick soupy stew
Soursop—*guanábana*
Squash—*auyama, calabaza, zapallo*
Squid—*calamar*

Stew—*guisado, sancocho*
Sunflower—*girasol*
Sweet bell pepper—*pimiento dulce, ají dulce, pimiento morrón*
Sweet chile pepper—*ají dulce*
Swiss Chard—*acelgas*
Tabasco—*ají picante, chile pequín*
Taro, tanier or dasheen, white starchy root plant—*malanga, yautía*
Tarragon—*estragón*
Tayote—*chayote*, water pear or christophine (pale green pear-shaped squash)
Thyme—*tomillo*
Tomillo—thyme
Trigo—wheat
Tuna—prickly pear
Tuna fish—*atún*
Vegetables—*verduras, hortalizas, legumbres, vegetales*
Vegetales—*verduras, hortalizas, legumbres*, vegetables
Verduras—*hortalizas, legumbres, vegetales*, vegetables
Water pear or christophine (pale green pear-shaped squash)—*chayote, tayote*
Watercress—*berro*
Wheat—*trigo*
Yam (large)—*ñame*
Yams—*camotes, batatas dulces*
Yautía—*malanga*, taro, tanier, or dasheen, white starchy root plant
Yuca—cassava root
Zanahorias—carrots
Zapallo—*Auyama, calabaza*, squash

INDEX

ABOUT THE AUTHOR

Maria Dolores Beatriz earned her master's degree magna cum laude from the University of Florida. In 1972 she founded Pierda Peso ("lose weight"), a state-of-the-art weight reduction plan, in Mexico. The program was a huge success, and Beatriz relocated the business to San Diego, California, and eventually re-christened it Esbeltez. By 1989, Esbeltez boasted centers from the 31 states of Mexico to Los Angeles to Yuma, Arizona. More than 50,000 people have lost weight and dramatically enhanced their lives through Esbeltez over the last 24 years.

Beatriz is fluent in Spanish and English and has spent her life divided between two countries. She and her husband currently divide their time between San Diego and Mexico.